Olivia,
    Congrats on
Class of 202

5/21/22

ant

Get the win!

Jeff Friday

Luke 2:52

CROSSING THE THIN LINE BETWEEN GOOD & GREAT IN SPORTS, BUSINESS & LIFE

SUPER BOWL CHAMPION STRENGTH COACH

JEFF FRIDAY

with Kevin Horner

CORE

Built 4 Winning
Crossing the Thin Line Between Good & Great in Sports, Business & Life
www.built4winning.com
www.jeffFriday.com

Copyright © 2021 by Jeff Friday

Published by The Core Media Group, Inc.
P.O. Box 2037, Indian Trail, NC 28079
www.thecoremediagroup.com

Cover & Interior Design: Nadia Guy
Cover photos provided by ESB Professional/Shutterstock, Topseller/Shutterstock,
Anatoliy Sadovskiy/Adobe Stock.

ISBN 978-1-950465-44-6

All rights reserved. No part of this publication may be reproduced, stored in a
retrieval system, or transmitted in any form or by any means—electronic, mechanical,
photocopy, recording, scanning, or other—except for brief quotation in printed
reviews, without the prior written permission of the publisher.

Unless otherwise indicated, scripture quotations in this book are taken from the *The
Holy Bible, New International Version*®, *NIV*®, Copyright © 1973, 1978, 1984, 2011
by Biblica, Inc.® Used by permission. All rights reserved worldwide.

Scripture quotation marked (NLT) are taken from the Holy Bible, New Living
Translation, copyright © 1996, 2004, 2015 by Tyndale House Foundation. Used by
permission of Tyndale House Publishers, Inc., Carol Stream, Illinois 60188. All rights
reserved.

Printed in the United States of America.

TABLE OF CONTENTS

BUILDING BLOCK 4: SPIRITUAL

PREFACE

In the spring of 2003, I spoke at a "Success Symposium" for Bridgeway Community Church in Columbia, Maryland. The goal of the event was for Christian professionals to share with the church family practical information for leading successful lives.

As a new believer, I felt honored to provide a faith-based message to a body of believers. I'd just finished my fourth year as the head strength and conditioning coach of the Baltimore Ravens, and the idea of using my professional education and experiences to teach a group of Christian men excited me. Although Bridgeway had multiple speakers lined up, my task was to address the question, "What does it take to be a healthy and whole man of God?" More specifically, I'd instruct a group of middle-aged men on how to implement a personal fitness program.

At that point in my career, I'd learned something: everyone knows the *benefit* of exercise. It's no secret that regular physical activity helps prevent disease, improve stamina, strengthen muscles, enhance flexibility, control weight and improve overall quality of life. The problem is, despite these obvious and well-touted advantages, many people still don't exercise regularly. Excuses like "I don't have enough time" or "I'm not getting any results" too often prevail. I knew my task was more complicated than showing these men statistics about the proven benefits of physical activity. I had to convince them *why*—why fitness was essential to living healthy, balanced lives as believers.

Given my audience, I knew I needed to explain the issue through the lens of Scripture. In my preparation, I went through plenty of verses on the human body, physical activity, health—anything that related to the importance of fitness—but one verse stood out: Luke 2:52. It's the last verse of Luke 2—the chapter many of us read at Christmas, about Jesus' birth—and serves as transition between Jesus' childhood/adolescence and his adulthood/public ministry.

"And Jesus grew in wisdom and stature, and in favor with God and man."

By itself, the verse is pretty simple. It's easy to breeze past it, almost as an afterthought, on your way to Luke 3. But to me, it captures the true purpose of physical fitness for followers of Jesus. It provides the "why," the inspiration, for implementing a personal fitness regimen. Of course, this isn't just my opinion or personal interpretation of the verse. In fact, the inspiration for that symposium presentation (and, ultimately, this book) came from the commentary in my *Life Application Study Bible*:

> "The second chapter of Luke shows us that although Jesus was unique, he had a normal childhood and adolescence. In terms of development, he went through the same progression we do. He grew physically and mentally, he related to other people, and he was loved by God. A full human life is not unbalanced. It was important to Jesus—and it should be important to all believers—to develop fully and harmoniously in each of these key areas: **physical, mental, social and spiritual.**"[1]

Jesus grew in all four of these areas—what I call the four "building blocks"—and to be like Him, we should do the same. As a Christ follower, I am driven to grow and nurture these four components of my personal development, so that I too can build a strong foundation as Jesus did. In doing so, I am able to experience my full potential and, ultimately, the life God wants for me.

So, on the basis of Luke 2:52, I presented "He Created Them Male: Exploring Issues in Health and Wellness" to a standing room only crowd at Bridgeway.

That symposium speech—and corresponding research—really provided the first impetus (of many) toward developing the content you'll find in this book. A few years later, I wrote an article on the same content for a Baltimore-based magazine, *SmartCEO*. In 2009, I almost included the building blocks in a manual I wrote as the strength and conditioning director of the United Football League (UFL). Although I ended up deciding against it, it led me to further develop the ideas. In 2010, I gave a short talk to a group of high school students on "Building the Total Athlete" through the Fellowship of Christian Athletes (FCA), which was the first time I really put these concepts into more detail. Over several more years—between more talks and presentations, football clinics, and finally, a colleague encouraging me to put my thoughts on paper—I built the template for this book.

This project has also been a fascinating reflection on my coaching career. For two decades, I've had the opportunity to witness many great performances by top athletes, including several NFL Hall of Fame players. In observing these elite athletes, I began to notice other contributing factors beyond mere talent and physical ability that influenced their success on and off the field. I noticed that the different energies an athlete devoted to the physical (regularity of training, effort level in the weight room, practice habits, diet), mental (film study, playbook recall, understanding assignments), social (accepting roles, being a good teammate) and spiritual (prayer, church, character, ability to remain grounded in a highly insecure and stressful profession) were equally effective indicators of overall success.

This book is a combination of both of those factors: 1) what I've learned, studied and researched on these topics, and 2) how the players I've coached and observed have successfully lived out these principles in their own lives. It's as much "my story" as it is a compilation of stories from all these different athletes.

Through the lens of story, this book uses biblical principles to teach you how to improve your performance both in sport and life—how to build your life on and off the field. That being said, this book isn't just for athletes and coaches. Although most of the stories come from the sports world, they could just as easily be applied to areas of business, family, personal development, etc.

This book *is* meant for people who have a heart for God—and for those who are searching. It's not a self-help book. These principles and strategies ultimately don't come from within ourselves, but from a higher power. To truly follow the recommendations in this book, you have to want to do better, to be better, as a follower of Jesus. This isn't about just "feeling good" or "feeling better about yourself;" it's about practical, tangible strategies for implementing *real* change.

Strengthening the mental, physical, spiritual and social building blocks has become an integral part of my life and work. I put my thoughts on paper to inspire others and provide tools for you to take your life to the next level. I can say confidently that the principles contained in this book have worked for me both personally and professionally. They've helped me and my family both grow closer to God *and* realize how much work we still have left to do. I pray God uses these stories and principles to bless your life and the lives of those around you.

THE FOUR BUILDING BLOCKS OF PERFORMANCE

"And Jesus grew in wisdom and stature, and in favor with God and man."
(Luke 2:52)

The first time I saw Kurt Warner throw a football was on opening day of the 1999 NFL season. His St. Louis Rams hosted my Baltimore Ravens inside of the Trans World Dome in downtown St. Louis. It was Warner's first NFL start at quarterback—and my first game as a head NFL strength coach. The anticipation grew with each tick of the pregame clock.

With a whole new coaching staff in Baltimore, we were ready to start a new season. After a full off-season of lifting, conditioning and game-planning, we had our first real opportunity to validate our training plan and efforts. And I knew the Rams felt the same. In pregame warm-ups, a St. Louis player turned to our bench and flexed his muscles. I smiled. Both sidelines emanated with the natural optimism that Week 1 in the NFL brings—that tangible sense of "this is our year"—and I was a part of it.

My confidence, in part, came from Warner. He wasn't supposed to be the Rams' Week 1 starter, but their lead quarterback, Trent Green, had torn his ACL just a week earlier.[1] We couldn't have asked for a much better situation to start the season. Not only was Warner a backup, but he was also completely untested—a lower-echelon, first-time NFL starter. Unknown to most football fans outside of Missouri, Warner had only thrown 11 NFL passes since going undrafted in 1994.[2] Leading an historically futile offense (they hadn't made the playoffs in 10 years) that had managed just four wins in 1998, the anonymous Warner stood no chance against our up-and-coming defense.

As you may know, that's *not* how this story unfolded.

As the game progressed, it quickly became clear that Kurt Warner would not remain anonymous for much longer. Playing with the poise and confidence of a veteran, he threw for 300 yards and three touchdowns to lead his Rams to an easy 27-10 victory.[3] In 48 frustrating minutes, the quarterback who'd spent the majority of his career in the Arena Football League, dismantled our defense and my confidence. I left the stadium extremely disappointed. What did a loss like this, to a team like this, to a quarterback like this, say about the future of our organization?

Well, as time would tell, not actually a whole lot. Ironically enough, the two teams that faced off in the Trans World Dome that Sunday—each finishing the previous season with losing records—quickly became two of the NFL's best. In that same season, with an offense that became known as "The Greatest Show on Turf," the Rams defeated Steve McNair, Eddie George and the Tennessee Titans to win Super Bowl XXXIV. The following year, anchored by *our* league-leading *defense*, the Ravens beat the New York Giants to win Super Bowl XXXV. Although we didn't know it at the time, that Week 1 game in 1999 also served as the launching point for many Hall-of-Fame careers—including the untested, anonymous quarterback wearing No. 12 on the opposite sideline.

Not only did Kurt Warner lead the Rams to the 1999 Super Bowl—winning the regular season and Super Bowl MVP awards along the way—but during his 12 NFL seasons, he also earned a *second* MVP award, two First Team All-Pro nominations and became the first quarterback to throw 300 or more yards in three Super Bowls.[4] These feats, along with several NFL records, eventually earned Warner a spot in the Pro Football Hall of Fame in 2017.

Warner's success didn't end on the field. On top of gracing multiple *Sports Illustrated* covers, he authored books, guest-starred on TV shows, won humanitarian awards, earned financial freedom and supported a loving, healthy family.[5]

So, what changed? How did Kurt Warner go from being undrafted in 1994 to NFL MVP, just five years later?

From Hy-Vee to the Hall of Fame: Point A to Point B

In 1994, after going undrafted and eventually getting cut from the Green Bay Packers' training camp, Kurt Warner fell a few steps short of his NFL dream. He'd earned the attention of NFL scouts—and was told he had enormous *potential*—but ultimately was dismissed because "he wasn't ready to be an NFL quarterback."[6] Warner began to question himself and his NFL dreams. In the meantime, he returned to the University of Northern Iowa—where he'd played college football—as a graduate assistant. Since the GA position didn't afford him a livable income, Warner took the night shift bagging groceries at the local Hy-Vee for a minimum wage of $5.50/hour.[7]

Between Hy-Vee in 1994 and the Trans World Dome in 1999, Warner developed four key areas of his life: physical, mental, social and spiritual.

In a matter of months, Warner had transitioned from NFL training camp to a grocery store in Cedar Falls, Iowa. Despite his humble financial position (his "Point A"), though, Warner held onto his vision of taking snaps in a sold-out NFL stadium (his "Point B"). "Something's got to change," he told himself.[8] And he went to work.

Between Hy-Vee in 1994 and the Trans World Dome in 1999, Warner developed four key areas of his life: physical, mental, social and spiritual. By focusing on all *four* facets, Warner created a solid foundation that propelled him to unprecedented success, both on and off the field:

- **PHYSICAL.** After rejection from the Packers, Warner played three seasons in the low-prestige Arena Football League (AFL), which allowed him to sharpen and develop his skills. Playing on a smaller field with fewer players required a faster pace of play, and the unique environment helped Warner develop a quicker, more accurate release.

- **MENTAL.** At the quarterback position, the AFL taught Warner to make fast reads and instant decisions. With less time in the pocket, he needed to rely more on his instincts for success. And with that success, his mental toughness increased by playing in a variety of key situations and pressure-packed games (including two ArenaBowl appearances).

- **SOCIAL.** As he trained himself physically and mentally, Warner also recognized the importance of relationships and the people with whom he surrounded himself. He expanded his "team" by becoming a husband and father—marrying his girlfriend of six years and legally adopting her two children.[9] His life, his dreams and his goals were no longer just about him. Even while pursuing his "Point B" of playing in the NFL, he went "all in" as a husband and father.

- **SPIRITUAL.** The most significant change Warner made was investing in his relationship with God. While playing in the AFL for the Iowa Barnstormers, Warner joined a Bible study with some of his teammates. After seeking answers to his spiritual beliefs in the Bible, he committed his life to Jesus.[10] As he invested in and strengthened this relationship with God, he developed a sense of peace and inner strength. As he put it: "Any power or peace I [felt], on the football field or otherwise, is because of my faith and my relationship with Jesus."[11]

All of these changes and developments moved Warner up what I call the "performance curve." As you'll see below, the chart segments a population by performance through a simple bell-shaped curve—the x-axis representing performance with the y-axis measuring volume, or number of people. Depending on the area of evaluation, "performance" might mean GPA, salary or max bench-press, but regardless, the same pattern exists. The majority of people land somewhere in the middle—average, slightly below average or slightly above average—with each end of the curve representing the extreme under- and over-achievers.

THE PERFORMANCE CURVE

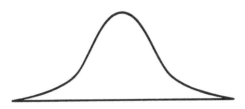

Among the NFL population, in terms of raw talent, skill level and *potential*, there isn't much difference between those on the far *left* of the performance curve (low performance) and those on the far *right* (high performance). To even earn a chance to *play* in the NFL, after all, you need a certain level of talent and ability, so everyone starts at a relatively similar "Point A." Yet, despite the minimal disparity in potential, overall *performance* can vary vastly from player to player.

Take salary, for example. In the NFL, a player's salary typically correlates with their performance level, as players get paid (mainly) for their productivity on the field. The more productive the player, the higher the salary. In the NFL population, the lower end of the curve might represent young prospects on practice squads or aging veterans on minimum salaries. In the center, at the peak of the curve, you'll find the majority of NFL players—dependable starters who are well-paid, but still land outside the realm of top-salaried players. Players to the far right of the curve are the game-changers—those at the top of their profession. Because of their performance on the field—and those intangible factors off of it—they earn the most lucrative contracts.

As most NFL players, like Kurt Warner, come to learn, making small tweaks to move up the performance curve can provide significant advantages. And this applies to all areas of life—not just football. Although you've probably never been featured on the cover of *SI*, most of us are more like Warner than we think. We all have goals we want to accomplish. We all have areas that need development. We all aspire to move up the performance curve, to reach that upper echelon of our profession or field of expertise. The first task in accomplishing those goals is to define reality (your Point A) and then determine your ideal performance goal (your Point B). After that, all you need to figure out is how to get there.

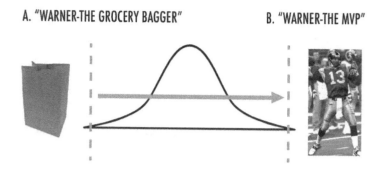

So, what will get us where we need to go? What separates the far left of the performance curve from the far right? What distinguishes elite, game-changing players like Kurt Warner, Ray Lewis and Cris Carter from the average NFL athlete? Or, in other words, *what fuels peak performance?*

The Four Building Blocks of Performance

For more than 25 years, I've trained athletes in the NCAA and NFL as a strength and conditioning coach. Since 1992, I've coached for Northwestern University (1992-1996), the Minnesota Vikings (1996-1999), the Baltimore Ravens (1999-2008), the Cincinnati Bengals (2010-2018) and two start-up professional football leagues (UFL and XFL). In the weight room, on the practice field and under the lights on game day, my career has centered around helping athletes move from Point A to Point B on the performance curve.

Along that journey, I've learned if I want to be successful at helping athletes achieve their goals, my focus needs to extend beyond the gym. For two decades, I've watched athletes grow and develop from "mediocre" to "good" and from "good" to "great." After coaching and observing every kind of athlete, the distinction between "good" and "great" slowly became clear—what sets great athletes apart and pushes them into the upper echelon goes well beyond mere talent and physical ability.

Think about it. You don't have to look far to find someone in peak *physical* shape but lacking in other areas, just drive to your local fitness center. On the other hand, you probably know plenty of people who've excelled in business or education or social status but seem to neglect physical fitness and nutrition. People's *strengths* are almost always matched by counterbalancing *weaknesses* and obstacles to achieving their overall peak performance.

This isn't just something I've passively observed in the athletes I've coached, either. I've had to learn this myself, right alongside them. For large parts of my life, I've hyper-focused on the physical—on training, conditioning and keeping my body healthy—all the while undervaluing and even neglecting key components of my development as coach, husband, parent and man of God.

There's a Bible verse at the end of Luke 2 that I think illustrates this well: "And Jesus grew in **wisdom** and **stature**, and in **favor with God** and **man**" (Luke 2:52). Notice the comprehensive nature of this description of Jesus. Although most of us would probably place Jesus in the "spiritual" category, Luke takes it a step further. Yes, he notes that Jesus is "in favor with God" (spiritual), but he also mentions his growth in "wisdom" (mental), "stature" (physical) and "favor with man" (social).

Being fully God, it's fairly clear why being "in favor with God" would be important for Jesus, but what about His social development in teaching His disciples and interacting with His followers? Or the mental fortitude He needed to engage the religious leaders? Think even about His physical development and what He endured on the day of His crucifixion. If Jesus is our example to follow—He is for me—then this is our roadmap. This is our guide to moving from "good" to "great," to achieving peak performance.

Kurt Warner exemplifies this well. To get from Hy-Vee to the Hall of Fame, he didn't build his foundation on *just* physical development, or even physical *and* mental development. He took a comprehensive approach in four key areas—what I call the "Four Building Blocks of Performance." As highlighted in Warner's life, they are the following:

- **PHYSICAL.** The physical building block refers to the body—how we train it, how we take care of it, what we put into it and how we let it recover. Through fitness, practice habits, nutrition and rest, developing the physical building block focuses on gaining the necessary levels of strength, power, speed, conditioning and flexibility to perform a given task. Depending on who you are, your ultimate goal might be throwing a football 50 yards, running a marathon or simply living long enough to watch your grandkids grow.

- **MENTAL.** The mental building block refers to the mind—how we understand it, develop it, control it and utilize it. Through goal setting, education, emotional development and positive self-talk, enhancing the mental building block increases the mind's ability to process available information, learn from it and make informed decisions. When we develop our minds, we increase our understanding of both ourselves and the world around us.

- **SOCIAL.** The social building block refers to relating and interacting with people. Through character, relationships, community and love, improving our social building block helps us understand ourselves, value other people's perspectives and respect our differences. It capitalizes on our innate desire for relationship, community and love—how to cultivate these things in our own life and help provide them for others. Social growth empowers us to follow our God-given purpose to love and live in relationship with others.

- **SPIRITUAL.** The spiritual building block refers to our relationship with God. It is the most important of the building blocks and the foundation on which all other growth is built. Spiritual issues examine the deep, underlying questions of life: Where did I come from? What gives life meaning? How do I determine right from wrong? Where do we go when we die?[12] Our spiritual growth determines our direction not only in this life, but also beyond.

The four building blocks are both essential and interdependent. They influence and rely upon each other. Like a chair, with its four legs, provides balanced support for the person who sits in it, so the four building blocks provide balanced development, growth and support in one's professional and personal life. To maximize performance and experience the best of this life (and beyond), all the building blocks need to be addressed sufficiently and comprehensively.

Unlike the NFL, there's no offseason when it comes to building a strong foundation. Throughout this book, you'll hear examples—from myself and from athletes I've coached—of how neglecting or over-focusing on one or multiple areas can lead to lack of balance and overall development. It's not enough to focus *somewhat* or *some of the time* on each of the building blocks; peak performance results from balanced, intentional, consistent time and effort.

Don't get me wrong, you can lack balance in your building blocks and still be a great athlete or top-performing salesperson. But, if you're not healthy in *all four areas*, you'll undershoot your potential. Have you ever met a person who was physically strong but didn't have the spiritual fortitude to sustain life's daily struggles? Their potential was thwarted. Or someone who was exceptionally intelligent, but not well-respected because their personal integrity was in question? Potential underachieved. Without focus on all four areas, you'll always fall short of your peak performance.

> *Throughout this book, you'll hear examples—from myself and from athletes I've coached—of how neglecting or over-focusing on one or multiple areas can lead to lack of balance and overall development.*

These building blocks have revolutionized and re-energized my coaching approach to be more holistic, maximizing success on and off the field for myself and the athletes I've coached. Because of what I've learned, I have committed to sharing the value in developing all four aspects of a strong foundation, not just the physical. This has led to dialogue about the importance of each key area and has created opportunities for athletes to assess strengths and limitations of their own performance. This is what I aim to teach you through this book.

The Journey Ahead

This book contains 16 chapters, divided into four sections based on the four building blocks. Each section includes four chapters, representing a different, essential aspect of that particular building block. In each chapter, I'll pull back the curtain to give you an inside look on the lives of athletes I've coached over the years—and lessons from their lives that relate to each principle. These stories will highlight how these extraordinary individuals used their well-developed building blocks to win in sport and life.

Beyond the stories of these college and professional athletes, the chapters are divided into four additional segments:

1. **Coach's Corner:** In this section, you'll find my personal perspective on that chapter's story and particular principle, as well as stories and practical application from my own life and coaching experience.

2. **Foundation Building Tip:** This is the one (or few) key takeaway(s) and application point(s) based on the lessons and truths of that chapter. As the name suggests, it's meant to help you *build your foundation* on the four blocks.

3. **Your Workout:** This section will provide a combination of thought-provoking questions, goal-setting prompts and tangible action steps all aimed at applying what you learn toward developing each of the four building blocks. If you're a coach, of any kind, you can use these questions for your players. As with most things in life, you'll get out of it what you put into it.

4. **Extra Workout Challenge:** The EWC is for those who want to dive deeper. In this final section, you'll be challenged beyond the basic action steps, to connect lessons from different building blocks and go the extra mile toward fulfilling your potential and achieving peak performance.

All of these sections are designed to provide you with steps to further grow and develop your building blocks. This book isn't an exhaustive review of the physical, mental, social and spiritual areas of life, yet through stories of athletes, personal reflection and practical application, you will learn more how to identify the areas hindering your performance and/or that of those you coach. As you read each chapter, you'll be able to evaluate whether potential cracks exist in your foundation. You'll also learn to enhance each building block, and to direct your focus on the areas that need the most attention.

Don't just view this as a book, but as a manual for learning, soul-searching and goal setting. Take notes to reinforce what you're learning. Growth requires action. Be proactive! Use the foundation building tips and workouts to create change in your life and fill in the gaps that keep you from experiencing a breakthrough in performance. If you listen and apply these principles and techniques, I promise you will grow physically, mentally, socially and spiritually. And, in doing so, you'll learn to maximize success on and off the field.

Don't just view this as a book, but as a manual for learning, soul-searching and goal setting.

In the end, this content is for YOU—it's designed to help you grow, develop and flourish in all areas of your life. But, as I've learned in my coaching career, almost anything you learn personally, you'll also bring into your interaction with others. In that sense, we're all "coaches." Whether it's as a teacher, parent, sibling, co-worker, friend or actual "coach," we all have opportunities to help others move up the performance curve alongside us. We all need others to help us travel from where we are to where we want to go.

Dedicating myself to developing these four building blocks has changed my life, both personally and professionally. It's kept me steady up the hills and down the valleys of my life and career. From the euphoria of winning a Super Bowl at the age 33 to the embarrassment of being fired—not once, but twice. From the accomplishment of being voted NFL Strength Coach of the Year by my peers to the rejection of failing to land a job in the NFL hiring cycle. From the elation of fathering a beautiful baby girl to the solace of watching her grow up with depression and anxiety. Without a strong physical, mental, social and spiritual foundation, I wouldn't have stayed the course in both the prosperous and difficult times of life.

I hope you enjoy this journey and reading the stories of some of the athletes I've had the privilege of coaching. I trust you will discover what I, and many of these athletes, have learned and experienced. Now it's your turn.

BUILDING BLOCK 1

SECTION 1: PHYSICAL BUILDING BLOCK

As a strength and conditioning coach, the physical building block seems like a natural place to start. Naturally, this building block is all about your physical body. Whether or not you're an athlete, physical growth and development is critical for achieving peak performance. Whether that's throwing a football, losing weight or living a long, healthy life, we all have goals that require intentionality in this building block.

Beyond performance, as human beings created in the image of God, we have a responsibility to devote attention to physical care and development. We only have one body, and as God's vessels, it's important we steward our bodies well. We accomplish this through:

- **Chapter 1: Fitness** - the capacity of an individual to perform sustained effort through the development of cardiovascular and muscular systems.

- **Chapter 2: Practice Habits** - the physical acts of self-preparation by repeating an activity or skill with intention.

- **Chapter 3: Nutrition** - the nourishment of the body and obtaining the essential nutrients in their proper amounts.

• **Chapter 4: Rest** - self-care and allowing the body to restore its proper and necessary energy.

The physical building block is both about *what we do* with our bodies as well as *what we put into* our bodies. Physical training, exercise, healthy eating and proper rest allow us to utilize our gifts and talents to execute our God-given purpose. We are better prepared to counteract the daily battles of life—anxiety, depression, fatigue, exhaustion, competition, etc.—when we are physically fit. In doing so, we increase our physical capacity, progress toward physical goals and boost our long-term health. Lack of physical activity and care increases our risk for a variety of health problems and outflows into all areas of our life and growth.

Physical development touches each of the four building blocks. Good physical health is part of a balanced lifestyle. Mentally, proper exercise, nutrition and rest boost our mental energy, productivity and attentiveness. Socially, physical growth can boost self-confidence, increase social energy and decrease irritability and impatience with others. Spiritually, our bodies are God's temples, so when we respect our physical state, we honor God.

Like the other building blocks, physical progress is only achieved through hard work, self-discipline and intentionality. You are responsible for your physical health—an essential facet of fulfilling your potential and achieving peak performance.

CHAPTER 1: FITNESS

"For physical training is of some value, but godliness has value for all things." (1 Timothy 4:8)

Everyone in the stadium knew what was coming, but it didn't matter. Every time, without fail, crowds gathered, both in the stands and on the field, as the electricity grew inside of M&T Stadium in Baltimore. As he danced his way out of the tunnel—despite it happening dozens of times before—the atmosphere exploded.

In one swift, powerful motion, he raised both arms in the air before throwing them down toward the ground and raising his right knee high in the air—fists clenched tightly, jaws open wide, balancing his body easily on his left foot. Fueled by the noise of the crowd and his teammates, No. 52 unleashed a roar that seemed to rise above the collective chorus of pandemonium. His teammates swarmed him—shouting, jumping and devouring his vivacity and pure love for the game. In an instant, everyone in the stadium wearing purple was cheering as if their Ravens had already won the game. On our sideline, I felt my own heart beating faster.

Ray Lewis had stepped onto the field.

During my tenure with the Ravens, Lewis was our leader. As the heart and soul of our team, Lewis set the tone for how hard the team worked, how prepared we were on game day and how much heart we left on the field. His high energy and strong passion for the game were contagious. For player, coach and fan alike, there was no better feeling than the presence of Ray Lewis.

During his 17-year career as a middle linebacker for the Ravens, Lewis earned All-Pro honors 12 times. He was also a two-time Super Bowl champion (XXXV and XLVII), Super Bowl MVP (2000), two-time NFL Defensive Player of the Year and member of the 2000s All-Decade Team.[1]

On top of the accolades and awards, Lewis electrified crowds and energized his teammates with his play-making ability on the field. For nine years, I watched him wreak havoc on great running backs across the league. In one game against the Cincinnati Bengals, our Lewis-led defense suffocated running back Corey Dillon to the tune of nine yards on 12 attempts. A few weeks later, Dillon set an NFL single-game record with 278 rushing yards.[2]

> **By developing his body, Lewis increased his physical capacity, progressed toward his goals and boosted his long-term health.**

Great leaders lead by example, and that's exactly what Lewis did. You'd only need to watch one game—or one quarter—to recognize that. But what some people may *not* realize was that, behind the scenes, underneath all of the success, show-stopping plays and leadership, was Lewis' commitment to physical fitness.

Physical fitness is the capacity of an individual to perform sustained effort through the development of cardiovascular and muscular systems. Physical training provides the endurance and energy required to perform daily tasks—and to perform the daily tasks of an NFL linebacker like Lewis, the intensity of training needs to match the desired output.

On several occasions, I found both seasoned and less experienced players circled around Lewis on the matted floor of our weight room. They were testing their grit against his infamous abdominal workout. What started as a handful of players eventually morphed into a full-blown competition between 10 to 20 guys who all wanted to keep up with Ray Lewis. Who all wanted to—sit-up for sit-up—match his extraordinary fitness regimen. Before they started, I always warned the players that, if they wanted to participate, they had to be willing to pay the price of stiff, sore abs the next day.

By developing his body, Lewis increased his physical capacity, progressed toward his goals and boosted his long-term health. This dedication and discipline started from a young age.

When he was 15 years-old, Lewis asked his mom for a deck of cards. She thought he wanted to gamble, so she said, "Junior, I don't gamble in my house. Ain't no cards coming in my house." But that's not why young Ray wanted the deck:

"I never saw a woman take so much physical abuse than the way I saw my mother beaten every day of my life. But I [couldn't] help her because I [wasn't] strong enough...I said, 'Ma, I need a deck of cards.'"

To fight the pain of what he saw, Lewis took that deck to the garage—he wasn't allowed to live in the house at that time—and started flipping cards. If the card was a six, he'd do six push-ups. If the next card was a face card, he'd do 10. An ace, 25. Joker, 50. Lewis went through the whole deck like this, reshuffled and did the same thing with sit-ups. That was his workout—and he stuck with it. He used the same workout throughout his NFL career—he just added more decks.

"I wanted to make sure sports weren't the reason I started training. It was to make sure a man never put his hands on my mom again...That's why I started doing what I started doing. Sports were a byproduct of what people started to see...If you can find a way to push through pain, there's something greater on the other side of it...The greatest pain of my life is the reason I'm standing here today."[3]

Out of love for his mother, Lewis dedicated himself to physical fitness. He had a unique endurance, an inner strength, that enabled him to face any difficulty without quitting. His growth in stature and physical capacity led to opportunities in sports. And in 1996, the Ravens gave Lewis the ultimate opportunity, drafting him with their second of two first-round picks and setting the stage for his Hall-of-Fame career as a middle linebacker in the NFL.

As a middle linebacker, he had to line up five, seven or ten yards in front of an offensive player and run into him at full speed. He had to dedicate his body for every play. To provide perspective on the intensity of impact, biomedical engineers at Tulane University did a study. The study compared a full speed hit by an NFL linebacker to that of a person balancing on the crossbar of a goal post and swan diving to the turf with nothing to absorb the impact but their flesh and bones. Repeat that crash 15 to 20 more times during a three-hour period, rotating the impact from your left side, right side, back and head, and that's the physical toll Lewis could deliver (and absorb) on any given Sunday. A 2,500-pound car generates the same amount of energy traveling at 5.75 mph.[4]

In one matchup against the Tennessee Titans, all throughout the game, Lewis pounded Titans' All-Pro running back Eddie George. For four quarters, Lewis hit George so hard that, after the game, our defensive back, Chris McAlister, told *Sports Illustrated* that George "folded up like a baby."[5]

How'd Lewis do it? Beyond the fuel from his childhood, beyond his dedication, beyond his work ethic—how did he properly train his body into a Pro Bowl, Super Bowl Champion, Pro Football Hall of Fame middle linebacker?

The strength, explosiveness and endurance Lewis possessed and exhibited on the field was acquired through strict training. He became a master over his body by developing the requisite amount of fitness needed to allow him to compete at the highest level. He developed his cardiovascular system to provide stamina, and he strengthened his muscles to protect his body and improve his speed and power. Lewis always went the extra mile. He consistently stayed after practice to run, particularly during training camp. His disciplined approach to intense exercise at uncomfortable levels built the mental and physical toughness required for NFL success.

> **"People only get old because [they] stop taking care of [their] bodies...We believe that once we get to a certain age, we shouldn't physically take care of our bodies. But you can be as strong as you want to be if you maintain."**

To fine-tune his off-season conditioning, Lewis constantly adjusted his exercise regimen to incorporate different modes of exercise. His workout schedule included weightlifting, running, kickboxing, wrestling, spin cycling and swimming.

"Every year it was a different challenge," Lewis told *Newsday* in 2012. "How do I want to challenge my body? How do I want to get better? It was always evolving."[6]

During the offseason, after finishing our workouts, Lewis would take a few guys to either run hills, swim or spin, before heading back to his house to watch film. Whatever methods he focused on, Lewis always showed up in great physical condition. It's something in which he took great pride.

"Nobody's as serious about health and fitness as me, and staying fit is my top priority," Lewis said. "How can I live longer? How can I feel better? If I can take care of my body when I am young, it will take care of me when I'm old."[7]

It's nothing short of remarkable Lewis lasted as long as he did, staying in Baltimore for his entire 17-year career. Not only that, but he *maintained* a high level of play every year from 1996 to 2012, when he retired.

"People only get old because [they] stop taking care of [their] bodies," Lewis told *Newsday* at age 37.[8] "We believe that once we get to a certain age, we shouldn't physically take care of our bodies. But you can be as strong as you want to be if you maintain."[9]

Ravens' general manager, Ozzie Newsome, had this to say about 37-year-old Lewis in 2012, "His change of direction, his burst and quickness, they're all there. I've watched the evolution of a young man over the years and seen how he continues to stay ahead of the curve."[10]

As a veteran, in 2011, Lewis earned his *13th* Pro Bowl nomination, and in his last game as an NFL player, he led the Ravens to victory in Super Bowl XLVII. With a deck of cards and an internal drive as his trainer, Lewis developed his body to become a playmaker, a leader and one of the greatest linebackers to ever play the game.

Coach's Corner

From an early age, we're taught the importance of physical activity. Whether in gym class or recreational sports growing up, the value of physical exercise is taught, emphasized and reiterated by our coaches, parents and role models from the moment we start walking. I'm guessing you've probably never questioned the importance of your physical health. And it's no surprise, either—talk to any doctor, and you'll quickly learn the short- and long-term benefits of exercising and training your body.

- **CAPACITY.** Physical training provides the necessary endurance and energy to adequately and exceedingly perform daily tasks. Beyond that, it helps us utilize our God-given talents to achieve greater purpose in our lives. In the case of Ray Lewis, his dedication to physical training allowed him to perform the "daily tasks" of hitting opposing players with the force of a moving car…for 17 straight years.

- **GOALS.** Physical fitness pushes us to meet and exceed our physical goals. Whether your goals are to run a marathon, bench-press 300 pounds or lose 15, these benchmarks are achieved through a commitment to fitness. For Lewis, as a teenager, his push-ups led to opportunities in sports, and as an NFL player, his continued dedication to exercise led to one of the greatest NFL careers of all-time.

- **HEALTH.** Most importantly, regular physical activity improves our health and reduces risk of heart disease, diabetes, high blood pressure, colon cancer, depression and anxiety.[11] Consistent exercise also helps control weight, builds and maintains healthy bones, muscles and joints, and reduces the risk of falling.[12] Even though our chronological age is fixed, we can adjust our *biological* age with physical training.[13] Researchers say inactive people may be up to 10 years older *biologically* than their active counterparts.[14] An exercise program, helps us feel better, sleep better and improves our disposition.[15]

Despite this awareness—and the medical evidence to back it up—the majority of people are physically undertrained. They don't get the proper amount of health-enhancing physical activity. According to a 2018 report from the Centers for Disease Control and Prevention, less than a quarter of Americans met all national physical activity guidelines.[16] So why the disconnect?

In short, excuses. Whether it's a lack of time to exercise, lack of effort to produce results or lack of patience to keep working until results are visible, physical fitness often takes a backseat to excuses and other priorities in life. Too often, people take a *reactive* rather than a *proactive* approach to physical health. We gain weight, *then* we start going to the gym. Our blood pressure increases, *then* we start exercising regularly. We wait for a negative consequence before we recognize our need for physical fitness—and sometimes, it's already too late.

Fortunately, a simple exercise program can help you achieve results with less effort and time than you might expect. Although most of us don't need to match Ray Lewis' exercise regimen, we can all learn from his example and approach to physical health. To establish a regular exercise routine, follow three simple steps.

First, identify your purpose for physical activity. Like Ray Lewis as a 15-year-old, you need to find something to motivate you toward physical fitness…beyond a last-minute New Years' resolution. If you have a set vision for *why* you're doing *what* you're doing—whether it's washboard abs, a starting spot on the team or living to see your grand-kids graduate college—you'll be able to more easily get started and maintain activity levels when your routine loses its initial appeal. For Lewis, his purpose was first rooted in protecting his mother. Then, after he grew and started playing sports, his purpose expanded to include playing college and professional football, and eventually, to holding the Vince Lombardi trophy.

In his book, *Twilight of the Idols*, German philosopher Friedrich Nietzsche said, "Those who have a 'why' to live can bear with almost any 'how.'"[17] If we have a vision for where we want to go—and we commit to aligning ourselves to that vision—we'll be able to push through those tough exercises, extra reps and early-morning workouts. Identify your purpose and it will motivate you to success.

Lewis understood this process well. He encouraged rookies to have a purpose—not just to train because they had to, but because it could make them better. Purpose not only motivates us toward physical health, but on the flip side, physical fitness allows us to achieve our purpose.

Second, find an activity you love—and do it! We handcuff ourselves when we think our only path to physical health is in the gym and on the treadmill. If we aren't enjoying what we're doing, motivation to persevere will only decrease. Fortunately for us, there are plenty of opportunities to find activities that 1) we enjoy and 2) keep us physically active. For Lewis, it was playing middle linebacker. For you, it might be walks with friends or family, recreational sports or biking to work. Whatever the case, there's no excuse to skip exercise because "we don't like running on the treadmill."

Finally, keep it simple and stay consistent. Lewis' use of playing cards to count reps of basic exercises, such as push-ups, sits-ups or body weight squats, is as simple as it gets. Physical activity doesn't require fancy equipment or large amounts of time. The American College of Sports Medicine suggests a person accumulate "150 minutes of moderate-intensity, or 75 minutes of vigorous-intensity aerobic physical exercise each week."[18] That's like an episode of T.V. per day. They also recommend muscle-strengthening activities on two (or more) days per week. Strength training prevents the loss of muscle tissue, enables us to burn more calories and leads to improved psychological well-being. Without strength training, you will lose between 5 and 7 pounds[19] of muscle and decrease your metabolic rate by 2 to 5 percent every decade.[20]

And once you get started, establish regular, consistent rhythms of activity. Results don't happen overnight; they're achieved over time. Anyone can set lofty goals, but without hard-work, preparation and self-discipline, those goals will fizzle out to nothing in a matter of weeks. For you, it might be helpful to set a regular schedule of 1) when you're going to exercise, 2) what you're going to do and 3) how long you're going to do it.

The importance of exercise shouldn't be undervalued, but it should also be taken in moderation. Like anything in life, if too much focus on an activity or behavior starts to negatively impact you or those around you, it may be more harmful than good. We need to remember: the physical is just *one* of the four comprehensive building blocks of performance. No, it shouldn't be ignored, but if we overcompensate and swing too far the other way, we risk neglecting a balanced, complete approach to growth and development.

Dr. Peter Ganshirt, sports psychologist who consulted for the Bengals when I was in Cincinnati, explains, "We go through the day to experience positive emotion." According to Dr. Ganshirt, some players spend too much time working out in the gym because they may not be getting positive emotional input elsewhere in their life. Growing up, I had to learn this the hard way.

It started in my early teenage years, when my mother saw me without a shirt and flippantly told me I had "a flat chest." Although she might not have meant much by it, that comment stuck with me—even to this day. Subconsciously, those words spurned me on to a lifetime of energy devoted to physical fitness. Building my body allowed me to mask my insecurity and low self-confidence. My body became my stronghold. I wanted to be good at something, so having a good physique allowed me to gain respect, be liked and feel good about myself. In one sense, that comment gave me a purpose for being fit, but because of my limited perspective, I let it get out of control.

In high school, my passion for physical fitness turned into an obsession. On one occasion, I remember one of my best friends, who was our high school's Spirit Committee chairman, organized a pep rally for the entire student body. It only happened once a year, and since we were seniors, this was our last chance to attend. He'd wanted me to be there, but because I just "had" to get in my weight-training workout, I chose to skip it. Since the weight room was located directly beneath the gymnasium, where the pep rally was held, I could hear and feel the roar of the student body while I lifted. In that moment, I realized I'd let my friend down. Everyone attended the pep rally except me. While I strengthened my physical building block that day, my social building block took a hit.

A few years ago, my pastor gave our congregation a challenge for the coming week. He asked us to sacrifice something in one area of our lives in order to grow in other areas. Right away, I felt the conviction to give up physical exercise, but I couldn't do it, even for a week. After I failed to meet my pastor's challenge, I realized the strain my commitment to physical fitness had caused in other areas of my life.

My inability to divert energy from one building block to another reminded of a verse in Paul's first letter to Timothy: "For physical training is of some value, but godliness has value for all things, holding promise for both the present life and the life to come" (1 Timothy 4:8).

Achieving peak performance is comprehensive—it's about dedication to all four building blocks—and without the full picture, we'll always end up short of our potential.

Physical training had become my idol. My loyalty to it was greater than my loyalty to God. My behaviors centered around the lure of the health benefits and positive emotions evoked from a workout. Had I substituted my weekly workouts by spending time with God that week, I would have gained spiritual health and improved my relationship with Jesus. Likewise, had I supported my friend and attended my high school pep rally, I would have invested in our relationship. Growth in these areas would have been more significant for the daily demands that lay ahead.

In all these areas of growth, it's critical we don't lose sight of the bigger picture. Achieving peak performance is comprehensive—it's about dedication to all four building blocks—and without the full picture, we'll always end up short of our potential.[21] Like Paul said to Timothy, physical fitness is valuable, but it loses its value if we forget our larger purpose in life.

In ancient Greece, athletes trained for ten months with purpose and discipline to compete in the Olympic Games. Their prize if they won? A wreath filled with wild olive leaves. After months of hard work and self-discipline, all they had to show for their efforts was a pile of withered leaves! Like that wreath, our bodies will all eventually lose vitality and deteriorate. If our only purpose for physical fitness is just that— the physical—then our prize will only be temporary. But if we train with purpose and endurance to achieve God's purpose for our lives, He provides a prize that will last for eternity.

Foundation Building Tip

By definition, physical fitness is the capacity of an individual to perform sustained effort through the development of cardiovascular and muscular systems. Fitness equips us with the necessary physical tools to work toward our God-given purpose.

Athletes train diligently to acquire the levels of speed, stamina, strength, power and flexibility required for peak performance. This is only achieved through hard work, self-discipline and grueling preparation. Take responsibility for your fitness level by identifying your purpose, finding activities you love and keeping it simple. In doing so, you'll increase your physical capacity, progress toward your physical goals and boost your long-term health.

Your Workout

1. Identify how much physical activity you currently get

each week. Include walking your dog, yard work and house cleaning. Adding up how many times you go up and down stairs to grab a snack doesn't count! If you're falling short of the national physical activity guidelines, develop a game plan to ensure you reach a minimum of 150 minutes of physical activity each week. Remember, be specific and reasonable. If you are currently involved in a structured fitness routine, that's great! Keep up the good work!

2. What is your struggle in maintaining good physical condition? Why don't you exercise how much/how often as you should? To help yourself, identify a purpose for your physical activity. Take some time to really think through and answer the question: *Why do I want to be physically fit?* Write it down and post it somewhere visible every time you exercise.

3. Find (at least) one activity you enjoy and incorporate it into your regular fitness plan. Whether it's hiking, softball or walking with a friend, allow it to motivate you to stay committed throughout the week. If you already have one, consider adding another. Push yourself to expand your physical capacity!

4. Never be out of shape. Stay active by performing some type of cardiovascular exercise three days per week. Muscles are inactive when seated for long periods of time (e.g., watching TV, studying, playing video games, working at a desk, etc.). Stay active by standing up, walking or riding a bike to promote blood flow and increase muscle activity.

5. Find a partner to join you in your commitment to fitness. Exercise together, set mutual goals, communicate regularly and hold each other accountable to stick to your game plans.

Extra Workout Challenge

1. Examine your motives behind physical fitness. For what crown or prize are you striving? Are you putting more weight on your physical appearance and what others think about you than the heart God desires for you? Are you aiming for a crown that will fade away or one that will last through eternity?

2. For me, I placed overemphasis on the physical building block. I sacrificed mental, social and spiritual growth because of my hyper focus on training my body. Where might you be focusing too much/not enough energy? Where might you need to invest more time? And where might you need to pull back?

PHYSICAL

CHAPTER 2: PRACTICE HABITS

"Whatever you do, work at it with all your heart, as working for the Lord."
(Colossians 3:23)

I stood next to the dummy, pressing a football into its arm—and waiting. Waiting for 300-plus pounds of muscle, speed and adrenaline to come barreling through and around a gauntlet of dummies and head straight for me—well, straight for the football I was holding. Another typical day at the office of the Minnesota Vikings.

As assistant strength coach, I helped the defensive line coach execute certain drills during practice. For this drill, my job was to hold a football to a Velcro attachment on the arm of a pop-up tackling dummy, which represented the opposing quarterback. Since the Velcro was so worn-down from years of drills, it couldn't actually hold the weight of the ball. That's why I had to stand there, until the very last possible moment, and hold it in place—effectively turning me into another tackling dummy if I didn't get out of the way in time.

Each defensive lineman would start by performing various pass-rushing techniques around a series of dummies, spaced five yards apart, representing potential blockers. After they made their way through, they came to the fifth and final dummy, where I was stationed. Their objective? Tackle and strip the ball from the "opposing quarterback." And those linemen didn't hold back. They were in *game* mode. In fact, because of the pure adrenaline and force of those tacklers, we had to put a crash pad behind the last dummy to keep them from getting injured.

On this particular day, the dummy donned a green-and-gold No. 4 jersey—identical to the one worn by the quarterback of our next opponent and division rival, the Green Bay Packers. The linemen always had a little extra juice when they had a chance to tackle Super Bowl champion and then-future Hall-of-Famer, Brett Favre. Every d-lineman in purple and gold wanted a piece of The Gunslinger!

As I held the football, I noticed the power with which each player hit the dummies, knocking them completely on their side. The players moved with such speed and agility that it seemed like only a fraction of a second before they arrived where I was positioned. I held the football to the arm of the quarterback dummy as long as possible before the linemen tackled and simultaneously stripped the football from the dummy quarterback. Each player attacked the drill in the same manner—with intensity and explosiveness, but also with precision and technique. By the grace of God, I made it out with all my arms and legs.

Day after day, across all the positional groups, we'd run through drills similar to this, channeling strength, aggression and power into minutely detailed movements. And practice after practice, we'd repeat many of the same drills, movements and exercises. Over time, these drills became second nature for our players, and perfection became the *expectation*, not the goal.

The level of intensity for any given drill usually depended greatly on the commitment and example of the leaders in each positional group. The first player in line set the standard. For the Vikings' defensive linemen, that player was John Randle.

Despite his smaller stature (6-foot-1, 240 pounds) and Division II college resume entering the NFL, Randle became one of the greatest and most feared defensive linemen in NFL history. During his 14-year career, he earned seven Pro-Bowl appearances, six First-Team All-Pro awards, a spot on the 1990s NFL All-Decade Team and became the 14th undrafted player in NFL history elected to the Pro Football Hall of Fame.[1] As a tackle, Randle lined up on the inside of the defensive line against offensive centers, guards and tackles. So, not only did Randle record 137.5 sacks (one of 11 NFL players to accomplish the feat),[2] but he made many of those plays against a double-team of blockers.

All after going undrafted. After playing for a D-II school. After being "undersized for his position."

Randle's career is evidence that he wasn't handed any of the accolades associated with his name. What he accomplished on the field didn't result from talent or pedigree alone. When the Vikings signed Randle as an undrafted free agent in 1990, the odds were stacked against him. But over time, he developed a reputation as a tireless worker on the practice field and in the weight room.

Randle didn't see practice like some others did. To him, it wasn't something to complain about—it was an opportunity on which to capitalize: "Some see practice as a nuisance, but I saw it as a way of getting better," Randle said. "I went so hard in practice that when the game came, it was so much easier."[3]

> **Great players aren't made on game day; they're built on the practice field.**

Practice habits are the physical acts of self-preparation by repeating an activity or skill with intention. Through repetition in practice, we develop specific motor patterns that improve our proficiency over a period of time. Using muscle memory and mental pathways, practice habits reduce the chance of making mistakes on the field and preserve physical and mental energy to allow us to overcome more challenging and unpredictable situations in the future.

In 2006, Duke University conducted a study that estimated up to 40 percent of our everyday decisions are habitual.[4] From how we get out of bed to how we drive to work, we make a sizable portion of our daily decisions without really thinking. If we—intentionally or unintentionally—develop negative habits, we can seriously limit our performance potential. Thus, practice becomes all the more important. Great players aren't made on game day; they're built on the practice field. As Pro Football Hall-of-Fame Coach Tony Dungy put it, this is what separates the "champions" from the rest of the pack:

"Champions don't do extraordinary things. They do ordinary things, but they do them without thinking, too fast for the other team to react. They follow the habits they've learned."[5]

This is what made John Randle a great football player, a champion. Through consistency and dedication in *practice*, Randle grew into one of the most successful defensive players *on the field* in NFL history. His technique and movements were automatic—they transferred seamlessly from practice to the game. Using specific drills and executing them with precision and purpose, he bulked up from 240 to 290 pounds and amassed an arsenal of pass-rushing techniques and maneuvers.[6] What Randle lacked in initial size and talent, he made up for through self-discipline and practice.

Even when he left the weight room or practice field, Randle didn't give himself any room to build up rust. He practiced his moves wherever he went—on doorways, in his yard, even in the grocery store. Vikings' defensive line coach, John Teerlinck, remembers this story about Randle:

> *"One year, he took the cushions from an old couch and duct-taped them to the trees outside his home in Texas. He made a gauntlet that he'd go running through in the forest."*[7]

And another, one of Teerlinck's favorites:

> *"One time he was at Cub Foods, and there was a woman coming toward him in the aisle. He came running up to her and put a stutter-spin move on her cart. She froze. She didn't know what to think, so she started screaming and yelling for the manager."*

Randle knew what it felt to be undersized, undervalued and under-appreciated, so he used every situation to improve and perfect his skill. "People thought it was weird," said Randle. "But it was just me trying to get better at my job."[8]

Beyond the work he put in on his own time, at practice Randle had Pro Bowl-caliber teammates who surrounded him, pushed him and kept him accountable. Players like Hall-of-Fame offensive guard, Randall McDaniel. Because of their opposite positions on the line of scrimmage, Randle and McDaniel would often line up across from each other in practice. McDaniel, a first-round pick, was in his third year when the Vikings signed Randle, and he'd already made the Pro

Bowl the previous year. Right off the bat, Randle had his work cut out for him.

One day, in Randle's third year, he finally beat McDaniel in practice. Later, McDaniel would say:

"Johnny made me a Hall of Famer. I knew if I ever took a play off in practice, he would have embarrassed me."[9]

Not only did Randle's teammates push him toward greatness in practice, but in turn, he did the same for them. When players saw Randle working extremely hard in practice, it encouraged others to follow suit. He raised the level of our team. That's how he ended up at the front of the line during the strip-sack drill, barreling toward me and pop-up dummy Brett Favre. He led by example, and the example he set was achieved through hard work, intentionality and establishing effective, consistent habits on the practice field.

And none of these habits were random—just muscle and adrenaline operating at a high intensity—they were all calculated and purposeful. They had to be. Yes, Randle worked hard, but more importantly, he worked smart. By establishing effective practice habits, he took the next step beyond physical fitness. He not only trained his body, but he trained it in such a way as to maximize growth, development and potential. He regularly exemplified an understanding of the difference between what's called the "practical limit" of practice and the "physiological limit," as introduced by sport psychologist, Coleman Griffith.

Coleman Griffith is known in the U.S. as the father of sports psychology. In his 1928 book, *Psychology and Athletics*, he made a then-revolutionary observation about practice—one that still rings true today: "Many people confuse the practical limit of practice with the physiological limit. The practical limit…means that most of us are willing to stop practice when our practice refuses to yield large measures of progress."[10] The physiological limit, on the other hand, is the nervous system's *actual* capacity to learn. In other words, most people aren't maximizing their potential growth in practice. They're stopping short (practical limit) of their bodies' capacity. This doesn't mean we should necessarily practice "until we drop" (physiological limit)—because, in reality, we might achieve similar results with far less time and effort. Without knowing it, we may be wasting repetitions and effort for no future reward.

Take shooting baskets, for example. Say I'm in the gym for 10 or 15 minutes, making the majority of my shots. But then, all of a sudden, I go through a spell where I start to miss. For whatever reason, I don't have the same success, and I begin to lose sight of the fruits of my labor. That's the *practical limit* of practice—the point when I stop seeing clear, positive results. Many athletes will stop there, but say, on this particular day, I'm feeling extra motivated and decide to push through this obstacle. I keep shooting. I may get back into a rhythm and progress some more, but after a while, my mental and motor processes will start to break down. I might lose focus, or my shooting technique might falter. Maybe I let my elbow stick out and become misaligned with the basket, or I stop short and don't extend it on my follow-though. That's the physiological limit. At that point, I've stopped benefitting from the practice at all. All I'm doing for myself is reinforcing negative practice habits that may actually *hurt* me in the future, on game day.

Ultimately, it boils down to being efficient with practice. You might still make progress with extra time in the gym, but it won't be as time efficient. For example, in the weight room, I may get similar results with a 45-minute strength program as I could with 60 minutes. I might push a player a *little bit* further with the extended practice, but is that worth the extra 15 minutes? It really depends on the individual— which is why it's so important for coaches to know their athletes—but in general, Griffith would say, "no."[11]

Almost every learning process—physical or non-physical—is broken up by a series of plateaus. Learning is not uniform throughout training. We progress in spurts and plateau while our nervous system automates a new set of habits upon which further progress can be based. We learn through quick bursts before running into a barren period during which there seems to be no progress at all. We can't just keep pushing and pushing and expect our nervous system to keep up—it needs time to develop and adapt.[12]

Because of this, learning occurs not only in the practice session itself, but in the time between sessions. It starts in an initial, within-session improvement phase. After the initial practice session, there is a consolidation period, which can last up to several hours. Then, after continued practice, "slow" learning emerges, consisting of delayed, incremental gains in performance.[13]

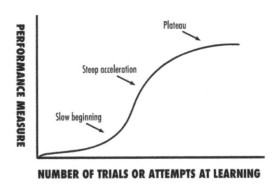

NUMBER OF TRIALS OR ATTEMPTS AT LEARNING

With physical training, especially, evidence of progress motivates us to keep going. That's why distributed practice (large gaps between sessions) has been found to be more beneficial than "massing" it all in one go (or, in other words, pushing until we hit our physiological limit). Griffith suggests that practice periods that exercise a *single skill* beyond 20 or 30 minutes without rest are unwise. For example, it's better to practice something for 15 minutes at the start of four separate hours—focusing on something else with the remaining 45 minutes of each hour—than it is to work on a skill for an hour straight through. In both cases, you're practicing for an hour, but distributing it through time creates a better memory of the skill—and more noticeable progress.[14] Just as you can change your biological age through physical fitness (see Chapter 1), you can also change your physiological limit through both fitness *and* effective practice habits. If the practice environment is structured in the most efficient manner, the physiological limits can be maximized and learning motor skills facilitated. This leads to longer, more effective practice void of undue mental and physical fatigue.[15]

In the 1910s, industrial managers, wanting their workers to be "maximally efficient," started insisting work be done in very particular ways. The problem was that, during the course of a long shift, these men couldn't maintain these new methods. Taking it upon themselves, the workers then made some changes—they rested some parts of their bodies while other parts carried the load. This shift allowed them to actually complete their work for the long hours required of them. The workers knew their own bodies better than their managers, and since no one person is proportioned exactly like another, there was no one routine that was "maximally efficient" for every worker. Practice—and work of any kind—needs to be individualized and to incorporate appropriate periods of rest.[16]

As coaches, it's important to know when to push past the practical limit to expand potential, but we also need to know our athletes well enough to keep them from diminishing returns and developing negative habits. No matter the practice schedule, it still comes down to putting in the time and repetitions that work best for the individual.

Instead of focusing on physical fitness alone—working and lifting and running until he physically couldn't continue—Randle aimed for the most efficient amount of practice required to master his specific skills. In doing so, he not only developed *those* skills, but he was able to dedicate the extra practice time to other areas that needed improvement. This is how he formed his practice habits. This is what led to the tackles, the sacks, the accolades. This is what made him a leader on the field. It all started in practice.

Randle found a practice regimen that enabled him to reach his body's unique performance limits because he was diligent and dedicated to his craft. He didn't end up in the Pro Football Hall of Fame by accident. He was rewarded because he put in an exorbitant amount of skill-specific training both with his team and outside of organized practices. He displayed the kind of work ethic and practice habits required for an undersized athlete to not only make it into the NFL, but also to become one of the premier pass rushers in NFL history. By tackling the pop-up dummy over and over in practice, Randle went on to sack Brett Favre—the *real* Brett Favre—12.5 times.[17]

Coach's Corner

As a strength and conditioning coach, most of my work was done in individual or small group workouts. It was a rarity for me to speak to the entire team. But on one occasion, when I coached for the Ravens, I had to present and demonstrate a simple drill for the whole squad. The content of my talk wasn't overly complex, but I took the situation seriously.

To prepare, I left the weight room through a back door to an isolated spot outside to practice my presentation. To my surprise, in the middle of my talk, voice frothing with emotion, one of our coaches turned the corner as he was going for a walk. He saw me rehearsing my speech. In my embarrassment, I quickly stopped speaking and pretended like I was just "enjoying the great outdoors." At the time, I felt ashamed for rehearsing something so trivial. In retrospect, though, I now realize my preparation reflected my commitment to my craft and desire to perform at my best. I practiced, quite literally, the same dedication I preached to the players in the weight room. If you want to achieve peak performance, you need to plan and execute in practice.

Last chapter, using the story of Ray Lewis, I talked about the importance of physical fitness—but physical fitness can only get you so far. Exercise *without* intentionality, preparation and consistency won't produce the same results as exercise *with* them. In order to maximize the effectiveness of physical activity and push closer to achieving your potential, you need to establish effective exercise rhythms and routines. You need a comprehensive, informed plan, and then stick to that plan.

John Randle provides us a good example in this arena. He was physically fit, yes, but more importantly, he was intentional, prepared and smart with his fitness. He designed and executed drills aimed at mastering hyper-specific skills. He understood the importance of the "in-between" times—on and off the practice field. He knew how to push through his practical limit when necessary, and how to pull up before his physiological limit. And his resulting production speaks for itself.

In *The Power of Habit*, Charles Duhigg explains the process that occurs when our brains establish a habit:

> *"This process within our brains is a three-step loop. First, there is a cue, a trigger that tells your brain to go into automatic mode and which habit to use. Then there is the routine, which can be physical or mental or emotional. Finally, there is a reward, which helps your brain figure out if this particular loop is worth remembering for the future."* [18]

The memorable loops, the habits that stick, are the ones that end in a positive neurological reward. If our minds connect a good outcome to a certain process, it will naturally repeat that process. Incentives are a critical part of the habit-forming process.

One of those incentives that works in the sports world, in particular, is competition. Most athletes perform better when there is competition. In my own coaching experience, I've established this principle by holding players accountable through detailed record-keeping. By charting repetitions and progress, after they performed an exercise, players knew instantly whether or not they improved. They either did more repetitions/weight than last time or they didn't. This created competition within themselves. Posting strength numbers on a grease board for all to see also drove competition within the team. When players improved and saw it on that board, it created a positive, habit-forming incentive.

This template can be carried over to the practice field, as well. Grading the performance of a player during a drill will let them know every drill is important and will intensify practice performance to more closely resemble game day. With every repetition, an athlete should strive for perfection, whether in the weight room or on the field. Even if perfection isn't achieved with every exercise, athletes will carry that practice habit onto the game field, and it will naturally lead to success.[19]

Effective practice habits happen when athletes execute in small, specific drills. This leads to performance on the big stage. Every NFL head coach I've worked for has preached the importance of consistent practice habits. Dennis Green of the Vikings encouraged players to work hard in every area of execution and preached the dependence of game performance on the effort placed in the locker room, training room, weight room, meetings, walk-throughs and practice. Brian Billick (Ravens) emphasized "self-analysis"—the process of always trying to improve—and encouraged players to identify what they needed above and beyond regular practice sessions (e.g., extra sprints, film study, weight training, etc.). Marvin Lewis (Bengals) asked his staff to pay attention to the details of everything we did, to leave no stone unturned, from our dress code to how hard we worked. Lewis understood the carry-over effect of loose boundaries:

> *Even if perfection isn't achieved with every exercise, athletes will carry that practice habit onto the game field, and it will naturally lead to success.*

"The discipline you show in your life is the discipline you should

have on the field. If you break down in your life, you are going to break down on the field."[20]

It's not difficult to see how this principle of developing good habits applies beyond the practice field to the other three building blocks of performance. If we train our minds through regular reading, processing and engagement, we'll grow in our critical thinking and mental capacity. Socially, if we consciously choose to offer forgiveness and grace, and regularly practice authenticity and vulnerability, it will come more naturally down the road. On a spiritual level, if we establish regular rhythms of prayer and Scripture reading, after a while, it will no longer feel forced. On the other hand, if we allow sin to creep into our lives unchecked and take control of our habits—even in the small things—it can lead us into destruction down the road.

> **None of us make decisions without consequences. Every tiny choice we make has an impact.**

In one of my daily devotionals, the author referred to St. Augustine's book, *Confessions*, and how the saint paid close attention to small sins. In the book, the saint devoted nine pages to the misdeed of a child climbing a neighbor's pear tree to steal its fruit. The child's pleasure was not in the fruit, for he wasn't even hungry, but rather in the sport of theft. By using this example to examine his own motives, St. Augustine arrives at a deeper truth—recklessness in small acts can open the door to larger sins down the road.[21]

In the same way, small victories—going to bed on-time, finishing that last repetition, choosing to forgo dessert—can establish life-changing habits that alter the course of our lives for the better. Regardless of our intentionality—distracted or focused—we'll form habits in practice, at work and in life, in general. One more quote from Charles Duhigg:

> *"Habits are powerful, but delicate. They can emerge outside our consciousness or can be deliberately designed. They often occur without our permission but can be reshaped by fiddling with their parts. They shape our lives far more than we realize—they*

are so strong, in fact, that they cause our brains to cling to them at the exclusion of all else, including common sense." [22]

None of us make decisions without consequences. Every tiny choice we make has an impact. We may not see it or feel it right away, but over time, if repeated enough, we'll experience the long-term implications of our habit-forming actions. If we navigate life carelessly, we'll lose control of our habits and ultimately, our lives. But if we have a focus, a vision, to align us and motivate even our smallest actions, we'll gain control and develop with intentionality. This, I think, is what the Apostle Paul is getting at in Colossians 3:23:

> *"Whatever you do, work at it with all your heart, as working for the Lord, not for human masters."*

Whatever you do—big or small—work at it with all your heart, as working for the Lord. And eventually, like John Randle, you'll grow into the person you've always desired to be.

Foundation Building Tip

Practice habits are the physical acts of self-preparation by repeating an activity or skill with intention. By establishing effective practice habits, we can overcome limitations and boost our performance. How we practice determines how we perform. Or, as you've probably heard from every coach/teacher in your life, practice makes perfect.

Practice habits aren't cemented in one session—it takes consistent time and intentional effort to get better at your craft. It takes years of practice and self-discipline to be your best. If we're careless and let our habits establish themselves, we'll see that come out on game day. But if we focus intentionally and consistently on the "small wins" in practice, we'll build positive habits and routines that, without thinking, will bring success on the field.

Your Workout

1. List (at least) three skills you want to develop. They don't have to be physical. It could be asking better questions, journaling more or reading more books. How can you be more intentional about practicing them? How might you

more effectively use this practice time?

2. List habits you've already established. Be honest and analyze them. Have they been effective in producing results? If so, what's made them effective? If not, how could you design them more intentionally?

3. Think of an example where practice led to success on the field, in the workplace, in life, etc. Reflect on the positive emotion you felt and how your preparedness, intentionality and effort led to a successful result. Write it down and use it as motivation for practice moving forward.

Extra Workout Challenge

1. What are some habits you've established, positive or negative, *beyond* the practice field and physical building block? Think through the other three building blocks—mental, social and spiritual. With what do you engage your mind without really thinking (social media, news, movies, TV, music)? What are some social phrases or clichés you use out of habit (e.g., "How are you? Good, how are you?")? Have you set up regular rhythms of prayer in your life?

2. For each building block, list (at least) one habit you'd like to establish, along with a specific plan to implement it over time.

CHAPTER 3: NUTRITION

"Do you not know that your bodies are temples of the Holy Spirit, who is in you, whom you have received from God? You are not your own; you were bought at a price. Therefore honor God with your bodies."
(1 Corinthians 6:19-20)

The difference between winning and losing, especially in close games, usually comes down to a few key plays. Even early in the second quarter, I knew this was one of those plays. It was the 2000 AFC Championship, tied 0-0, and the Oakland Raiders had pinned us (Ravens) deep in our own territory. After a first-down sack and a second-down run of no gain, we faced a third-down from our own four-yard-line. We needed 18 yards to keep the drive alive.

I wasn't the only one who realized the importance of this play. Inside of the Oakland Coliseum, the noise of "Raiders Nation" grew to a deafening level as our quarterback, Trent Dilfer, lined up under center. On the sideline, I was nervous. Our team identity centered on our defense, not our offense, and on this play, the odds were clearly stacked against us. Anything less than a first down would likely set up the Raiders with great field position to break open the scoring. The stakes were as high as they'd been all season—a trip to the Super Bowl on the line.

The play happened fast. After a three-step drop, Dilfer got the ball out quick. He zipped a bullet through the Raiders defense into the hands of our veteran tight end, Shannon Sharpe, cutting across the field. What at first looked like a safe option—a play designed to give our punting team a few more yards of breathing room—Sharpe turned into a game-changing play. In an instant, he burst through the Raiders' secondary and past the first-down marker. He wasn't done. He split the last two defenders and exploded into the open field, nothing but green grass between him and a six-point lead. Just 10 seconds after he caught it, Sharpe raised the ball in victory as he completed his 96-yard touchdown, setting a new NFL postseason record.[1]

Our sideline erupted into hysteria as we celebrated the improbability of the situation. Not only was Sharpe a 32-year-old NFL veteran, in year 11 of his 14-year career, but also, tight ends weren't known for running 96-yard touchdowns. Then again, Shannon Sharpe was no normal NFL tight end.

Sharpe rewrote the record books for players of his position. During his 14-year career (1990-2003), Sharpe became the NFL tight-end leader in receptions (815), receiving yards (10,060), and receiving touchdowns (62).[2] He ushered in a new era of the NFL tight end— setting the stage for pass-catchers like Tony Gonzalez, Jason Witten, Antonio Gates and Rob Gronkowski. In his two-year stint with the Ravens (2000-2001), Sharpe was a key contributor to our Super Bowl XXXV championship team, and in 2011, he was elected to the Pro Football Hall of Fame. The three-time Super Bowl champion was a physical specimen and a dominating force on the field. But that's not how his NFL career started.

Coming out of Division I-AA (now-FCS) Savannah State University, Sharpe entered the NFL Draft as a wide receiver. In a draft class that included other Hall-of-Famers like Randle, Junior Seau and Emmitt Smith, the Denver Broncos selected Sharpe in the seventh round.[3] And, as any late-round pick knows, your spot on the roster is never guaranteed.

Before the Broncos' last preseason game in 1990, one of Sharpe's coaches approached him: "Shannon, I'm not supposed to be sharing this with you, but your name is on the board for being one of the final cuts." In other words, just a few days before the Broncos had to submit their final 53-man roster, Sharpe was on the chopping block.

"I think you should go out there and give it your all tonight because not only are you playing to make *this* team, but everybody else is going to get tape of this game. So maybe you can flash something, and somebody else can pick you up if we release you." Not the most encouraging message for a rookie NFL hopeful to hear before his last chance to prove himself on the field. Nonetheless, it motivated Sharpe.

To his dismay, as Sharpe drove to the field that day, it started to rain. In football, rain means heavy doses of the run game, and Sharpe knew his chances to showcase his receiving abilities would be limited. He turned his focus to special teams.

"Bodies are made in the kitchen, not in the gym."

"As the rain started to build, I knew I was going to be on special teams," Sharpe said. "And I knew I was going to probably play late in the ball game—probably the fourth quarter, after the starters came out. I needed a flash."[4]

And a flash is just what Sharpe provided. Not only did he make plays on special teams, but he also impressed his coaches with his work on offense late in the game. The next morning, his coach told him his name was off the board. Sharpe had secured his spot, but his motivation to prove himself didn't stop there. He made the team, but he still had plenty of mountains between his performance and his ultimate goals.

In his rookie season, Sharpe caught only seven receptions, so the following year, head coach Dan Reeves moved Sharpe to h-back (a cross between tight end and full back). Being undersized for his position (6'2", 230 pounds),[5] Sharpe had to rely on other aspects of his game to prosper on the field.

"I remember thinking, 'I need to go to practice every single day and give them one reason to keep me,'" Sharpe said.[6]

With a new job description that included heavy doses of running routes and blocking opposing defenders, Sharpe focused his training on conditioning and strength building. Although he did spend an above-average amount of time in the weight room and on the practice field, the cornerstone of Sharpe's training program was nutrition—what he put into his body.

A common misconception about physical health is that "if I just exercise enough, I can eat whatever I want." That's far from the truth. As Sharpe often said, "Bodies are made in the kitchen, not in the gym."[7] In other words, in order to stay in shape, you not only need appropriate physical activity, but also proper eating habits. A general guide to follow for taking care of your body is the 80/20 rule—80 percent diet, 20 percent exercise. That means, for the 16-18 hours you're awake each day, you might only need 2-3 hours of physical activity, but the intentionality doesn't stop there. For the remaining 80 percent, you need to prioritize proper nutrition.

> **What we put into our bodies either helps or hinders—there is no in-between.**

Nutrition focuses on the nourishment of the body and obtaining the essential nutrients (protein, carbohydrates, fats, vitamins, minerals and fluids) in their proper amounts to fuel us toward physical success. Proper nutrition equips our bodies to combat our own genetic weaknesses and empowers us to reach our full physical potential.[8] What we put into our bodies either helps or hinders—there is no in-between. Your diet and lifestyle either cause disease or prevent it. And, as nutritionist Robert Crayhon said in his book, The Carnitine Miracle, "Optimal health is the state in which the cells of the body have enough of each nutrient to give them the freedom to do what they want."[9]

Sharpe was definitely well ahead of his time when it came to fueling his body, but his philosophy proved to be on-point. Between the years 1980-2000—during the majority of Sharpe's NFL career—fitness club memberships more than doubled in the U.S. Yet during the same period of time, obesity in the U.S. also doubled. A decade later, two out of every three Americans were either overweight or obese.[10]

In his Hall-of-Fame induction speech, Sharpe credited his success to traits that he called "The Three D's": Determination (firmness of purpose), Dedication (commitment) and Discipline (follow-through). Through this triad of focal points, Sharpe created a purpose behind what he ate, stayed committed and stayed consistent with his dietary choices.[11]

Like most NFL teams, the Ravens supplied breakfast, lunch and sometimes dinner for their players and coaches. Sharpe was disciplined about what he consumed. He monitored what he put in his body so judiciously that, instead of eating whatever was in front of him, he brought his own food to the complex. He planned his meals—a crucial element of nutrition. While a lot of people eat when they're hungry or when it works best with their schedule, Sharpe meticulously scheduled out his meals and hydration to guarantee a nutrient-rich and balanced diet.[12]

Just how regimented was Sharpe with nutrition? Like John Randle's practice habits (in chapter 2), Sharpe had a similar arsenal of habits for what and *how* he ate:

- **Eat breakfast.** Sharpe sometimes ate his first meal as early as 4:30 a.m., and it was always consistent: egg whites, one whole egg and one-and-three-quarters cups of oatmeal.[13] *Why?* Lean protein and diet-friendly whole grains take longer to digest. This helps one feel full and comfortable throughout the day and reduces mid-morning cravings for sugar, starches and high-calorie foods which lead to weight gain. Soluble fibers like oatmeal may also lower total cholesterol levels by lowering low-density lipoprotein (LDL), or "bad cholesterol," levels.[14] Early-morning protein and fiber also help maintain steady blood sugar levels to fuel the brain and the body.[15] As you increase your fiber intake, you'll also need to increase your fluids. Always choose water as your first fluid.

- **Eat lean or plant-based protein with each meal.** For his specific performance, Sharpe typically ate five small(er) meals throughout the day—each centered around lean protein. Two-and-a-half hours after breakfast, Sharpe would eat six ounces of turkey or chicken. For lunch, he would eat the other protein. Meals four and five might have been turkey or chicken again, six ounces of bison meatballs or sea bass.[16] Why? Protein is a nutrient that helps to build new tissue and repair torn/worn tissue (muscles and organs).[17] Protein is the building block for strength and muscle growth.[18] If you're a vegetarian or vegan, you can replace lean proteins like turkey and chicken with plant-based proteins like tofu or chickpeas.

- **Eat fruits and vegetables with each meal.** Sharpe consistently ate golden beets or broccoli, sweet potatoes, and fibrous vegetables such as arugula, spinach and kale.[19] *Why?* Fruits and vegetables control free radical damage (high energy molecules that damage DNA, protein and cells throughout the body). Fibrous vegetables have the added benefit of promoting movement of material through the digestive system and increasing stool bulk that can aid with constipation.[20]

Throughout his career, Sharpe made a living off beating opposing linebackers and safeties to catch the football. He not only needed physicality to block in the trenches, but also speed and elusiveness to get out into the open. In order to do his job effectively, he needed to maintain an ideal bodyweight. By filling his body with proper nutrients, Sharpe increased his body's energy and efficiency before, during and after periods of increased physical activity.[21] All of this moved him up the performance curve and led to a long, successful and relatively healthy career.

> **Every person is different and requires different nutritional needs based on age, activity level, emotional condition and body composition.**

Sharpe's training program absolutely incorporated fitness and practice habits, but it revolved around what he put into his mouth. He stayed consistent with his diet and focused on what his body needed to achieve peak performance. Sharpe discovered and stayed committed to eating habits he claimed were tried and true. Eating breakfast, small meals throughout the day, along with protein and vegetables, is a commonsense approach to a healthy diet.

Philosophies around nutrition vary based on the individual. Every person is different and requires different nutritional needs based on age, activity level, emotional condition and body composition. For Sharpe, depending on the stage of his career, he had to adjust his body weight and energy levels accordingly. He crafted a diet that met these needs and thus improved his performance. Maintaining an optimum body weight and low percentage of body fat enabled him to make plays like that 96-yard touchdown in the AFC Championship, and others like it, throughout his 14-year Hall-of-Fame career.

Coach's Corner

Despite the allure of certain food and drinks, improper nutrition is one of the leading ways we deplete our body of energy. It's also one of the easiest areas in which to slip up when it comes to the physical building block. Whether out of boredom, anxiety or just being over-responsive to cravings, our bodies often seem hardwired to neglect proper nutrition. And much of this actually has less to do with our physical state and more to do with our psychology—what's influencing and guiding our eating habits.

We acquire eating habits at a young age. If Fruit Loops and French toast were a staple as a kid, chances are these items will become staples for your family, too. As we learned in Chapter 2, we tend to stick with those habits that produce positive psychological results. Eating sugary cereal may produce happy childhood memories and temporary satisfaction, but they likely won't give you the energy and momentum you need for your day.

Unfortunately, most people don't correlate what they're eating with how their body is performing. Often, we're so accustomed to eating a certain way we don't recognize the signals of poor nutrition. If health problems run rampant in your family history, we may take it a step further by believing our fate has been predetermined—which is far from the truth. Shannon Sharpe has a family history of diabetes and heart problems, yet through nutrition and exercise, he fought the trend and maintained optimal health throughout his NFL career and beyond.[22] Studies have confirmed a healthy lifestyle—healthy diet, physical activity, weight control, avoiding tobacco and alcohol—have a greater impact on overall health than genetics.[23]

The food-body connection becomes even more allusive when we simply "accept" how we feel. We may convince ourselves our low energy levels are due to aging or reduced physical activity. While these factors may contribute to lower energy levels, they may not be the root of what's causing them.

It's easy to make poor food choices when our only nutritional education comes from parental guidance, advertising, and our own cravings and insecurities.[24] When our minds (and habits) set us up to neglect proper nutrition, many of us will ignore physiological evidence of how we might be harming our bodies. How many of us truly eat based on our physiological needs? How many of us even know what those needs are?

Even in the NFL—where physical health is critical to on-field performance—nutrition can take a backseat to other priorities, like tradition. As a longstanding NFL ritual, rookie players purchase food for the veteran players and the rest of their position groups. Often, this tradition is practiced the day before a road game. Despite the physiological harm, the menu almost always includes fried food, which is high in fat (a poor food choice 24 hours before intense physical activity). Foods high in saturated fats raise LDL (bad cholesterol) levels.

If we don't understand our physiology, even if we're in the gym regularly, we may be limiting our physical potential.

Higher LDL levels restrict proper blood flow and impede the transportation of oxygen to muscles.[25] Instead of optimizing their bodies' fuel before competition, by neglecting their physiological needs, these players may have ultimately hurt their performance.

Nutrition involves supplying our bodies with proper nutrients, based on our physiological needs, to promote immediate and long-term health. If we don't understand our physiology, even if we're in the gym regularly, we may be limiting our physical potential.

So, given already established eating habits and motivations, how can we effectively implement a nutritional plan based on our physiological needs? I'll defer to Shannon Sharpe on this one and refer back to the "Three D's" of his Hall-of-Fame induction speech. Maintaining proper nutrition requires determination, dedication and discipline:

- **DETERMINATION.** Determination involves firmness of purpose. Like physical fitness (as we discussed in Chapter 1), proper nutrition requires a purpose and a commitment to that purpose. Sharpe found his purpose in achieving success on the field, whether he was playing wide receiver, h-back or tight end. Personally, I know God values my body and so do I. My purpose for proper nutrition is found in the truth David proclaims to God in Psalm 139:14, "I praise you because I am fearfully and wonderfully made," I also believe what the Apostle Paul wrote when he said, "For we are God's workmanship, created in Christ Jesus to do good works, which God prepared in advance for us to do" (Ephesians 2:10). God is my Creator, and I am His vessel. Because of that, I do my best to take the necessary steps to put things into my body that will honor God and allow me to be the person He desires.

- **DEDICATION.** Dedication is all about commitment to your nutritional plan. When we dedicate ourselves to nutrition, we're not dipping our toes in the water—trying to eat fruits and vegetables every now and then—we're going all-in. For me, this looks like incorporating a "rainbow diet" every day. The rainbow diet involves eating lots of colorful fruit and vegetables on a daily basis. Each color carries its own unique vitamins and minerals. I start my morning with a smoothie which includes as many different colors of fruit and vegetables as I can get my hands on (i.e., strawberries, blueberries, banana, spinach, kale, celery, apples, oranges, cantaloupe, watermelon, carrots, etc.). I mix it with water, a little protein powder, honey, cinnamon and chia seeds for a fortified breakfast. I continue the same process at lunch by incorporating carrots, lettuce and other colors I may have missed during breakfast.

- **DISCIPLINE.** Discipline revolves around consistent, repeated follow-through regarding your nutritional plan. Never fall into the "diet trap." Diets are only temporary and rarely produce long-term results. A large portion of the weight lost through low-calorie diets is muscle tissue, which actually *reduces* resting metabolism, and after a year, about 95 percent of all dieters replace that lost muscle with regained fat.[26] The key to attaining and maintaining good health is through disciplined lifestyle changes. This requires a daily commitment, making one change at a time and sticking to it. Whether it's eliminating a specific food or adding healthier foods to your diet, start slow and add on. You will be compelled to make further changes once you notice the benefits of taking the first step.

You only have one body. Like the other building blocks, nutrition will affect the outcomes in all areas of your life. For example, unbalanced sugar or glucose in our bodies can lead to instability in our moods and difficulty concentrating. When our bodies have the *proper* nutrients, however, we feel good and think clearly.[27] Beyond the mental building block, nutrition is one way we can practice stewardship according to God's design.

If you trust Jesus as your Savior, the New Testament says God "makes His home" within you (Ephesians 3:17).[28] Like the *physical* temple was for the Israelites in the Old Testament, your body is God's dwelling place. It's a temple given to you by God (1 Corinthians 6:19). Many believe they can do what they want with their bodies (or any number of God's gifts), but as followers of Jesus, we're called to stewardship through exercise, good habits, nutrition and rest. Just as we're called to steward our resources (finances, gifts and talents, etc.), so too are we to steward our bodies. Not only does proper nutrition lead to higher energy, greater performance and long-term health, but it also brings us into closer alignment with God's purpose for us as followers of Jesus.

Foundation Building Tip

Nutrition focuses on the nourishment of the body and obtaining the proper amounts of essential nutrients to improve performance and promote long-term health. Proper nutrition increases energy, builds and repairs our tissues, and regulates body processes before, during and after physical activity. In order to implement an effective nutrition plan based on our physiological needs, we need a purpose, commitment and self-discipline to follow-through with small, consistent changes every day.

Nutrition not only affects our physical state, but all other areas of our life as well. If we're fueling our bodies correctly, we'll benefit our mental, social and spiritual building blocks. Our bodies are God's temples. In order to steward His temple effectively, we need to carefully and intentionally monitor what we put into our bodies.

Your Workout

1. Write down three foods or beverages in your current diet that have a negative impact on your health.

2. From that list, circle one food or beverage you are going to eliminate this week. Make it a daily practice to remove this item from your diet. To keep you on track, replace what you've eliminated with a healthier alternative. For example, if you are going to eliminate sugary drinks, replace them with water (add lemon, mint, basil or berries to enhance the flavor of your new beverage of choice). Likewise, when removing starchy foods such as white bread, replace it with whole wheat varieties or lettuce. Skip the McMuffin and make a smoothie. Simply choosing an organic option will be a win!

3. Make a point to pray before each meal this week. Thank God for what has been provided. Ask him to use your meal to provide nourishment for your body.

4. Keep a food journal. Take note of how you feel after removing the chosen item from your diet. Jot down any improvement in energy, digestion, memory, etc.

5. Repeat. Go down your list and continue to remove other items from your diet that may be negatively impacting your health. As you remove these items, you will naturally replace them with healthier options.

Extra Workout Challenge

1. Through Scripture (1 Corinthians 6:19-20), we know God values our bodies. Our bodies are said to be a temple of the Holy Spirit, and we are called to take care of and honor God's temple to fulfill His will. How does this passage change your view of your eating habits?

2. How might your diet be keeping you from following God's purpose for your life?

CHAPTER 4: REST

"Come to me, all you who are weary and burdened, and I will give you rest." (Matthew 11:28)

In 2015, 13 years into his tenure as head coach of the Cincinnati Bengals, Marvin Lewis made a dramatic change to our weekly practice schedule. To end the practice week, Lewis replaced our traditional 90-minute practice with a one-hour walkthrough, followed by an up-tempo practice the next day. Under this new format, the hardest part of the practice week finished 72 hours before each game.

Lewis' wanted to give his players an opportunity to focus on restoring their bodies—to have them at their best, physically and mentally, on game day. According to Lewis, the practice week progressed "from the physical focus to the mental focus to the personal focus, for [the player] to get his body back to peak shape, to play his best football on Sunday."[1]

Lewis worked intentionally with our strength and conditioning staff to create individualized plans for players to maximize recovery from the rigors of an NFL season. He believed our unique schedule and plan provided us a competitive advantage. The intent was to limit physical preparation to a degree that prevented unnecessary fatigue on game day. Lewis wanted to maximize growth while minimizing risk of overtraining, exhaustion and injury. Not coincidentally, the 2015 Bengals led the league in the least games missed through injury,[2] propelling us to a division title and franchise-record-tying 12 wins.

Lewis wasn't the first advocate for proper rest and recovery in the NFL. That title belongs to a coach 35 years his predecessor and the founder of the team Lewis spent the majority of his career coaching, the Bengals. That man was legendary Hall-of-Fame coach Paul Brown.

During his 30-year professional coaching career, Brown not only won seven League championships, but he also won seven different Coach of the Year awards. Before that, he won a NCAA championship coaching at The Ohio State University, seven high school state championships (one in Maryland, six in Ohio) and four high school *national* championships—the first of which came at the young age of 27. In 1967, Brown was elected to the Pro Football Hall of Fame,[3] and in 2009, *Sporting News* named him the 12th greatest coach of all-time—of any sport.[4] Today, Brown is known as undoubtedly one of the greatest men to ever coach the game of football, and like Lewis, he had a secret weapon.

Considered an innovator in the coaching field, Brown's rule was to spend no more than 90 minutes at a time on the practice field.

In the 1940s, when he began his professional coaching career, Brown noticed a pattern among other pro football teams. Across the League, coaches kept their players on the field for 150 minutes or longer, working them to the point of physical and emotional fatigue. Coaches focused so intensely on having their teams at their best on gameday that overtraining players became the common practice around the League. Later on, several studies conducted in professional football came to an interesting conclusion. The average player was most fatigued *before the first game of the season*, not at the end of the season when most people might expect. This was attributed, primarily, to two-a-day practices and excess repetitions.[5]

Brown noticed this pattern ahead of his time and saw the opportunity for a competitive advantage. Considered an innovator in the coaching field, Brown's rule was to spend no more than 90 minutes at a time on the practice field. Contrary to common practice at the time, Brown believed a player's attention span and ability to learn diminished if practice exceeded that amount of time. He also observed that players got tired just standing around for long periods of time.[6] In response, Brown limited practice time, minimized unnecessary repetitions and physical exertion, and prioritized rest and recovery—all with the end goal to avoid overtraining and exhaustion. Like Marvin Lewis, Brown's philosophy revolved around understanding and monitoring one key factor: stress.

One of the main ways we grow as humans—physically, mentally, socially and spiritually—is responding, adapting and recovering from stress. Essentially, this is what life is. Whether it's physical stress from football practice, mental stress from a long workday or social stress from an interpersonal argument, our bodies respond the same way.[7] The General Adaptation Syndrome (GAS), theorized by Austrian scientist Hans Selye, advocates the body has only one system to respond to and recover from stress, regardless of the source. It happens in three steps.

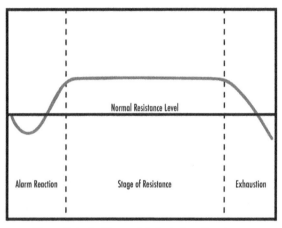

Hans Selye's General Adaptation Syndrome

First, after the body perceives an outside threat, or stressor, it goes through what's called an "alarm reaction." In this stage, the body sends a distress signal to the brain, which in turn, releases stress hormones throughout the body that increase heart rate and raise blood pressure. The stress hormones prepare the body to respond to the stressor—"fight or flight." In earlier times, these hormones increased energy levels for the purpose of greater physical effort like running from danger, hunting for food or fending off an attack from a neighboring tribe. Today, our stresses are different, yet our bodies still create the same "alarm reaction." Instead of helping us, though, this physical reaction often leads to anger and other negative emotions.[8]

If the stress continues, the body then moves into the "resistance" stage, attempting to counteract the physiological changes that occurred during the alarm reaction stage. Our nervous systems try to return our bodies back to normal, and if the stress diminishes, it works. Our bodies, having successfully conquered the stressor, come out stronger on the other side. If proper adaptation occurs, we'll incrementally improve every workout, practice, project, etc. This is the main goal of physical exercise and strength training. These periods of rest not only include *physical* restoration, but also *psychological*. They are the "barren periods" I talked about in Chapter 2 that allow our nervous systems to develop new sets of habits. If the stress continues without rest, however, our brain continues to produce stress hormones faster than our bodies can keep up. We approach the body's physiological limit and become irritable, struggle to concentrate, and we move into the third and final stage of the GAS: exhaustion.

If we don't create space for rest, our muscles will overload to the point of exhaustion, and we'll fail to maximize the output of our physical training.

In the exhaustion stage, we've depleted our bodies' energy resources, and we're no longer equipped to fight stress. As we've all experienced, this leads to tiredness, anxiety and feeling unable to cope. On the football field, this is overtraining, and it translates to fatigue, higher risk of injury and overall decrease in performance. When stress isn't managed at this level, people can develop stress-related health conditions (physical and mental) such as obesity, heart disease, diabetes and depression.[9]

In the first two chapters of the physical building block, we covered fitness and practice habits. Yes, these are at the foundation of this block and critical to physical growth, but ultimately, they're stressors. And stressors, while essential to increases in performance, need to be properly monitored and managed. As we learned in Chapter 2, unregulated practice time won't lead to peak performance. Instead of working until we drop (physiological limit), we need to target efficiency in practice in order to maximize growth. To avoid overtraining, injury risk and diminishing returns, one needs to balance training and exercise with proper amounts of recovery and rest.

In exercise, work and relationships alike, rest is self-care, caring for your own needs. Rest means stopping our many daily obligations, distractions and activities to restore energy and provide space to recover from fatigue, problems, fears and anxieties. Although often overlooked—in all areas of life—rest and recovery ultimately allow us to be energetic, alert and productive. Caring for ourselves allows us to, in turn, care for others.

In strength training, high intensity work creates stress to our muscles and breaks down muscle fibers. After the appropriate amount of recovery, the muscles will come back stronger. However, if we don't create space for rest, our muscles will overload to the point of exhaustion, and we'll fail to maximize the output of our physical training. We might regress, get injured or, at best, plateau in weight lifted. From a physiological standpoint, humans adapt to stress in the same way. Without proper rest, we'll never give our bodies time and space to grow.

So how can we apply this? How do we find the balance between training and recovery? Although each person is unique and can find personalized methods of recovery, I'll highlight three I've witnessed (and experienced personally) throughout my coaching career.

First, routines. Like I mentioned in Chapter 2, establishing effective practice habits is a prime example of balancing training and rest. If we understand our physiology and build practice plans around it, we'll maximize physical output while avoiding overtraining and exhaustion.

Paul Brown passed down his coaching philosophy to other legendary coaches like Bill Walsh, Don Shula and Chuck Noll, who in turn, passed it down to other coaches on their staffs. I've been fortunate to work with three coaches who were a product of the coaching tree Paul Brown created. In addition to Lewis, both Dennis Green of the Minnesota Vikings and Brian Billick of the Baltimore Ravens implemented their own version of Brown's methods and approach in practice.

NFL teams typically conduct three types of practice during the season, distinguished by varying degrees of physical contact: full pads (helmet and shoulder/thigh/knee pads, heavy contact), shells (helmet and soft protection over shoulders, controlled contact) and shorts (helmet, no contact). It takes proper planning by coaches, mixing the various types of practices throughout the week to minimize undue mental and physical fatigue.

Billick, who developed his coaching philosophy from both Walsh and Green, made sure the schedule of required practice sessions did not place undue physiological demands on the players. He carefully structured practice to avoid overtraining due to excessive hitting or running. In order to protect his players from exhaustion, Billick maximized the amount of "shorts" practices throughout the season. If a player could get in great position with minimal contact and show that he could make a play, that was a success. If the team went through repetitions of an exercise, they were *meaningful* repetitions. In doing so, Billick extended the physiological limits of his players and maximized efficient motor learning in practice.

Billick's teams learned valuable techniques and skills without over-exerting themselves physically. Often, two out of three weekly practices during the season were in shorts. And the number only increased as the season progressed. By late November, all three practices were free of shells and pads.

"We are built for November and December because of the way we prepare," Billick would say. And it worked—the evidence is in the numbers.

From 1999-2001 (Billick's first three years as head coach), the Ravens boasted the best regular season record in November and December (18-5), picking up a Super Bowl win along the way in 2000. On that Super Bowl-winning team in 2000, every starter, key contributor and top reserve on the team in July was available for action in the Super Bowl. On a roster of nearly sixty players, with the exception of one rookie, we had no major injuries. Billick knew keeping his players at full strength throughout the season was of utmost importance.

It takes meticulous planning and educating of players to ensure just enough stress is applied in practice to produce favorable results without overtraining. Billick knew the importance of keeping his players at full strength, mentally and physically, so he dedicated the time and focus to balance training and exercise with proper rest and recovery. Now, he has a Super Bowl XXXV ring to show for it.

Second, recovery methods and technology. Beyond establishing effective habits and routines *in* practice, proper rest can be achieved by incorporating different recovery methods before, between and after time on the field. As with practice, this rest is enhanced by monitoring physical loads and energy levels. In sports, these can be tracked by coaches (e.g., observation of appearance, behaviors, performance), individual athletes (e.g., self-evaluation), and/or the help of sports science and medicine (e.g., heart rate monitors, Global Positioning Systems).[10]

In the NFL, to inform decisions such as which recovery methods to incorporate, how many repetitions to complete or what muscles group to prioritize, coaches and players use technology that monitors players' workloads and energy levels. Heart rate monitors and GPS give coaches concrete, real-time data to back up what they see and what athletes feel to help reduce injury

Usain Bolt–a.k.a. "Lightning Bolt," eight-time Olympic Gold Medal winner and "Fastest Man Who Has Ever Lived"– typically sleeps up to 10 hours each night.

and improve recovery. Tracking workloads lets athletes and coaches know how much is too much. If a player strays way outside of the norm during a workout, they can implement recovery strategies to reduce overtraining and prevent injury. Coaches can also step in and adjust practice repetitions accordingly.

Throughout the season, NFL players monitored and managed stress by incorporating certain recovery modalities into their daily rhythms. Based on training loads—either measured or perceived—athletes chose methods based on their needs. Bengals Pro Bowl defensive end Carlos Dunlap spent ten hours per week on different rest and recovery techniques during the season. These included massage therapy, acupuncture, stretching techniques and chiropractic adjustments. Like Shannon Sharpe in Chapter 3, Dunlap also prioritized nutrition and had a private chef provide breakfast, lunch and dinner five days per week during the season.[11]

Third—and by far, the most important—sleep. Sleep plays a foundational role in both our rest and recovery and our overall physical and mental health. Usain Bolt—a.k.a. "Lightning Bolt," eight-time Olympic Gold Medal winner and "Fastest Man Who Has Ever Lived"[12]— typically sleeps up to 10 hours each night.[13] After a poor performance eight weeks prior to the 2012 London Olympics, Bolt blamed it on a lack of sleep. Known for his power naps, Bolt caught up on sleep during the next two months and, as a result, improved his 100-meter time by four percent in London, setting yet another Olympic record.[14]

Sleep benefits us in three main areas—physical recovery, weight control and memory consolidation:

- **PHYSICAL RECOVERY.** Nearly 50 percent of Human Growth Hormone (HGH), which repairs and builds muscles and connective tissue, is released during deep sleep. Sleep deprivation can increase injury recovery time by days, weeks, even months.[15]

- **WEIGHT CONTROL.** Insufficient sleep is associated with both a drop in the hormone that curbs appetite (leptin) and a rise in the hormone that makes you hungry (ghrelin). Researchers found subjects with a four-hour sleep session ate 22 percent more calories the next day than they did after eight hours of sleep.[16] Those deprived of sleep have an increased appetite and crave sweets and carbohydrates.

- **MEMORY CONSOLIDATION.** Memory consolidation is the merging of motor and perceptual (vision, hearing and touch) skill memories. Proper sleep allows you to bundle memories of information, experiences and feelings appropriately and effectively.[17]

To fully reap the benefits of proper sleep, you need to not only get enough of it, but you also need to find a steady rhythm based on your individual body clock. Our bodies operate on regular sleep cycles, which means you should go to bed and wake up at the same time every day, even on weekends. This pattern, known as your "body clock," or circadian rhythm, is a natural part of human life. It's based on waking up with the light and falling asleep to the dark. Before Thomas Edison invented the light bulb in 1879, the average person slept 11 hours per night.[18]

The body clock sets off a regulated pattern of activities by controlling hormones, body temperature and other functions that make us feel tired or wide-awake. There are hundreds of biological processes that repeat themselves once every day according to our circadian rhythm.

Below is a diagram showing the peaks and valleys of a typical body clock cycle.[19]

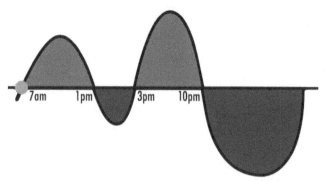

A day in the life of your body clock.

The diagram looks at the rest and work cycle during a 24-hour time period. The higher the line, the more your clock is telling your body to work, and the higher your energy level, reaction time and flexibility will increase. In the scenario laid out in the diagram, you wake up at 7 a.m., and your clock starts telling your body to work, reaching its peak in the late morning. It then declines and signals your body to take a light rest in the early afternoon (Can you say "siesta"?). The late afternoon and evening are the height of the body clock's workday. Not surprisingly, this time of day is when almost all athletic world records are broken. As it gets dark outside, your body releases melatonin, telling you to rest and recover from the day. It stays elevated for about 12 hours, until the light of morning.

Circadian rhythms are relative to the individual and based on age and genetics. The times of work and rest patterns differ from person to person. Optimal sleep times also change with age. In general, your body clock winds down latest around age 20 and moves slightly early every year until age 50 or 60.[20] It's important to listen to your body about what bedtimes feel natural knowing that, as we age, going to sleep earlier is beneficial. When your body clock is telling you it's time to sleep, it's in your best interest to listen.

All sleep is not created equal. When sleeping, we go through different stages distinguished by changes in our brain waves. The sleep cycles, all of which are important for physical and mental recovery, consist of REM (Rapid Eye Movement), light sleep and deep sleep. A typical sleep cycle lasts around 90 minutes. If our sleep pattern is disturbed or we don't go through enough cycles, our body will fail to maximize the restorative effects of sleep. In general, deep sleep occurs closer to the beginning, usually within the first four or five hours of sleep. Consequently, the amount of time you spend in deep sleep correlates with how closely your sleep pattern matches your circadian rhythm. The closer you align falling asleep with your body's natural release of melatonin, the more likely you are to align with your body clock, increase your sleep cycles and maximize your body's recovery.[21]

An easy goal to aim for is one hour of sleep for every two hours you are awake. That's eight hours of sleep—say 10 p.m. to 6 a.m.—for 16 hours of being awake in any given day. According to the National Sleep Foundation, 67 percent of people with "less than good sleep" report "fair" or "poor" overall health.[22] Beyond physical recovery, weight control and memory consolidation, proper sleep increases life expectancy and reduces risk for serious health problems.[23]

Whether it's sleep, practice habits or recovery methods, rest is essential for combatting stress, minimizing fatigue and achieving peak performance. It's true that you need to push yourself to grow (fitness and practice habits), but if you don't counteract that training with rest and recovery, you'll end up pushing yourself into exhaustion and anxiety. Decades after Paul Brown's coaching career began, his philosophy still rings true—and extends far beyond the practice field.

Coach's Corner

When I coached the XFL for the D.C. Defenders, I put a picture of a piggy bank on our whiteboard. I had the players' attention, so I explained how the piggy bank is like our body. We lose money (debit) as our body encounters stress throughout the week in games, practice, meetings, relationships and other energy-depleting activities. To reach a balance, we need to add money back into our account (credit) through restoratives activities like sleep, proper nutrition, massage, stretching, etc. Throughout the week, I'd place a different money value on all of the debit and credit activities, based on how much an activity depleted or restored energy. (Sleep was the number-one credit with sound nutrition coming in a close second.) The goal was to, at the end of the week, have the debit equal the credit, ensuring the athlete was 100 percent ready for game day.

Rest is the often forgotten, yet critical element of the physical building block. From a young age, we hear the importance of fitness and exercise, but far too easily, we neglect the importance of allowing our bodies to recover. But, as we learned above, rest is essential to physical growth. It provides energy, increases productivity, combats exhaustion and fatigue, and helps keep us fresh and alert throughout the day.

Coaches continually adjust their weekly practice structure to find a model that ensures their team is as fresh as possible to compete on game day. If you don't have a coach, be your own coach! Every minute of rest you get is an opportunity to increase your performance and quality of life. Pay attention to your body and get appropriate rest. Continually make adjustments to find a model that works best for you.

One technique I've coached players on during weight training sessions is a deep breathing exercise also known as diaphragmatic breathing. It's a relaxation technique to release stress and tension in the muscles. To do the exercise properly, I have the players lie on their backs with knees bent, feet flat on the ground and hands on their belly, and I encourage them to breathe in through their nose, into their belly and out through their nose. Only the hands on their belly should rise and fall, not their chest.

Breathing through the chest is far less efficient than breathing through the belly. Chest (or thoracic) breathers will average from 16 to 20 breaths per minute compared to belly breathers who average 6 to 8 breaths per minute.[24] The cardiovascular system has to work much harder when we breathe through the chest as less oxygen is drawn to the lungs. When you face anxiety or stress, your tendency may be to breathe through your chest. To reduce that stress, concentrate on applying this diaphragmatic breathing technique.

In life outside of work, I've noticed exercise—whether it's lifting weights, running or a leisurely walk—also provides me with restoration. A walk with my wife is a great respite for me to clear my mind, exchange thoughts and become renewed. Spending quiet time reading in the morning and before I go to bed also provides mental, physical and social rest.

You might not have the resources to hire a private chef or get a daily massage (like Carlos Dunlap), but you can still invest in your recovery with creative methods that align with your unique lifestyle. Some examples include stretching with a foam roller, taking a hot and cold shower to increase blood flow or even just going for a light jog. Give your body rest periods that match your interests, schedule and stage of life.

Rest is a practice commonly and easily applied across all four building blocks.[25] Socially, lack of rest leads to irritability, impatience and shortness with others. Mentally, we need rest to maintain focus, stay productive and avoid mistakes. In a study of hospital staff nurses, shifts longer than 12 hours and work weeks of more than 40 hours correlated with significantly higher rates of error and have raised questions about patient safety. Another study concluded that medical interns were significantly more likely to be involved in motor vehicle crashes if they had just worked extended shifts. Similar reports have been made about airline pilots, police officers, truck drivers and soldiers.[26]

> **Rest is a practice commonly and easily applied across all four building blocks.**

Spiritually, we need look no further than the man on whom the entire Bible centers. The life of Jesus provides a perfect, practical template for how to rest.

Jesus' ministry matched the busyness we often see today—in Western culture, especially. As a teacher, preacher, storyteller, healer, miracle worker and comprehensive "giver of life," no other individual has had more responsibility or been more influential in the world than Jesus. And he accomplished this in only three short years of ministry.

As word of Jesus' teaching and good works spread, crowds began to form. Everywhere he and his disciples went, people wanted to hear Jesus speak and perform miracles. He had to always be "on." Being fully God *and* fully man, Jesus was subject to the physical and mental tolls of his ministry, and rest wasn't easy to find. He needed to intentionally seek out rest and recovery to avoid exhaustion.

In Mark 1, there's a story that exemplifies this well:

> *"Very early in the morning, while it was still dark, Jesus got up, left the house and went off to a solitary place, where he prayed"* (v. 35).

In the middle of the busyness of his ministry, Jesus took time and space to be alone. After days of constantly giving and emptying himself for the sake of others, Jesus recognized his need to be filled by his Father. And, after the disciples scrambled to figure out where Jesus went, he returned—refreshed, and with a new agenda from the Father:

"Let us go somewhere else—to the nearby villages—so I can preach there also. That is why I have come" (v. 38).

Jesus did this often. He unplugged. To rest, he'd go to a solitary place (Mark 1:35, Luke 4:42), a lake (Matthew 14:13) or a mountain (Matthew 14:23, John 6:15). He even took a nap on a boat during a storm (Mark 4:38). Jesus recognized the importance of deliberate and scheduled rest to better love and serve others. Not only did it provide him *physical* rest, but it re-centered him mentally, socially and emotionally. When people's demands of him grew and he reached his physical and mental limitations, Jesus sought the Father for rest and realignment with the truth.

In a culture of instant gratification, short attention spans and the glorification of busyness, Jesus provides a refreshing example and reminder. Whether it's advertising, social media or TV, we're always being told to "try this" or "travel more" or "work harder"—it's an onslaught of things vying for our attention, promising satisfaction but leaving us in what John Mark Comer (pastor of Bridgetown Church in Portland) calls a "chronic state of restlessness":

"Ultimately, nothing in this life, apart from God, can satisfy our desires. Tragically, we continue to chase after our desires ad infinitum. The result? A chronic state of restlessness or, worse, angst, anger, anxiety, disillusionment, depression—all of which lead to a life of hurry, a life of busyness, overload, shopping, materialism, careerism, a life of more...which in turn makes us even more restless. And the cycle spirals out of control."[27]

Without Jesus to keep us grounded and centered, we'll remain pulled in every other direction except rest in the present moment. Many of us, myself included, jump forward to the future or backward to the past instead of staying in the moment. To remain centered, I too, need to unplug and pull away from my daily tasks to find solitude with God. Only then can I learn from the One who is gentle and humble—the One who says, "Come to me, all you are weary and burdened, and I will give you rest" (Matthew 11:28).

Rest comes when I am focused on my heart's relationship with God rather than my earthly status. When I take my eyes off Him, self-seeking ambitions like approval and recognition from others become my goal. When I keep my eyes on Him, selfless behaviors like sacrifice and teamwork come into focus. When I take my eyes off Him, comparisons and envy overtake me. When I keep my eyes on him, appreciation and happiness overflow from me. When I take my eyes off Him, anxiety, fear and stress take priority. When I keep my eyes on him, peace and contentment overtake me.

> **Rest comes when I am focused on my heart's relationship with God rather than my earthly status.**

It's in this state of abiding in my heavenly Father—not in stress, anxiety and busyness—that I can begin to follow my God-given purpose. If I'm going to reach my potential, it will be because of God's work in me.

Foundation Building Tip

Essentially, rest comes down to self-care. Proper rest means seeking healing and recovery through energy-restoring techniques and activities—whether that's going for a walk, taking a nap or praying on top of a mountain. As you encounter regular stressors in your life, pause from your many daily obligations, distractions and activities, and provide a reprieve from your fatigue, problems, worries, fears and anxieties. And as you establish those regular rhythms of rest and recovery, you'll notice you're more energized, productive and attentive on the other side. Daily, weekly and annual periods of prolonged rest promote well-being and productivity.

Stop what's weighing you down. Pause and enjoy life. Put your feet up and relax. Have fun. Laugh. Just be. Then get back to work—refreshed, and with a smile on your face.

Your Workout

1. **Get rest daily.** Write down different ways (walking, qui-

et time, reading, massage, meditating, sleep, etc.) you can rest and relax each day this week—one technique/activity for each day. These are your personal recovery methods.

2. **Get rest monthly.** Write down more extended forms of rest you can apply once a month. Because this won't be something you do all the time, it should place a larger, specialized emphasis on rest and recovery. It may be a special date night, overnight trip, spa day or camping weekend.

3. **Sleep.** Go to bed early. If you're waking up to an alarm, you're probably losing out on valuable muscle and mental growth. Make it a point to wake up before your alarm. It will take some time to develop the habit and get in tune with your body clock. To make it happen, you might need to give up late-night trips to the gym and binges on Netflix. Shut off all electronics at least 30 minutes before going to bed.

4. **Chart your progress.** At the end of each day (and month), record your success at following through with your goals. If you can, take note of your energy levels, productivity and attentiveness. If you stay consistent, you'll begin to see the effectiveness of intentional rest over time.

Extra Workout Challenge

1. In the 10 Commandments (Exodus 20), God said, "Remember the Sabbath day by keeping it holy." Once a week, take a day (or part of a day) and dedicate it to restful activities and practices. Journal, pray and seek the Father like Jesus did—that you might be refreshed and re-centered on the Truth.

2. Are you sacrificing rest for productivity, success and/or money? Write down (at least) one motivation holding you back from proper rest and what you can do to remedy it.

3. Sometimes we can't sleep because of anxious thoughts,

worry or guilt. In Psalms 4, David sleeps in peace (v. 8) because God has filled his heart with great joy (v. 7). What's on your plate currently that you can give up to God?

BUILDING BLOCK 2

M
MENTAL

SECTION 2: MENTAL BUILDING BLOCK

As I stated earlier, none of these building blocks exist in a vacuum; they're all critically and inseparably interdependent. Nothing I covered in the physical building block—fitness, practice habits, nutrition and rest—would be possible to develop and utilize without the mental. While the physical block covered the body, the mental, by definition, explores the mind. Underneath every physical, social or spiritual action—one or several layers down—is a thought, and without control and understanding of those thoughts, we're hopeless to grow in any of these areas.

Throughout the biblical story, the authors emphasize and re-emphasize the importance of mental growth and development: "be transformed by the renewing of your *mind*" (Rom 12:2), "…love the Lord your God with all your heart and with all your soul and with all your *mind*" (Matt 22:37), "take captive every *thought* to make it obedient to Christ" (2 Cor 10:5). As with our bodies, we have a responsibility as bearers of God's image—to steward and serve God with our minds. We accomplish this through:

- **Chapter 5: Education** - the process that combines learning and memory to acquire knowledge that is encoded, stored and later retrieved.

- **Chapter 6: Self-Talk** - the continual, ongoing dialogue we have with ourselves that encompasses whatever we repeatedly tell ourselves.

• **Chapter 7: Emotion** - strong feelings deriving from one's circumstances, mood or relationships with others.

• **Chapter 8: Wisdom** - the combination of knowledge, discipline and humility that informs our decision-making.

The mental building block is about compiling, understanding and utilizing what's inside our minds. Education fuels our mental capacity. Self-talk refocuses our thoughts. Emotions empower our behaviors. Wisdom (or lack thereof) informs all of our decisions. Without mental dexterity, we *can't* develop effective practice habits. We *can't* learn social cues and techniques. We *can't* grow in knowledge and understanding of God. Although the spiritual building block is the most important, the mental block may be the most difficult for the average person to live without.

As we develop mentally, we empower ourselves to overcome shortcomings or other obstacles between us and our peak performance. You might not receive ideal athletic genes from your parents (e.g., a short basketball player), but with a sound mind and understanding of the game, you can still set yourself apart (e.g., NBA point guards who orchestrate the offense). Maybe you didn't grow up in a Christian household and weren't immersed in God's truth early in life, but with discipline, dedication and humility, you can *learn* about that truth and still grow spiritually in God's wisdom.

Although we all start life in different places, our minds give us opportunities to achieve peak performance regardless. If we take responsibility to learn, understand and apply, we'll begin to see the natural benefits across all four areas of our development.

CHAPTER 5: EDUCATION

"Hold on to instruction, do not let it go; guard it well, for it is your life."
(Proverbs 4:13)

One of the first things I noticed upon arrival at Northwestern University was its lack of athletic success—specifically in football and men's basketball. It was 1992—I'd just finished grad school at Illinois State University—and to that point, NU had yet to qualify for the NCAA Men's Basketball Tournament[1] and hadn't won a Big Ten Conference Championship in football for half a century.[2]

With an enrollment around 7,000,[3] plenty of seats remained empty at sporting events—especially on the "Home" side. It wasn't uncommon for more than half the crowd to consist of visiting fans who'd traveled to support their team—creating a kind-of "reverse home field advantage."

When I walked onto NU's campus for my first day as a professional strength coach, I was well-aware—from an athletics perspective—I wasn't at Ohio State or Michigan. Yet, what Northwestern lacked in athletic prowess, it more than made up for in academic excellence. Because of NU's high academic standards and esteemed alumni network, I always felt the athletes who walked through the weight room door would become leaders in their chosen fields and communities. And, among many others, a basketball player from Ohio named

Evan Eschmeyer proved me right.

From an early age, Eschmeyer had a vision to attend Northwestern. On family trips from their home in New Knoxville, Ohio, the Eschmeyers often passed NU's campus in Evanston, where Evan's aunt had attended school. When they did, Evan's parents would remind him: "If you study really hard, you can go to school there someday, too." Their encouragement gave Evan both the motivation and the method for accomplishing his vision.

As time told, Eschmeyer received a bit of extra help toward achieving his goal from his genetics. By his senior year of high school, Eschmeyer was 6-foot-11 and one of the top 50 prospects in the nation for his class, averaging 30.2 points, 14.5 rebounds and 3.5 blocks per game.[4] While he did put in the academic work to get there, Eschmeyer's ultimate ticket to Northwestern was a full-ride *basketball* scholarship in 1993—pushing him closer to another one of his childhood dreams: playing in the NBA. As a prized recruit, Eschmeyer chose NU to fulfill both his athletic and academic goals.

> **Without education, we have no intellectual ground on which to stand and walk.**

While playing in the Big Ten allowed him to compete at the highest level, Eschmeyer never lost sight of his original motivation to attend NU. During his time as a Wildcat, he kept a balanced approach to basketball and his studies. As Evan once told me, "Your education is the one thing that no one can take away from you. It is another tool in your toolbox to attack life."

Education is the process by which we acquire knowledge that is encoded, stored and later retrieved. It's a combination of both learning and memory that starts from the day we're born and continues until we die. Education is the foundation of the mental building block—everything we learn and use to grow intellectually results from education, whether formal or informal (e.g., experience). When used correctly, education boosts critical thinking and decision-making, develops our minds, and empowers us to pursue our God-given purpose. Without education, we have no intellectual ground on which to stand and walk.

Our brains are not static organs. From the moment we're born, they're constantly changing and developing in response to education and experience. This adaptability is known as brain plasticity. As we grow, our nervous system modifies and restructures the brain accordingly, resulting in psychological change (a.k.a. "learning" or "memory"). When you learn a new motor skill—like playing an instrument, for example—there are plastic changes in the structure of your brain cells that underlie the motor skill. But learning doesn't happen in a vacuum. Obstacles such as distraction or lack of intentional focus can prevent these plastic, underlying brain changes from occurring. Without these changes, motor learning won't occur.[5]

Our brains actually *need* new information to survive and grow. The more we exert our brains through consistent mental stimulation, the more neurological branches and connections form, and the higher our brains can function. According to *Your Miracle Brain* by Jean Carper, neurological investment through education can prevent long-term mental complications:

> *"The brain is like a muscle—using it makes it grow and expand; disuse causes it to atrophy. Thus, education makes brains more resistant to deterioration and disease, because people who earn degrees tend to exercise their brains more, building a more lively, resilient, and complex brain."*[6]

Eschmeyer's time at Northwestern counteracted what has become a persistent problem in college athletics—a *neglect* for education. Many student-athletes—top recruits, in particular—have become so focused on "making it pro" that they often push aside anything in their way to achieving that end goal. Because of confidence in their ability to succeed athletically, many neglect an (often-free) opportunity at a quality education. They might attend classes, but their focus, energy and effort are elsewhere. And, in doing so, they ignore the clear, but discouraging facts about the reality of their situation.

Take men's basketball, for example. In 2019, more than 540,000 boys played high school basketball. Of that group, only 3.5 percent competed at the NCAA-level (less than 19,000). Of those college players, only 0.28 percent (52 players) made it to the NBA. That's one NBA player for every 10,400[7] high school players (or, less than one one-hundredth of a percent). Not to mention that the average NBA career lasts less than five years. Hall-of-Fame wide receiver Cris Carter (whom you'll read about next chapter) offered this perspective on ESPN Radio:

"People are losing perspective. There is a thing called player development, athletic development, and then there is human development. From a maturity standpoint, [coaches need to] keep [students] in college as long as you can. Get your education because, one day, you're definitely going to need it. Maybe we need to start pushing that more than sports, and even if he makes it to the NFL, the League's telling him 3.4 years. So get your education, kids. Give yourself another option. Don't put all your eggs in one basket."[8]

Because Eschmeyer understood this problem, he took a long-term approach to his professional career and planned for life *after* basketball accordingly. Education wasn't just something to "get through" on Evan's path to the NBA; it was an opportunity to mentally grow, expand his opportunities and set himself up for future success. And not even a year into his college basketball career, it looked as if this post-basketball plan would start much earlier than expected.

Just three weeks into his freshman season, foot pain Eschmeyer had experienced in high school resurfaced in practice. Doctors first diagnosed him with a stress fracture, before later revealing he had avascular necrosis, a rare nerve and bone condition. He was told he'd never play basketball again. Eschmeyer's NU athletic career—the one fans hoped would lead to the Wildcats' first NCAA Tournament appearance in school history—seemed to be over before it really even began.[9] But Eschmeyer wasn't quite ready to let that dream die.

As the assistant strength and conditioning coach at NU at the time, I spent a great deal of time with Eschmeyer. Through multiple operations and setbacks, Evan and I focused on developing his muscles in the weight room and conditioning his heart in the swimming pool. Day-in and day-out, I witnessed his great work ethic and vision to return to the court.

On one occasion, Evan was traveling and had to miss his in-person workout with me—but that didn't keep him from an opportunity for physical growth. In the middle of a road trip, *in the back of a van*, Evan performed a partner resistance workout I'd taught him with a fellow athlete. Inside of a moving car, with a teammate using his strength as resistance, Evan successfully completed exercises for his chest, back, shoulders and biceps. Maybe it wasn't the safest decision in the world, but talk about dedication! As proof, he even sent me a picture.

In the fall of 1995, after two seasons of rehabilitation, Eschmeyer proved the doctors wrong. With his foot fully recovered, he stepped back on the court and his path to professional basketball. By the end of his Northwestern career in 1999, Eschmeyer had filled the school's record books. At the time, he finished second in career points (1,805), first in field goal percentage (.595), first in free throws made (595), second in blocks (132) and first in rebounds (995).[10] Eschmeyer was also named a three-time All-Big Ten selection and second-team All-American in 1999.

> *Education wasn't just something to "get through" on Evan's path to the NBA; it was an opportunity to mentally grow, expand his opportunities and set himself up for future success.*

Because of the time he missed with his injury, the NCAA awarded Eschmeyer a fifth year of athletic eligibility—and then a rare sixth year. As his basketball stats show, Eschmeyer took advantage of his two bonus years at NU—and that was true in the classroom as well. With the extra time, he completed pre-med coursework, majored in secondary education for the sciences and began working towards an economics degree. His mental fortitude mirrored the work ethic he exhibited in the gym. If the NBA didn't work out, Eschmeyer had his education to not only fall back on, but to propel himself toward a successful career in a variety of different fields.

To give you a glimpse into Eschmeyer's relentless pursuit of education, here's a sampling of his comments from the 1996-97 Northwestern Basketball Media Guide:[11]

- *My advice to youth: "Study!"* Like on the court, Eschmeyer had to study to survive as he competed with some of the top students in the world at a rigorous academic institution.

- *When I want to get away from basketball: "I go to the library."* Eschmeyer spent two to three hours each night in the library—a.k.a. the gym for his brain.

• *If I could change one thing in the world: "My GPA."*
As a Division-I athlete, Eschmeyer managed a workload comparable to simultaneously balancing a full-time job (basketball) and a full-time college education. Despite his success—both on the court and in the classroom—he always had motivation to improve.

In 1999, the New Jersey Nets fulfilled Eschmeyer's childhood dreams by selecting him in the second round of the NBA Draft. Again, although basketball directed his new major life step, Eschmeyer didn't let his education go to waste.

> **Eschmeyer used his education and corresponding skills to not only benefit himself, but to help others and pay forward the gifts he'd been given.**

In the NBA, he served as a representative on the player's union and helped negotiate a collective bargaining agreement on behalf of the highest-paid union members in the world (average annual salary of $4 million).[12] He also helped players plan out their financial futures—an area many struggled with, especially when it came to early retirement. For high schoolers, Eschmeyer co-founded a free online recruiting service to help them acquire scholarships by providing real-time data—statistics, honors, test scores—to recruiters.[13] Eschmeyer used his education and corresponding skills to not only benefit himself, but to help others and pay forward the gifts he'd been given.

After four years between the Nets and the Dallas Mavericks, four knee surgeries in a three-year period cut Eschmeyer's NBA career short. But because of his education, he had a back-up plan. Faced with early retirement at age 29, he returned to where it all started. Eschmeyer enrolled in Northwestern's law-business double-degree program, and three years later, he had two more degrees to add to his resume.[14] Eschmeyer's friend and former Northwestern teammate, Nate Pomeday, had this to say about Evan's decision to continue his education:

"All of us are better off that Evan's going to Kellogg (NU's business school) instead of sitting on a beach somewhere. Anything he's going to do is going to be to help people."[15]

Pomeday's prophecy proved true. In his post-NBA career, Eschmeyer's roles ranged from angel investor—investing his own money and expertise into start-up companies—to working in the U.S. Senate on food and agricultural issues, to serving as a legal fellow, advocating for cleaner water and air through sustainable business development. As a CFO for a telecommunications company, Eschmeyer also played a lead role in delivering enhanced cell phone connectivity to rural areas. In everything he did, he committed to bettering communities through creating jobs and boosting economies.[16]

From New Knoxville to Northwestern to the NBA and beyond, education was Eschmeyer's common thread. He knew and capitalized on the value of developing his mental building block through education. One of his mottos was, "If you work hard and work smart, you can accomplish anything."[17] With education as his base, Eschmeyer's drive and rigor led him to Northwestern, unique roles in the NBA and significant career opportunities afterwards. His hunger to learn—and continue learning—set him apart and allowed him to not only change himself, but to impact others.

Coach's Corner

Following the 2005 season with the Baltimore Ravens—during which we finished 6-10—the team reported for our voluntary off-season training program. Typically, we sent the training schedule and program requirements out ahead of time, and players would show up at different times throughout the day to run or lift. Younger players were expected to participate—they relied on the extra income (yes, players were paid to work out) and needed the structure of the organized team program—but it wasn't uncommon for others, especially veterans, to refrain. So, when I arrived at our facility in the spring of 2006, I wasn't surprised or concerned to see a few players absent—that is, until I heard the reason why.

As I was told, certain players felt their training needs weren't being met by our strength and conditioning department—led by me—so they'd decided to pay out of their own pockets to hire an outside personal trainer. On top of that, when our offseason minicamp came around in May—with greater time commitments for meetings and practices—they requested to be coached by this outside trainer *at our team complex* after hours, and our front office gave them permission.

So, to sum it up, players I'd been *paid to train* felt I wasn't serving them well, so they personally funded someone else to do *my* job in *my* gym. Talk about a humbling experience.

Looking back, I can see the lack of attention to my mental building block and what led me to that point. The problem wasn't necessarily my training program—its success was proven—it was more so my lack of awareness to the specific needs of the players. I failed to stay ahead of the curve.

At that point in my life—although I'd been a strength coach for more than a decade—I was evolving in different ways. Jen and I had just started a family, and I was learning to be both a husband and a father. I was also a new Christian—and growing rapidly in my faith. When the workday finished, I would stay in my office to read the Bible or transcribe notes from a recorded sermon. Although I still dedicated time and effort to my job as a strength coach, I just didn't have the spare time I had before starting my family. I no longer stayed up late reading books and periodicals like I did earlier in my career and life journey. None of these changes and developments were bad—I was developing my mental building block in other ways—but the reality was they'd cost me a sense of understanding of some of my players. I hadn't kept up with the latest performance trends.

In hindsight, I can honestly and confidently say my program was working, but after a losing season, everything gets magnified. In an already insecure profession, losing amplifies a player's search for answers. It's in a pro athlete's nature to seek innovative and creative trends, whether it be diets, supplements, recovery methods or brain exercises. Even Tom Brady—arguably the greatest quarterback of all-time—developed a performance training and lifestyle approach (called "TB12") that he turned into a business. These aren't average athletes, after all—they're the world's best. They're always looking for a competitive advantage, and rightly so. In my case in 2006, it was a personal trainer.

It was a very tumultuous time in my career. I remember head coach Brian Billick coming down to my office to tell me to give the other coaches a presentation on the strength and conditioning program. "Explain it or change it," he said, referencing his mantra for our entire coaching staff. Not only was my leadership being questioned by my athletes, but I also had to prepare and provide my thoughts on the program to our coaching staff. There was dissension on two fronts, both players and coaches. I could've easily been fired. I'd arrived at a crossroads in my career.

Although I survived that offseason, it did cause me to self-evaluate. *Was I leading well? Did the players trust me?* I had a choice to make. Although I didn't want to sacrifice the other developments in my life (family, faith, habits, etc.), I needed to find a way to redistribute my time—to keep my priorities in order while also dedicating more time to my professional development. If players were searching for their next secret weapon, I needed to find it before they did. That was my job, and in order to help those players, I made it a priority to pursue continuing education in my field.

The 2006 season, thankfully, was a successful campaign. We finished the regular season with the second-best record in the AFC at 13-3, earning us a first-round bye in the playoffs. Unfortunately, we lost to the future Super Bowl champs—Peyton Manning and the Indianapolis Colts—in the divisional round.

Not wanting to repeat the previous offseason with regards to player backlash, I appealed to the organization to invest in my education. I asked them to bring in Charles Poliquin, a world-renowned strength coach who'd coached many medal-winning Olympians and actually mentored the personal trainer whom the players had worked with during minicamps. It was a big ask and a financial investment for the Ravens, but they agreed, and Poliquin visited for a week to teach myself and our staff innovative approaches to training prior to the 2007 season. The extra education enabled me to incorporate additional techniques to complement what we were already doing.

During his visit, Poliquin introduced us to Active Release Techniques[18] (ART), a soft-tissue management system. During a workout with myself and two of our players, Charles noticed each of our movement patterns was restricted because of tightness in various parts of our bodies, so he used ART to increase our flexibility. The results of ART impressed me so much that I made it a point to get certified myself.

During the 2007 season, I sent a proposal to the Ravens to fund and support my continuing education. I requested approval to participate in courses that would allow me to become ART certified. In order to do so, I needed to become a licensed healthcare professional (or enrolled student), and the prerequisite I thought would benefit me (and the players) the most was massage therapy. Sure enough, the Ravens agreed to my proposal.

Due to time commitment, financial investment and rigorous coursework, this was a unique certification for a strength coach to obtain. In God's perfect timing, though, the Ravens released our coaching staff in 2008, at the end of our disappointing 5-11 season. The time away allowed me to begin my massage therapy coursework and weave in my ART classes throughout the year. The different ART seminars involved three days of teaching and practicing, and a fourth day of testing. I remember pulling near all-nighters practicing and preparing for those tests, but at the end of those two years of education, it was all worth it.

From a professional standpoint, with so many qualified people chasing the same few NFL jobs, the added training expanded the scope of what I could offer. Like Evan Eschmeyer, it was another tool in my toolbox that opened doors for me to serve and impact athletes at various levels of the physical spectrum. It prepared me well for my return to the NFL in 2010.

This, I feel, is true of all my educational experiences. From my undergraduate program at the University of Wisconsin-Milwaukee to the biomechanics lab at the Illinois State University grad school, my education helped me develop and improve a variety of skills and gave me opportunities to accomplish my personal and professional goals. Through early and consistent investment in my brain through education, I was empowered to become the person for whom I strived.

> **Because we're neurologically blank canvases when we're young, every action, every experience, every bit of education significantly impacts our brains. The process of learning is creating order out of chaos.**

The human brain has incredible capacity—both for success and for destruction. Unlike other mammals who have very hard-wired neurological connections from birth, humans are effectively born with a blank slate. How we learn is not set in stone. That's why, after a few hours, a horse can stand up, walk and gallop, whereas humans need multiple months before they can even crawl. Essentially, our brains sacrifice security and independence in early youth for the opportunity to develop a large diversity of skills as we grow.[19] That's where education and experience come into the picture.

Because we're neurologically blank canvases when we're young, every action, every experience, every bit of education significantly impacts our brains. The process of learning is creating order out of chaos. Over time, as we repeat actions, and learn and re-learn certain things and skills, those thoughts and habits become deeply ingrained, deeply embedded neurological pathways. While we begin life as purely plastic potential, as we grow and develop, our brain structures begin to limit us through the patterns and connections we create through learning.[20] Whatever habits we establish in life's developmental stages will most likely stick with us into adulthood and old age.

> *If we don't challenge ourselves to mentally grow and develop, we'll eventually settle for the intellectually comfortable and habitual, falling short of our potential for comprehensive success.*

This why being a lifelong learner is essential. Learning involves two parts: breaking old connections and creating new ones. As you learn, your brain builds structures of what you perceive the world to be. It creates the world as we know it.[21] If we aren't consistently promoting positive neurological change through education, our brains will create habits that will become harder and harder to change and overcome. Your brain is going to change either way. If it's not getting better, it's getting worse. You go back to chaos. If you don't take care of your car, it starts breaking down. If you don't take care of your brain, it starts to get weaker; it gets slower. If we don't challenge ourselves to mentally grow and develop, we'll eventually settle for the intellectually comfortable and habitual, falling short of our potential for comprehensive success.

It doesn't have to be formal education, either. For Evan, a large part of his educational growth came from formal, in-class instruction, but it also came from conversations with more-experienced peers, reading books and studying his teammates. For you, it can be as simple as asking questions of someone older and wiser in your chosen field. We all have to start somewhere, and not all of us have the same access to or quality of formal education. We need to use what's around us to challenge ourselves to learn and grow intellectually. It's the starting place not just for the mental area of life, but for all other building blocks as well.

Physically, proper education has been linked to greater life expectancy and long-term health.[22] Better educated individuals are more likely to exercise and obtain preventative care.[23] Socially, as we educate ourselves about family, friends and other individuals, we become more relationally adept. When we ask questions and remember others' likes, dislikes, habits and passions, we learn how to be better spouses, supporters and encouragers. Spiritual education—through reading the Bible, listening to sermons/podcasts and getting involved in community—leads to a better understanding and knowledge of God, ourselves and our purpose.

> We need to use what's around us to challenge ourselves to learn and grow intellectually.

As Scripture affirms, seeking the truth through education is critical to mental growth. Look at Proverbs 4, for example. In verse 13, it says, "Hold on to instruction, do not let it go; guard it well, for it is your life." Even for the Bible, that's some strong language. *It is your life.* But how true is that? Our instruction, our education, determines our neurological development and ultimately, our mental growth and development. If we neglect education, we also neglect opportunities to positively impact ourselves and others. But if we dedicate the necessary time, effort and energy to education, we'll move one step forward toward achieving our mental (and overall) potential, both as a human being and as a child of God.

In 1 Corinthians, Paul speaks to another motivation for educating myself. In chapter 9, Paul says he "made [himself] a servant to all, that [he] might win more of them" (v.19, ESV). To the Jew, he became a Jew. To the Gentile, he became a Gentile. To the weak, he became weak. For the sake of the gospel, he became "all things to all people so that by all possible means [he] might save some" (v. 22).

Like Paul, one of my main goals as a follower of Jesus is building connections with as many people as possible. Education opens doors for those connections, for those common bonds. Our understanding of different people and their unique needs and motivations allows us to connect with them in ways others can't. Because of my strength and conditioning education, I could build into the lives of professional athletes and coaches, and my certification in ART and massage techniques expanded those opportunities. Some of the best conversations I had with players were not actually in the weight room, but on the treatment table. For Evan, the same was true in his many post-NBA career ventures.

Education can be a tool to "win others," as Paul said—which, ultimately, is to win their hearts and minds. When we use education to understand others' needs, we can also then step in to help *meet* those

> **If we neglect education, we also neglect opportunities to positively impact ourselves and others.**

needs through relationship. As a Christian, this might mean encouraging others, offering wisdom or even sharing with them the hope I have in Jesus. Ultimately, education equips us to follow God's call in the unique contexts and spheres of influence of our lives.

Foundation Building Tip

By developing our minds, education allows you to acquire knowledge and utilize it when necessary. It improves general skills, such as critical thinking and decision-making, and opens doors to positively impact yourself and others. Proper education boosts long-term health and life expectancy, leads to stronger, deeper relationships and gives us knowledge and understanding of our Creator.

Be a lifetime learner. Education should be a process that continues throughout your lifetime. What we feed our mind is just as important as what we feed our body. Never let your formal education, or lack of it, be used as an excuse for where you want to go in sport and life. Continue educating yourself through books, podcasts, local or online courses, seminars, etc. Use the instruction to make yourself and others think and do better. Always be receptive to learning, so, like Paul, you might "become all things to all people."

Your Workout

1. How has education (formal or informal) helped you achieve your personal and professional goals? List at least three examples.

2. How has a lack of education (formal or informal) prevented you from growing in certain areas of your life? Again, if you can, list three examples.

3. What are some practical ways you can grow physically, mentally, socially and/or spiritually through education? Maybe it's a conversation with someone you respect, listening to a podcast or reading a book. List three practical action steps you can take this week.

4. How can you use your education to not only benefit yourself, but also to help other people, like Evan Eschmeyer? If you can, write down three examples.

Extra Workout Challenge

1. Think of three friends and/or family members. Write down their names. Then ask yourself: What could I learn to deepen and strengthen my relationships with these people? Maybe it's researching about their profession or asking questions about their family history. Be creative and think of intentional action steps for implementing your ideas.

2. 1 Peter 3:15 tells us to "Always be prepared to give an answer to everyone who asks you to give the reason for the hope that you have." How might you better prepare yourself to "give an answer" through spiritual education? What could you learn about God (His character, His promises, His commands) that could more firmly establish your trust and confidence in Him?

CHAPTER 6: SELF-TALK

"Whatever is true, whatever is noble, whatever is right...think about such things." (Philippians 4:8)

Just three years into my NFL coaching career, I was a win away from the Big Game—Super Bowl XXXIII in Miami. I'd only coached for one team, the Minnesota Vikings, but all I knew to that point in my NFL coaching career was success.

In my first two years with the Vikings (1996-1998), we'd ended our season in the playoffs. In 1996, we squeaked into a Wild Card spot at 9-7 before being blown out by Troy Aikman, Emmitt Smith and the Cowboys, 40-15, in Dallas. In 1997, we had the same record (9-7), but this time, we won our Wild Card game...only to lose to the San Francisco 49ers a week later. But in 1998, when we clinched the playoffs for the third consecutive year, we knew it was different.

This year, we didn't squeak into the playoffs with a barely above .500 record—we won our division, the NFC North, by four games, finishing with a franchise-best *15-1 record* (which had only been done twice before).[1] This year, we beat our opponents by an average of 17.5 points per game and set an NFL record for most points in a single season (556).[2] This year, we didn't even have to *play* in the Wild Card game (we earned a bye week). After a 20-point win over the Arizona Cardinals in the Divisional Round, we were now set to host the Atlanta

Falcons in the 1998 NFC Championship game—winner headed to Miami. And by all accounts—best record, No. 1 seed, home-field advantage—we were the favorites.

A few weeks earlier, we celebrated the team's success at the annual holiday party—I can still hear our players and staff singing along with Will Smith, "I'm goin' to Miami"—but now was not the time for celebrating. Now, the pressure was on. For an overwhelming majority of our players and coaches, this was their first (and maybe only) opportunity to play in a game of this magnitude. I've coached for teams where only a handful of players and coaches even made it to the playoffs, much less a chance to play for football's biggest prize. Earning the top seed in the playoffs is one thing, but winning when it matters most is entirely another. From the fans to the media to the intensity on the field, the weight of this game was on a whole new level.

Although we were the favorites—playing in our Metrodome with a roster of 10 Pro Bowlers and four future Hall-of-Famers—the Falcons weren't your traditional underdog. They'd lost only one fewer game than us (14-2), had five Pro Bowlers of their own and led the League in turnover differential (+20).[3] Even in front of our home fans, behind an offense led by Randall Cunningham, Randy Moss and Cris Carter, none of us expected the next 48 minutes to be anything less than the most intense game of our careers.

Every player on the field—from the last player on the roster to the superstar with a high-paying contract—felt the pressure. And since conference championships were such a rarity for most players, that pressure was magnified. No one knew when (or if) this opportunity might come around again. Nothing could be taken for granted. This was especially true for the veterans. For them, it was essentially sudden death. Win or go home—and probably never come back.

Despite his accolades—to that point, six straight Pro Bowls, two-time receiving touchdowns leader—Vikings' All-Pro and future Hall-of-Fame wide receiver Cris Carter was by no means immune to the weight of that '98 NFC Championship Game. Reflecting back, Carter had this insight of playing in such a high stakes game:

"I don't think people give credit to the amount of pressure that guys were under. Just the normal thing becomes very, very difficult under that situation...My body has never felt the type of

pressure that was in those games." [4]

But to channel his focus and fuel his performance, Carter had a secret: self-talk.

"As the game went on, I had to talk to myself, to let myself know, 'Ok. *This is what I was born to do.*'" [5]

Self-talk is the continual, ongoing dialogue we have with ourselves. It's statements or thoughts addressed to the self—you know, those conversations we have in our heads. Self-talk encompasses whatever we repeatedly tell ourselves through conscious thoughts, unconscious beliefs and behaviors, and emotional responses to events and experiences. [6] A 2007 study found that 95 percent of athletes use either overt or subvocal exercise-related self-talk. [7]

"As the game went on, I had to talk to myself, to let myself know, 'Ok. This is what I was born to do.'"

As with all dialogue, self-talk can be positive, negative or neutral. Positive self-talk ("You can do it!") is personal encouragement, a belief in your ability to succeed. Negative self-talk ("I'm going to mess this up") is personal criticism, a *lack* of belief in your ability to succeed. Whatever method you choose (or use by default) has the potential to significantly impact your performance.

Turns out *The Little Engine That Could* is more than just an inspirational children's book—it's science. In a study conducted on insurance salesmen, those who labeled themselves as optimists sold 37 percent more in their first two years than did their pessimistic counterparts. [8] By countering negative self-talk and redirecting our focus to our goals, positive self-talk ("I think I can") actually makes performance easier. [9] Another study found self-talk reduces perceived exertion and improves performance by 18 percent. In other words, self-talk is comparable to the performance-enhancing impact of psycho-stimulant drugs. [10]

Studies show that athletes utilize self-talk at specific times—when they're tired, want to quit, at the hardest part of an exercise or near the end of an exercise. All four scenarios share a common characteristic: fatigue. We use self-talk when we need a little something extra—when we have nothing left in the tank. And it works. [11]

In the same 2007 study I mentioned earlier, researchers found that positive self-talk actually significantly reduces our rating of perceived effort, or RPE. In other words, when we use prepared positive phrases, we convince our minds that a task is easier—that we're giving *less effort*—than we previously thought. As a result, our perception of our maximal effort also increases. Because we think we still have more in the tank, it takes longer for us to reach exhaustion. Positive self-talk enhances our physical (or mental, spiritual or social) endurance and stamina.[12] When you tell yourself, "I can do this," it becomes a self-ful-filling prophecy.

> *When we use prepared positive phrases, we convince our minds that a task is easier—that we're giving* less *effort—than we previously thought.*

Although most people know Cris Carter for his success—eight-time Pro Bowler, three-time All-Pro, 1999 Walter Payton Man of the Year, Pro Football Hall-of-Famer—few seem to remember his starting place. After the Phila-delphia Eagles drafted him in the fourth round of the 1987 supplemental draft, Carter failed three drug tests during a three-year period. He'd drank heavily and used drugs like marijuana, cocaine and ecstasy on a regular basis, and in 1990, Eagles' coach Buddy Ryan cut Carter before the preseason even started.[13] But Carter wasn't going to let his life turn into a forgettable footnote.

After the Vikings claimed him off waivers for $100, Carter took advantage of his second chance.[14] He stopped drinking and doing drugs, and he began a process of physical and psychological detoxifica-tion. He dramatically upgraded the intensity of his fitness routine by working out harder, conditioning his body and losing weight. Carter even became a part-time owner of a sports performance facility and invited other NFL players to train with him in the offseason.[15]

With his new team, Carter recognized the importance of making small changes to move up the performance curve. He did all the little things to improve his play—most of which revolved around the most important asset for an NFL wide receiver: his hands. On a regular basis, Carter would play with Silly Putty to develop hand strength, place his hands in paraffin wax to soothe his muscles and catch thousands of footballs, one-handed, from all different angles, from a JUGS machine. On ESPN Radio, Carter once said that one of his greatest assets was that he "didn't have a dominant hand" because his left was just as good as his right.[16]

In Carter's mind, he went back to a time when he was eight years old:

> *"[Legendary Indiana basketball coach] Bobby Knight was recruiting my oldest brother Butch, and he was the best player in the state, one of the best players in America. I had three other older brothers who played basketball and all went on to play on basketball scholarships," Carter told ESPN Radio in 2015. "I was upstairs, and Bobby said, 'Man, you have a really talented family', and my mom said, 'Bobby, I got a youngest son. His name is Cris. He's eight years old. He's the most talented kid in our family.' And I never forgot that. I remembered that when Buddy Ryan cut me. As I was riding home in my car, I remembered what my mother said."* [17]

From that disappointment in the summer of 1990, Carter used that memory to fuel him to become one of the greatest wide receivers in NFL history. At the base of his motivation, he had this positive phrase of self-talk, engrained in him by his mother as an eight-year-old kid: *"This is what I was born to do."*

Back at the Metrodome in 1998, we had a seven-point lead with just over two minutes left in the game. At the Falcons 22-yard-line, we had a field goal attempt to give us a 10-point lead and all but seal our

When you tell yourself, "I can do this," it becomes a self-fulfilling prophecy.

trip to Miami. On top of that, our kicker, Gary Anderson, had yet to miss a field goal as a Viking (35-for-35 in 1998).[18] On the sideline, I was so convinced we were headed to the Super Bowl, I asked our equipment manager to save me a game ball as a keepsake.

I'll let the Falcons radio broadcast take the story from here:

> *"Here's the snap, the kick is up, and it is…no good! No good! Gary Anderson has missed a field goal for the first time in two years!"* [19]

We missed plenty of opportunities to put the game away—the blame can't be placed on one play or one player—but long story short, the Falcons tied the game with 49 seconds left and eventually won in overtime. In devastation, I watched the Falcons celebrate on our field. Stunned and disappointed, I was one of the last people to leave our sideline. It was unquestionably the worst loss of my professional career. After a record-breaking 15-1 season, with the highest scoring offense in NFL history, leading by seven with under three minutes to play, we ended our season in front of our shocked home fans.

Out of respect for the organization, my wife and I stopped by the post-game party at a nearby hotel to "celebrate" what was supposed to be a Super Bowl berth. The room was nearly empty. To add to my embarrassment, a few days after the game, our equipment manager handed me the game ball I had requested in the fourth quarter. Talk about insult on top of injury. That ball has since served as a reminder for me of the difference between optimism and overconfidence——arrogance never guarantees a win!

Despite the disappointing loss, Carter tied all players in that game for receptions (six, on nine targets) and went on to play four more years, attending his eighth consecutive (and final) Pro Bowl in 2000 after tallying 1,000 receiving yards for the eighth straight season.[20] In 2002, when he retired, Carter was only the second receiver in NFL history to finish with more than 1,000 career catches (1,101).[21] His hard work, dedication and discipline fulfilled the prophecy of his positive self-talk. Cris Carter was born to play football.

"What [the Vikings] invested in me was more than money," Carter told the *Star Tribune* after being inducted into the Pro Football Hall of Fame in 2013. "What they taught me was how to live the rest of my life. I didn't have to be a prisoner to the things that held me back before. That I could finally, finally tap into my athletic ability. That was the first time that I really feel like the car was running 100 percent."

Coach's Corner

I'm not a huge TV fan—I rarely watch anything other than sports—but a few years ago, Jen and I were trying to find something to watch together. Soon enough, we got hooked on a series about a politician clawing his way up the ladder in search for power. The more we watched, the darker the show became—and the more it affected us.

We had trouble falling asleep as violent and scandalous thoughts raced through our minds. We allowed evil thoughts from the show's grim and demoralizing scenes to enter our consciousness and chip away at our sense of peace.

Most of us have heard the phrase, "garbage in, garbage out." If we absorb negative thoughts and energy, that is exactly what we'll produce in our words and actions. Jen and I learned this the hard way with our Netflix routine. The people you surround yourself with, the music you listen to, the social media you partake in, and the television you watch all influence your demeanor. Perhaps this is why the Bible says, "Above all else, guard your heart, for everything you do flows from it" (Proverbs 4:23). Far too easily, we fall into the trap of rooting evil in our heart.

> **The way we think about ourselves is how we behave, and the more we're exposed to a statement, the more likely we're to come to believe it's true.**

By our nature, we move toward what we think about. The way we think about ourselves is how we behave, and the more we're exposed to a statement, the more likely we're to come to believe it's true. The book, *Personal Coaching for Results* by Joyce Quick and Lou Tice, puts it like this:

> *"Where the thought goes, the energy flows… The more thought, the more energy, and the more energy, the more likely a reality becomes. If you can clearly see yourself being and achieving what you want, you're far more likely to be and do those things. If you can't see it, how in the world can you expect to be it? You can only grow as far as you can imagine yourself growing."* [22]

Unfortunately for many, negative self-talk is deeply engrained from a very early age. From birth, we develop what are called "psychological scripts." Essentially, these scripts tell us where we are going in life and how we'll get there—and they're based on deep, emotional responses to certain events in our lives. For example, when children are neglected, ignored or negatively addressed by their parents—especially when it comes to meeting basic needs—they begin to subconsciously write things like "I'm not good enough" or "I'm unlovable" or "I'll never amount to anything" into their psychological scripts.[23]

Primarily, a person's script deals with three questions involving identity and destiny: "Who am I?", "What am I doing here?" and "Who are all these other people?" Positive personal scripts might tell us, "I've got a good head on my shoulders. I can accomplish whatever I put my mind on. Other people will help me," whereas negative experiences might lead to messages like, "I'm a bum. I'll never amount to anything. Other people are out to get me."

> While your psychological scripts may tell you "You're unlovable" or "You're worthless," Jesus says, "You are loved" (John 3:16) and "You are valuable" (Matt 5:26).

Most of the time, we're not even consciously aware of the control our psychological scripts have over us. On a deep psychological level, we're practicing self-talk that affects our actions and future, but until we actively process through those memories, we'll never actually be able to change those messages. Until you hear your script telling you, "I'm not good enough" or "I'm not going anywhere," you'll never be able to replace that negative self-talk with positive truths about yourself.[24] This is why it becomes key not only to evaluate our emotions and our past, but also to be constantly filling our minds with positive biblical truth.

What we put in our mind determines what comes out in our words and actions. Be careful and intentional about what you spend time thinking about. As the Apostle Paul says in Philippians, "whatever is true, whatever is noble, whatever is right, whatever is pure, whatever is lovely, whatever is admirable—if anything is excellent or praiseworthy—think about such things" (Philippians 4:8). The word "think" is from the Greek word, *logidzamai*, from which we get the mathematical term "logarithm." Logarithm means "a deliberate and prolonged contemplation as is if one is weighing a mathematical problem."[25] We are to purposefully think positive things (a.k.a. positive self-talk).

While your psychological scripts may tell you "You're unlovable" or "You're worthless," Jesus says, "You are loved" (John 3:16) and "You are valuable" (Matt 5:26). Replace the lies of the Enemy, intended to hold you back, with the truth of your Creator, meant to give you life and freedom. Pour over words that motivate. Let them marinate in your mind. Let them simmer. Prepare positive phrases, based on God's truth, and repeat them over and over again in order to push yourself to succeed.

As Cris Carter's life reflected, to perform at optimum levels, you must be intentional about what you feed your mind. In a profession that demands your peak performance regardless of circumstances, self-talk can mean the difference between winning and losing. It's the difference between getting the sale and losing the deal. Hitting your goals or missing the mark. Getting the job or missing another opportunity.

To help improve the self-talk of athletes, I've incorporated motivational phrases into my coaching. For example, as the athlete is preparing to perform an exercise or starting their first few repetitions, I may use a statement such as, "be strong today." As he or she progresses closer to their goal, I'll change the statement to something like, "finish strong." The objective is to help facilitate their positive thinking to push past pain, delay the point of exhaustion and increase endurance and overall performance.

Sometimes thoughts just need to be redirected. With self-talk, tuning out the negative is just as important as dwelling on the positive. On occasion, athletes complain for the sake of complaining. When I see it isn't productive, I may say, "Stop! Switch your thoughts to something positive." They might think I'm just disciplining for the sake of discipline, but in reality, I have their own self-confidence and performance in mind. I've found myself using this same approach with myself and my family.

Personally, praying and reciting truths from Scripture helps me remember I am not alone and that I can trust in God. A common phrase I return to is from Luke 1: "For nothing will be impossible with God" (Luke 1:37, ESV). When I face difficult situations, I say "Lord, be with me," to shift my thoughts from being discontented or worried to being courageous and thankful, or "You are my God," to acknowledge God's sovereign authority over everything. Whenever I can, I try to use gospel truth to be grateful in all circumstances. I've found it's difficult to be angry, anxious, depressed, disappointed or upset when you are grateful for God's goodness, grace and love. The two attitudes can't coexist. When times are tough, focusing on God's blessings of health, family, provision and purpose allows me to view my circumstances with a new perspective.

In Luke 6:45, Jesus says, "A good man brings good things out of the good stored up in his heart, and an evil man brings evil things out of the evil stored up in his heart. For the mouth speaks what the heart is full of." Garbage in, garbage out. Whatever we fill our hearts and minds with—whether through television, social media, relationships or self-talk—will determine our attitudes and actions. None of us are immune to the impact of external influences, so be intentional. Fill your mind with what is noble, right, pure, lovely, admirable, excellent and praise-worthy, and let the self-fulfilling prophecy work itself out.

Foundation Building Tip

We become what we think about. Studies show that what we fill our minds with, specifically through self-talk, affects our overall psychology. And our psychology, in turn, affects our physical, mental, social and spiritual actions. Positive self-talk makes performance easier, whereas negative self-talk hinders performance.

Controlling self-talk is a skill that must be repeatedly practiced and developed into a habit. Learn to gain control by following this two-step process:

1. **Stop the negative.** Identify when you are using negative self-talk. Learn to intervene by visualizing a stop sign and saying to yourself, "stop it!"

2. **Replace the negative with positive.** Make a list of pre-pared positive phrases you can keep in your toolbox. Use these statements to replace negative thoughts with positive ones. For example, replace "I can't hold this speed" with "Hold this speed."

Your Workout

1. Your behaviors reflect your self-talk. What do other people (your friends, teammates, coaches, family) say about your behavior? Think about what these people might say, and reflect on where that behavior might stem from. For example, my family would say I'm cheap and don't like to spend money, which stems from years of self-talk phrases

like, "I'm going to lose it all" or "I don't have enough."

2. Use facts to disprove a faulty belief you may have about yourself. Write down a negative perception you have about yourself. Then write down a fact to counter or refute this perception.

3. While most of us won't experience the pressure of winning a championship game like Cris Carter, we all go through stressful situations. Whether you have a fear of going to the dentist or speaking in public, you can use self-talk to help you. Create prepared, positive statements to shift your focus from negative to positive.

4. Use positive statements to help a family member, co-worker, neighbor or friend. For example, my daughter is a grown adult, yet I still often reminder her she "is my princess." Likewise, my wife wrote on both of our children's bathroom mirrors the statement, "I am enough" to eliminate self-doubt of who they are.

Extra Workout Challenge

1. Read Philippians 4:8. Mediate on what you read. Throughout the week, do your best to write down different thoughts on which you find yourself dwelling. At the end of the week, review. Compare your thoughts to Paul's criteria in Philippians.

2. Find three truths in Scripture about who God says you are. Write them down, keep them with you and/or memorize them. When you feel worthless, unloved or empty, remind yourself of God's truth about your identity and ultimate destiny.

CHAPTER 7: EMOTION

"Better a patient man than a warrior, a man who controls his temper than one who takes a city." (Proverbs 16:32)

On a beautiful, sunny September day in Baltimore, Ravens' running back Jamal Lewis was *in the zone*. It was Week 2 of the 2003 season, and on the second offensive play of the game, Lewis broke through an opening in the Cleveland Browns defense—cutting, sidestepping and eventually outrunning every Browns defender on the field. Eighty-two-yard touchdown. 7-0, Ravens.

Lewis had played well before—he finished each of his first two healthy NFL seasons (2000 and 2002) with more than 1,300 rushing yards[1]—but this game was different. Lewis put everything on display— his seemingly effortless combination of balance, power, speed and determination. As the game progressed—and our lead grew—I could sense some special brewing in M&T Bank Stadium. With each carry, the sea of purple and black in the stands grew louder.

By the end of the first quarter, Lewis had already eclipsed 100 yards (118). At halftime, he was just 20 yards away from 200. In the third quarter, Lewis managed only 15 more yards—bringing his total to 195—but in the fourth, he turned things up again. On the first play of the final quarter, he ran for a 63-yard touchdown, and by the time the game ended, Jamal Lewis had set a new single-game NFL rushing record: 295 yards. It was the greatest single-game rushing performance in the NFL's then-83-year history.[2]

Three years before, in 2000, Lewis capped off his rookie season by becoming the youngest player in NFL history to score a touchdown in the Super Bowl (21) in our championship victory over the New York Giants.[3] But before the 2001 season even started, Lewis tore his ACL in training camp and spent the year rehabbing and recovering. Returning from the knee injury in 2002, we monitored Lewis' body composition on a weekly basis to find the optimal level for peak performance. He finished the season with a respectable 1,327 yards.

But, as evidenced in the Week 2 matchup with the Browns, 2003 was an entirely new chapter in Lewis' career. He entered his record-breaking season in terrific shape and maintained an ideal body composition level throughout the season. Not only that, but Lewis also became a more patient runner, trusting his offensive line to create holes for him to run through. He studied film, asked questions of his offensive linemen and learned how defenses tried to defend him. In all areas of performance, Lewis had set himself up for a career year—and it showed.[4] He finished the 2003 season with 2,066 rushing yards—at the time, the second-most in NFL history—and was named the NFL Offensive Player of the Year.

Many other NFL players have returned from injury like Lewis, with ideal body composition, more film study and better understanding of offensive schemes, yet, to that point, only Eric Dickerson had put up single-season rushing numbers like Lewis did in 2003.[5] With games of 134, 180 and 205 rushing yards (on top of Week 2's 295), the future All-Pro clearly operated on an historic level.[6] So, what was the difference?

As I mentioned earlier, the evidence is in something Lewis told reporters after the Week 2 matchup against Cleveland:

> *"The big thing I took away…was how well we executed. If we can get that kind of penetration every game, with everyone blocking downfield, there's no reason we can't do that again.* I feel like I'm in a zone, *and I want to stay in it."*[7]

Twenty-six years earlier, when Bears Hall-of-Fame running back Walter Payton set the same NFL record (single-game rushing) with 275 yards against the Vikings, funny enough, he said something similar:

> "It was like being in a zone... *There are times when you got out on the football field and you never tire. Every move that you make is just like the last one, with the same speed, with the same enthusiasm. Every time the play is called, you know exactly what you are supposed to do, and you do it. It happens.*"[8]

As much as you've probably heard it used, especially in sports, "the zone" is actually more than a clichéd phrase that athletes use when they're feeling particularly good. There's some psychology behind it. While there's not consistency in exact terminology, "the zone" is the area of mental focus in which someone will most likely reach peak performance. It's that state of heightened sensory and physiological awareness—affected by many external and internal factors—in which you feel essentially unbeatable.[9] The book *Inner Skiing*, by Timothy Gallwey, defines it like this:

> "*Everything seems to click, and we ski so much better than usual that we surprise ourselves. Turns we struggle with are suddenly easy. Frustrations vanish, and we become totally absorbed in the joy of the moment. The usual mental struggle— trying to do everything right, worrying about how we look or about falling and failing—is forgotten. Enjoyment is so intense that we don't even think of making a mistake—and we don't. The thinking mind is in a state of rest; awareness is at a peak. For a time, self-imposed limitations are forgotten; we are skiing unconsciously.*"[10]

Gallwey then goes on to point out the implications of this reality:

> "*But the breakthrough (Gallwey's terminology for "the zone") confronts us with an undeniable and somewhat uncomfortable truth: we can perform much better than we usually do.*"[11]

In other words, we get in our own way. No one knows exactly why— some days everything clicks inside of us; other days, we're awkward and off-balance.[12] Despite the obvious benefits, even the best athletes only achieve this mental state about 15 percent of the time.[13] So why is zone performance so rare?

For most athletes, especially at the professional level, the starting point for peak performance is something called "the flow." Flow is the mental state of performance in which an athlete's (or anyone's) challenges and skills are completely immersed in three things: 1) positive thoughts, 2) positive beliefs, and 3) positive behaviors.[14] Let's break that down using a sports psychology model from Dr. Peter Ganshirt, who worked with me in Cincinnati.

1. Thoughts

Thoughts are the starting place for our values, beliefs and behaviors, and they're based on what we learned or were taught in the past (See "Chapter 5: Education"). As we learned in Chapter 6, in order to control and utilize these thoughts, or self-talk, we need to first be aware of our thinking patterns. When our thoughts distract from our main goal, in any way, performance suffers. Is your thinking naturally more uplifting or does it lean more toward self-criticism? Examples of positive and negative thoughts include:

Negative –	Positive +
"I blew that catch."	"I'll make the catch."
"What if we lose?"	"I think we will win."

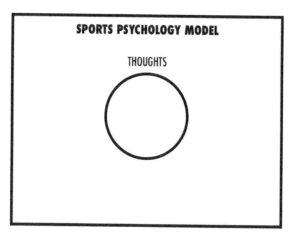

Ganshirt's Sports Psychology Model: Thoughts

2. Beliefs

Beliefs are based on our value system. They're firm convictions about someone or something, and stem from both internal (thoughts) and external variables. Depending on factors like parents, mentors, coaches, teammates, referees, field conditions, etc., our minds influence our beliefs, thus having an effect on our emotions, both positive and negative. Examples include:

Negative –
"I am not responsible"
"Practice is too long"
"I don't like football"

Positive +
"My teammate has my back"
"We have a good game plan"
"I like football"

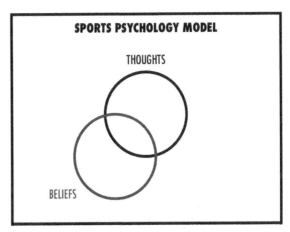

Ganshirt's Sports Psychology Model: Beliefs

3. Behaviors

Behaviors, simply, are the physical manifestation of our thoughts and beliefs. Examples include:

Negative –
Head down
Eyes down
Throwing helmet
Yelling

Positive +
High five
Running
Hitting pads of teammate
Helping player get up

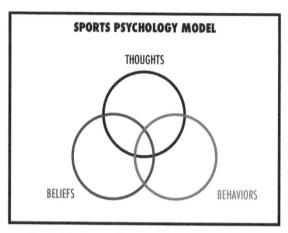

Ganshirt's Sports Psychology Model: Behaviors

As I mentioned earlier, in order for someone to achieve a "flow state," all three of these areas must be positive.[15] Positive thoughts, positive beliefs and positive behaviors. Before kickoff, an NFL player "in the flow" might look something like this:

- Thought: "I think I'll play well today."
- Belief: "I have the skills and talents to perform on the field."
- Behavior: Head up, chest out, standing tall.

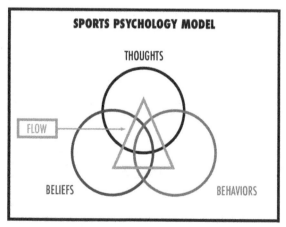

Ganshirt's Sports Psychology Model: Flow

Because of their training, most professional athletes can get into the flow very easily, yet, as you've probably noticed, most athletes don't perform with the consistency and success of Jamal Lewis in Week 2 of the 2003 NFL season. That's because something's missing. While the flow state is a critical starting point, by itself, flow doesn't actually elevate performance. You need a fourth and final element to truly get yourself "in the zone": emotion.[16]

When we infuse constructive emotion into the flow of positive thoughts, beliefs and behavior, we step into that coveted 15 percent. Emotion is the difference-maker. That's what separated Jamal Lewis from the rest of the NFL running backs in 2003. Not only did he set himself up for success with training, education and self-talk, but he channeled his constructive emotions—confidence, enthusiasm, determination—into success on the field.

> *Not only did he set himself up for success with training, education and self-talk, but he channeled his constructive emotions— confidence, enthusiasm, determination—into success on the field.*

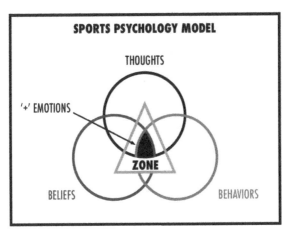

Ganshirt's Sports Psychology Model: The Zone

Emotions are strong feelings deriving from one's circumstances, mood or relationships with others. They represent our internal evaluation and response to how certain events in our lives affect our well-being (a process called "appraisal").[17] That's why the flow state focuses on maintaining positive thoughts, beliefs and behaviors—because if one of these slips into the negative, it opens a door for negative, destructive emotions. Not only do emotions *result* from thoughts, beliefs and behaviors, they also *inspire* them. Emotions differ from feelings in that emotions elicit the impulse to act. When we're confident (constructive emotion), we think positive thoughts, believe positive things about ourselves and model positive behaviors. Constructive emotion brings consistency to the flow state and, in turn, pushes us toward peak performance.

> **When we're confident (constructive emotion), we think positive thoughts, believe positive things about ourselves and model positive behaviors.**

On the other hand, negative emotions—anger, frustration, fear, doubt, anxiety—may *prevent* an athlete from getting into the zone.[18] First, they can interrupt the accomplishment of personal goals with another agenda.[19] Take anger, for example, which produces "a powerful impulse to counterattack in order to gain revenge for an affront or repair a wounded self-esteem. This is what makes anger such a dangerous emotion." Think of athletes who end up fist fighting the opponent instead of playing the game.[20] Also, through various physiological changes, negative emotions can narrow our perceptual field, decrease our ability to shift attention, diminish our fine motor functioning, disrupt blood flow patterns, impede decision-making and cause our muscles to tense up.[21] Any emotion, except those that promote enhanced concentration and focus, can lead to a serious adverse effect on performance.

As a longtime coach, I've, unfortunately, observed this firsthand. In one game alone in 2005, my team (Ravens) had *21 penalties*—one short of the NFL record![22] To put that in perspective, the most-penalized team that year—the Oakland Raiders—averaged *just 9.2 penalties per game*.[23] The game spiraled out of control as one of our defensive players threw a ball at the opposing receiver after an interception. Another player threw a ball at a wall because the referee turned his back on him. Another received a personal foul for giving an obscene gesture to the crowd. Two more were ejected for bumping into the referee.

It should come as no surprise that we lost that game—by 18 points.

After the game, head coach Brian Billick summarized our performance by saying, "Clearly, what happened out there was giving in to the emotion of the situation."[24] If not for the abundance of negative emotion expressed in inappropriate ways, we might've won that game against a team we very well should've beaten.

According to Dr. Ganshirt's model for zone performance, emotional targeting and regulation is the bedrock for consistent, peak performance. If we can monitor and protect ourselves from negative, destructive emotions (anger, fear, insecurity) while channeling constructive ones (confidence, optimism, excitement), we'll set ourselves up for consistent, high-level performance. And while Dr. Ganshirt's model focuses on athletes, this process can be applied to anyone.[25]

The next question then becomes: *How do we do this? How do we block out negative emotions and infuse positive ones into our flow state?*

Of course, this is easier said than done. When destructive emotions take over our minds, it often leads to short-sightedness and loss of perspective, which makes it difficult to act rationally.[26] While there's no simple answer to this question—keep in mind that we're condensing a complex, multifaceted issue into a simplified process—Dr. Ganshirt does offer a solution for infusing emotion and boosting performance. He calls it the mental loop for zone performance.

Essentially, Dr. Ganshirt's model is a method of "coping"—a way of responding (positively or negatively) to uncomfortable, destructive emotions. Coping is how we manage or regulate our emotions.[27] We use anger to cope with feeling hurt. We use hope to cope with despair. Some emotions (like shame or defeat) are more difficult to cope with than others.[28] When we suppress these emotions or try to avoid them through entertainment and distraction, we end up stunting our emotional awareness and development. Dr. Ganshirt's mental loop, though, provides a positive alternative. To get in the zone, you need to follow a three-step process of recognizing, regrouping, and refocusing your thoughts, beliefs and behaviors—from negative to positive:

Recognize

The first step in the mental loop is to recognize the negative. Before you can take any steps forward, you must first be aware of what's there. You need to identify potential destructive self-statements like "I am going to lose" or "What if I miss?" that may be lurking on or underneath the surface of your active thoughts. According to Travis Bradberry, the author of *Emotional Intelligence 2.0*, self-awareness—understanding what makes you behave in a certain way—is one of the most important skills to controlling emotion. Of the 500,000 people Bradberry tested, only 36 percent could successfully identify their emotions as they occurred.[29]

As a coach, it's crucial to recognize negative beliefs and behaviors in athletes to keep them from dwelling on destructive emotions. To understand their thought process, asking open-ended questions like, "Can you tell me more?" or "What was your experience like when you didn't perform the way you expected?" gets the athlete talking. Then, as you listen to the athlete, try to pay particular attention to the emotions (or lack thereof) they experienced when not performing up to expectations. These may include doubt, uncertainty, fear or anger. From there, an effective strategy may be to develop a list of negative thoughts and write them down, bringing them from the subconscious to the conscious. Now, instead of these thoughts being repressed and continuing to produce negative emotions, the athlete has awareness, and they begin to develop confidence in managing and controlling their performance.

Destructive thoughts may be harder to recognize when we activate our Freudian defense mechanisms. These are psychological defenses outside of a person's conscious control that protect one from facing uncomfortable unacceptable thoughts or feelings. These may include denial ("this isn't a problem"), projection ("it's your fault, not mine"), rationalization (making excuses), repression (holding feelings in), regression (escaping to earlier developmental stages), and reaction formation (behaving the opposite of how one feels). While these mechanisms *do* protect us (temporarily) from uneasy realities, they also inhibit our awareness of subconscious destructive thoughts.[30] As a result, these defenses perpetuate those thoughts and keep us from peak performance. Without awareness, we can't make substantial emotional progress.

Regroup

After recognition, the next step is to regroup *away* from neutral or destructive thoughts, beliefs and behaviors. This is where self-talk becomes important. Since negative thought patterns typically lead to negative emotions, it's important to break the cycle and prevent negative thoughts from stacking on top of each other through regrouping statements. These are simply words or phrases (think "prepared positive phrases" from Chapter 6) that disrupt negative thoughts. Some examples might be, "Let's go!", "Come on!" or "I got this."

I arrived at Northwestern University the same year as head football coach Gary Barnett. In 1992, Coach Barnett walked into a football program that had last finished with a winning record in 1971—21 years. Go back 23 *more* years, to 1948, and that was the last time the school had made a bowl appearance. That all changed with Coach Barnett.[31]

To create his own culture, one of the first things Coach implemented was a regrouping phrase: "Expect Victory!" He wanted to change the culture through how players thought about themselves and the program. "Expect Victory!" became so integrated at Northwestern that it eventually spread to the entire athletic department, transforming the mindset of athletes, staff and administration. This positive self-talk prominently decorated all athletic facilities and media publications. By 1995—just Coach Barnett's fourth season at NU—the Wildcats went 10-1, claiming a Big Ten title and earning a trip to the Rose Bowl.[32]

Refocus

Once you've disrupted destructive thoughts, refocusing uses positive thoughts, beliefs and behavior to infuse constructive emotions, such as confidence, optimism or enthusiasm, to optimize zone performance. Here, self-talk becomes *even more* important. In addition to redirecting focus away from the negative, you're also intentionally targeting positive emotion. You can do this by inserting an adjective or description into your self-talk that stimulates an emotion such as:

- Confidence: "I'm going to be great!"
- Optimism: "We're going to kick butt!"
- Enthusiasm: "I'm *pumped* about this chance to prove myself."

Unfortunately, this third step is where many coaches (and athletes) fall short. You've probably experienced this yourself. You'll hear (or use) regrouping phrases like "C'mon!" or "Let's go!", but it stops there.

Refocusing statement in team meeting room at Paul Brown Stadium

The self-talk never takes that next step to infuse constructive emotion through refocusing—and thus, athletes and coaches miss out on this piece of "coaching gold," as Dr. Ganshirt likes to call it. Refocusing is a powerful way to move players into the "zone" to get an additional five to 15 percent of physical potential.[33] This seemingly small boost could be the difference between winning and losing—or moving up the performance curve.

+++

In my opinion, emotion is one of the most important skillsets to develop. Think about it. Think about the things for which you're striving. For an NFL player, he might say he wants to score a touchdown or intercept a pass or sack the quarterback, but what he really craves is that positive emotion—joy, excitement, enthusiasm—that *results* from that positive action. For you, it might be having a hard conversation with a loved one or finishing a project at work or going on vacation. Is your end goal *actually* the accomplishment itself? Or is it the resulting emotions of relief, satisfaction and relaxation?

Emotions connect us with our deeper selves. Our minds measure every life event's impact on our well-being, and the result is emotion.[34] Whether we recognize them or not (conscious or subconscious), our emotions are always there. They enhance (or lessen) attention and concentration,[35] and they motivate action. Confidence, enthusiasm and love for the game led Jamal Lewis to put together one of the greatest rushing seasons in NFL history. God created us with a wide spectrum of emotions that provide us with abundant life, and fully experiencing them makes life worth living.

On the other hand, when we lose control of our emotions, we create the possibility of hurting ourselves and others. You might've heard the phrase, "Hurt people hurt people." This is a tangible reflection of this concept. I've worked with players who had troubles off the field, and often times, those resulting negative emotions carried over to practice and game day. Because our emotions are so engrained and influential, it's almost impossible to prevent them from impacting our actions.

What makes things more complicated is not all emotions are created equal for each person. For example, typically positive emotions like confidence and enthusiasm might increase performance for one athlete but lead to complacency in another. On the flipside, anger (a typically "negative" emotion) might be destructive for one person—leading to distraction, lack of focus and sporadic behavior—while increasing focus and energy for another. Some children who are put down and made to feel they're "not good enough" by their parents actually *use* that pent-up anger to focus, work harder and prove their parents wrong.[36] Psychologist Richard Lazarus sums it up like this:

> *"The lesson is that we have to be careful not to presume that negative thinking is always damaging and that positive thinking always facilitates performance. Simplistic thinking like this is not what we need."*[37]

Our 2000 Ravens team was known as one of the most underrated teams to ever make the Super Bowl. As much as we believed in ourselves, no one outside of our locker room seemed to believe we had a chance at a successful season—much less, the Super Bowl. And although disrespect is, again, typically a "negative" emotion, there's no doubt that it fueled our performance and led us to victory in Super Bowl XXXV.

Unfortunately, there are no absolutes. There's no one, sure-fire way to regulate emotions. Although Dr. Ganshirt's model for zone performance provides a helpful, simplified model for many athletes, even he recognizes the importance of individualizing emotional management.

The art of coaching involves targeting the specific emotions of each athlete. You have to understand the player, their position and their personality. For example, the job of a middle linebacker in football is to make tackles. Targeting more aggressive emotions—such as confidence, fortitude and determination, would be appropriate for these players. The mentality of a running back is to "hit the hole with all your might," because tackling typically results in violent collisions. A kicker may require a different set of emotions, such as calmness and confidence to "kick the ball smooth and easy."

Dr. Ganshirt implemented this by prioritizing a list of three primary emotions for each athlete, based on their personality and position. He would then help athletes infuse these individualized emotions into their flow state to move them into zone performance. For example, with one Bengals' running back, Dr. Ganshirt targeted his confidence, anger and happiness—two typically "positive" emotions and one typically "negative." When this player ran with confidence in his abilities, anger to break through tackles and burst through gaps, and happiness to be playing the game he loved, he maximized his performance.[38]

> **Until we truly recognize and embrace our emotions, we can't effectively move forward.**

Unfortunately, not all of us are professional athletes—and thus, not all of us have professional psychologists creating personalized plans for recognizing and utilizing our emotions. That's OK. Ultimately, it all goes back to step one in the mental loop—recognition. Until we truly recognize and embrace our emotions, we can't effectively move forward. That's why awareness is so critical.

In order to get in the zone—to reach that state of mind in which we not only appreciate our sport, but also perform at our best—we need to be aware of what thoughts, doubts and fears might be limiting us. According to *Inner Skiing*, our "greatest possibilities lie in overcoming the self-imposed mental limitations, which prevent the full expression of [our] physical potential."[39] It's our mental state, not our physical, that provides the greatest threat to achieving peak performance.

As *Inner Skiing* addresses, fear is a great example of this. When we're driven and controlled by fear, we become consumed by things that might happen in the future. We're pulled out of the present moment—and away from awareness—because we're worried about what might happen, how we might fail, what disaster might strike. Then, as Gallwey puts it, "the skier who decides that he is having a bad day inevitably will have one. The person who decides that he has reached a plateau will stay there until he decides that he is off it."[40]

This goes back to why positive self-talk and confidence are so important—why Dr. Ganshirt always targets confidence in his athletes and why Jamal Lewis had such success in 2003. When we infuse positive, helpful emotions into our flow state, we increase awareness and acknowledge fear. Instead of worrying about what might happen, we can acknowledge the risks while preventing that fear from actually controlling us. When we're confident, we view failures and mistakes not as sources of anger and frustration but as opportunities to learn and grow.[41]

That's why, even after Lewis started of his historic 2003 with a disappointing 69 yards on 15 carries in a 34-15 loss to Pittsburgh in Week 1, he could bounce back with the greatest rushing performance of all-time.

Coach's Corner

As any NFL player knows, the 17-week season gets *long*. Week after week, day after day, these athletes put their bodies on the line, sacrificing their physical state to violently collide with other super-athletes for 48 minutes on a Sunday afternoon. As the season wears on, the physical toll becomes more and more prevalent—perhaps at no clearer a time than mid-season, early-morning workouts.

In the middle of the season, it's not uncommon for players to report as early as 7 a.m. on any given workday. It's also not uncommon for them to be tired, fatigued and often unmotivated. In these moments, I have a choice. I can either give into my own frustration at the players' lack of motivation and energy, or I can choose to counteract their negative emotions with positive emotions of my own. Although I've fallen into both camps, as I've learned, only when I choose the latter can I really bring out the best in an athlete.

As humans, we feed off each other's positive and negative emotions, so as a strength coach, I consider my emotional state part of my job. It's critical for me to maintain a positive mental framework. For the sake of those I'm coaching—and effectiveness in my own techniques and instruction—I need to be encouraging, excited and positive. In the weight room, I've tried to implement Dr. Ganshirt's principles to generate positive energy daily. I'll smile to get a player to smile, or I'll give a high-five or shake a player's hand after they achieve a goal. To further elicit positive emotions, I'll strategically place refocusing statements like "get better today," "be precise" and "violent" on benches, dumbbells, kettlebells and barbell racks. As Proverbs 12:25 says, "Anxiety weighs down the heart, but a kind word cheers it up." A good word from a coach, friend or even the word of God can be comforting, uplifting and even inspirational.

On the other side, any crack in the foundation of the four building blocks can create negative emotions. Broken relationships, lack of mental preparedness, physical limitations, or a lack of faith or relationship with God, can create a downgrade of positive emotion and decrease the possibility of zone performance. In turn, performance becomes inconsistent, which generates more negative emotion. According to Dr. Ganshirt, "All negativity in [one's] personal life may proportionally decrease the ability to consistently perform in a zone capacity."[42] For example, if a player feels as if he is not a good father, husband or teammate, this may inhibit him from experiencing true joy when he makes a great play. The result, then, is inconsistent performance.

> **When emotions reach our identity, it affects everything we think, say and believe.**

Emotions not only impact our actions, but they also affect our identity. How we feel about ourselves often informs what we believe about who we are as human beings. If we're driven by fear of not being lovable or never being enough, those negative emotions can lead us to believe "I am unlovable" or "I'm not enough." These feelings about our identity are often difficult to compartmentalize. If you feel shame and disappointment about our job as a spouse or a parent, you'll have trouble keeping that from affecting your performance at work or on the field.[43] When emotions reach our identity, it affects everything we think, say and believe.

Negative emotions can also have direct consequences on our physical building block. When we're doubtful and afraid, our bodies become rigid, tense and awkward. When we experience anxiety—conscious or subconscious—our bodies follow suit by moving our shoulders and jaw forward, increasing our breathing rate and limiting the ability of the internal organs and muscles to utilize oxygen. And just as positive emotions can lead to positive physical effects, the reverse is also true. We can combat our body's response to anxiety through deep, controlled breathing that lowers our heart rate and fends off negative emotions like anger and fear.

On a social level, emotional awareness helps us communicate with others. When we understand, feel and connect with our emotions, we're then able to adequately express those feelings to others. It also allows us to properly react to and relate with others. For example, when you're arguing with a friend or a spouse and they say something that targets an insecurity, your gut reaction might be to respond in anger. However, if you're aware of the fear underneath your insecurity that triggered the anger as a coping mechanism, you can communicate that to your friend or spouse instead of lashing out and risking hurting them in the process.

Spiritually, the Bible gives us countless examples of the importance of emotional awareness in expressions. In the Psalms, the authors paint a surprisingly unfiltered and vulnerable picture of how emotions impact prayer. In the book of Job, amid his anguish and bitterness toward God, Job said, "Therefore I will not keep silent; I will speak out in the anguish of my spirit, I will complain in the bitterness of my soul" (Job 7:11). God provides us with an open door and listening ear to express and process through our emotions with Him. Instead of suppressing and eventually becoming overwhelmed by what's underneath the surface, we gain an eternal perspective and the ability to constructively deal with the situation.[44]

Another model for emotional health comes directly from the Source—Jesus Himself. In John 2, during the Jewish Passover, Jesus goes to Jerusalem, enters the temple and sees people using His Father's house for their own financial gain. And he *responds*:

> *"So he made a whip out of cords, and drove all from the temple courts, both sheep and cattle; he scattered the coins of the money changers and overturned their tables. To those who sold doves he said, 'Get these out of here! Stop turning my Father's house into a market!'" (John 2:15-16).*

Many of us know Jesus as the loving, gentle man who heals the sick, forgives the sinner and saves the lost. And while He *is* all of those things, He also got angry—not an uncontrolled, fear-based anger, but a righteous, zealous (passionate, energetic, devoted) anger for the holiness of God. Before this scene, Jesus had just come from joyfully celebrating a wedding in Cana. After the temple, Jesus exhibits deep empa-

> *Not only does Jesus provide a perfect example for emotional expression, but He also provides the antidote for the effects of destructive emotions on our identity*

thy and care for a Pharisee named Nicodemus.[45] While we might often see Jesus as one-dimensional, the biblical account tells a different story: Jesus lived an abundant life by experiencing and expressing the same wide range of emotions as us.

Not only does Jesus provide a perfect example for emotional expression, but He also provides the antidote for the effects of destructive emotions on our identity. When our fears tell us, "I'm not enough," He says, "my power is made perfect in your weakness" (2 Cor 12:9) When we hear, "I'm unlovable," He says, "You are loved" (John 3:16). When that inner voice says, "I'm nothing," He says, "You are my child" (1 John 3:1).

Foundation Building Tip

Emotions both influence and are influenced *by* our thoughts, beliefs and behaviors. In the same way, constructive emotions are both critical to peak performance and to living a full, abundant life. We live not to climb mountains, run races and earn degrees—we live to experience the emotions that result from them. And experiencing and communicating those emotions is foundational to the human experience.

Take steps to boost your emotional awareness. Journal, pray or talk with close, trusted friends about your thoughts, feelings and reactions to different internal and external influences. Use that knowledge to combat the destructive, channel the constructive, build a healthy physical, mental, social and spiritual life.

Your Workout

1. Can you think of a time when you were "in the zone"? Journal through what you can remember. What factors contributed to your success? What emotions were you feeling? What may have led to you feeling those things? What took you out of the zone?

2. What fears, anxieties or doubts keep you from zone performance? Take some time to examine your deepest sourc-

es of fear and stress. Where do they come from? How can you combat and redirect them?

3. Think about a time, place or situation when you tend to feel more negative thoughts. How can you utilize the mental loop of zone performance to combat those thoughts and promote positive emotions? Write down 1-2 regrouping and refocusing phrases to use.

4. How we feel about ourselves affects our identity. What lies are you believing about yourself because of deep-seated fears or insecurities? Maybe it's "I'm not good enough" or "No one wants to be my friend." Address those fears with God's truth about you. Write down each of those insecurities and next to it, write down what God would say in response.

Extra Workout Challenge

1. Memorize and practice Proverbs 16:32: "Better a patient man than a warrior, a man who controls his temper than one who takes a city." Write it down somewhere that you'll see it every day.

2. List three ways that you can elicit positive emotion from those you come in contact with at home or at work. Be specific in your examples.

CHAPTER 8: WISDOM

"Fear of the Lord is the foundation of true knowledge, but fools despise wisdom and discipline." (Proverbs 1:7, NLT)

Fresh off his best season in 10 years, Ravens kicker Matt Stover headed into our Week 1 home matchup against the Indianapolis Colts with confidence. He'd only missed three kicks the season before (2004) and made offseason adjustments to improve his leg strength and power to get that number even closer to zero. Unlike every other NFL position, a perfect season wasn't out of the question for a kicker, so Stover wasn't leaving room for any mistakes.

The Sunday night lights shined bright inside of M&T Stadium for the season opener, and the star power on the opposing sideline seemed to match them. Coming off two 12-win seasons (and two division titles), the Colts had yet to miss the playoffs under head coach Tony Dungy.[1] In 2005, they'd send eight players to the Pro Bowl, including an offense led by Marvin Harrison, Edgerrin James and five-time MVP quarterback Peyton Manning.[2] We'd drawn the short straw with our Week 1 matchup, and Stover knew every kick would be critical.

Stover's first chance came near the end of the first quarter. We'd just turned the Colts over on downs and had driven down to their 20-yard-line before our own drive stalled. Stover lined up his 38-yard field goal attempt. On a clear September night in Baltimore, it was a chip shot to give us an early lead. The snap and hold were clean, Stover drove the ball what looked right down the middle…but it hooked left, just outside the goal post. He jogged off the field in frustration.

Stover's second chance didn't come until the second half. It'd been a low-scoring game to that point—the Colts had a 3-0 halftime lead—so when Stover had a 47-yard attempt on the half's opening drive to tie the game at 3-3, the crowd felt the weight of the kick. Again, the snap and hold were perfect, and again, Stover hooked the kick wide left. As the ESPN announcer commented:

"The reliable 16-year veteran has missed—*twice!*"[3] Stover unhooked his chin strap and jogged off the field.

Stover's third and final attempt came two possessions later. After our defense gave up touchdowns on two consecutive drives to Manning and the Colts, our offense responded with a 15-play, six-and-a-half-minute drive that stalled on Indianapolis' 27-yard-line. The fourth-and-16 we faced left us only one choice—send Stover back out there. Snap, hold, kick…pushed wide right. Head coach Brian Billick's look of frustration and unbelief said it all.

"Stover has missed three! 38, 47 and 45," the ESPN announcer said. "The boo birds are out in Baltimore."[4]

In our highly anticipated start to the season, we didn't manage to put any points on the board until our last drive of the game. The game finished in a 24-7 loss, and we headed to our locker room defeated.

In practice the next week, Stover went back to the drawing board—which, for him, was his notebook. Throughout his career, Stover studied film and took copious notes to identify any possible errors in his technique. For example, for kickoffs during games and practices, he mentally charted his kicks and wrote them into his journal. He watched video of every kick and recorded the ball's air time, distance traveled and location on the field (left, right or middle). Stover's notebook gave him a vehicle to retrace his performance and focus on the aspects that needed improvement.

So, leading up to Week 2 in 2005, Stover returned to his notes from the previous year—the season in which he'd made 90.6 percent of his field goals and every one of his extra points. It didn't take long for him to find the key he'd been missing. In a journal entry from 2004, Stover had written: "go slow, hit it easy." It was a goal he'd written for a specific game that season. After reviewing his film from Week 1 against the

AFC Championship Week (1-20-10)
Vs Jets

Wed 1-20-10
F6's
① ㉖ mL   1.30
② ㉜ mR   1.32
③ ㉜ R H   1.30
④ ㊷ m   1.31   Pushed a little hard with clb step, had longer Drive Step
⑤ ㊽ R H   1.31   & Pushed Right a little. Still made it
Coaching : Do not Push too hard with clb. Stay Down
             Hips Back, yelled Short Drive Step
A few Teammates Chattered at me during F6's. It definitely
helps/makes me focus more.

Stover's practice notes ahead of the 2010 AFC Championship game.

Stover's notebooks corresponding to each year he played in the NFL.

Colts, Stover recognized the disconnect. In each of those three kicks—since he'd been so focused on his power to drive the ball further—he'd neglected his goal from the previous year. He wasn't hitting the ball slow and easy.

Registering the advice from his past self, Stover made the adjustment to his kicking routine. The result? He missed only one more kick—a 43-yarder on Halloween in Pittsburgh—for the remainder of the season. Stover finished the season 30-for-34—third in the NFL in field goals made and sixth in field goal percentage (88.2).[5]

> *Unless we actively observe our experiences, we'll live a life without purpose.*

In sports and beyond, the best performers examine themselves closely. In Stover's case, he used self-observation and evaluation to learn from his past and move him toward success. His notebook allowed him to retrace his steps, mentally visualize his kicks and analyze what happened—and he was better because of it. Like many before (and after) him, Stover knew the importance of observation.

Before his death in Ancient Greece, Socrates allegedly said these famous words: "The unexamined life is not worth living." As a philosopher, Socrates understood that unless we examine and learn from our lives—our mistakes, successes and failures—we won't grow. We won't move forward. Unless we actively observe our experiences, we'll live a life without purpose.

Biblical truth tells us we are fools to expect different results if we don't learn from our past mistakes. As Proverbs 26:11-12 says, "As a dog returns to its vomit, so a fool repeats his folly. Do you see a man wise in his own eyes? There is more hope for a fool than for him."

Observation and learning from our past are the first steps in obtaining and growing through **knowledge**. Knowledge is the compilation of facts, information and skills acquired through experience. As one anonymous source said, "Knowledge is the treasure of a wise man." As we gain more knowledge, we give ourselves more opportunities to learn, grow and move up the performance curve. Think about the last three chapters: Education, Self-Talk and Emotion. Knowledge encompasses all of these. Through education, we learn about the world, how it works and our place within it. Through self-talk, we learn to motivate ourselves and boost performance. Through emotion, we learn to connect with our deeper selves and experience a full, abundant life.

As we've learned in the past few chapters, though, knowledge by itself falls short. Yes, knowledge gives us more *opportunities* to move up the performance curve, but knowledge alone won't actually push the needle forward. What if, after finishing this book, you decided you were satisfied with the *knowledge* of these concepts alone? What if you stopped at, "that's interesting," but made no effort to apply or contextualize that knowledge? What good would this book actually do you?

Obviously, that scenario—learning without any attempt to understand or apply—seems wasteful. But, in reality, how many times have you done that in the past?

> **Without discipline, we'll keep missing kicks wide left and wide right.**

How many classes did you take in school where you were so focused on "just passing" that you neglected actually understanding and applying what you learned? How many conversations have you had with parents, teachers, coaches, friends in which you listened, but you didn't try to appreciate what was being said? How many podcasts and church sermons have you listened to without any effort to understand and apply? I know I'm guilty of all these things.

Knowledge is only the first step, the first "treasure of a wise man." But that's just what knowledge is—a treasure. A treasure of a person who has used it for a greater end: wisdom.

Wisdom adds two other elements to knowledge, and the first is action-oriented. It's about taking what you've learned—education, experience, self-awareness—and applying it. For that application to occur, you need **discipline**—a dedicated, action-based approach to seek improvement. Without discipline, we'll keep missing kicks wide left and wide right.

Stover used discipline to improve his craft, to apply his knowledge and observation. His journal contained not only practice and game notes, but other pertinent information for virtually every one of the 19 seasons for which he kicked in the NFL. It's not abnormal for kickers to monitor and chart their kicks, but Stover took it a step further. Based on what he'd recorded, he set realistic, achievable goals for himself.

Stover developed this successful routine during his second season, after his position coach had him set goals for every game. Even as a seasoned veteran, Stover never took this exercise for granted, and now he ranks in the top-10 all-time NFL kickers list for field goals made.

Discipline through goal-setting is directly related to performance— but it's more than just, "I'm going to do this." Geoff Colvin, author of the book *Talent is Overrated* put it like this:

> *"Mediocre performers set goals that are general and are often focused on simply achieving a good outcome—win the order; get the new project proposal done. The best performers (like Stover) set goals that are not about the outcome, but rather about the process of reaching the outcome."* [6]

Instead of setting the goal to make a kick, Stover aimed to "have fun" and "want the kick." He also focused on the specifics of his technique, striving to "stay down" and keep his "hips back."

Colvin goes on to say, "The poorest performers don't set goals at all; they just slog through their work."[7] Likewise, King Solomon warns against the danger of not disciplining yourself or creating a vision for the future in the book of Proverbs:

> *"Go to the ant, you sluggard;*
> *consider its ways and be wise!*
> *It has no commander,*
> *no overseer or ruler,*
> *yet it stores provisions in summer*
> *and gathers its food at harvest.*
> *How long will you lie there, you sluggard?*
> *When will you get up from your sleep?*
> *A little sleep, a little slumber,*
> *a little folding of the hands to rest—*
> *and poverty will come on you like a bandit*
> *and scarcity like an armed man."*
> *(Proverbs 6:6-11)*

The sluggard lives the unexamined life. He wastes time and neglects the present moment, failing to learn from his experience. The result is poverty, scarcity and lack of direction. The ant, on the other hand, is

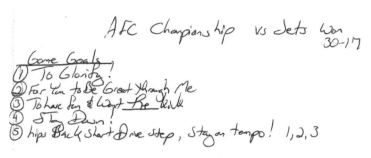

Stover's goals for the 2010 AFC Championship game.

the example. Compared to the human, ironically, the ant is the wise one. Without any prompting, this wise little insect plans ahead, stores provisions and collects food while it's plentiful, in preparation for the upcoming winter. Wisdom requires us to be disciplined and proactive!

Solomon, the author of this proverb, was known for his wisdom. The Old Testament tells us that he was "greater…in wisdom than all the other kinds of the earth" (1 Kings 10:23). Earlier in 1 Kings, while Solomon is presenting an offering to God, God says to him, "Ask for whatever you want me to give you" (v. 5). Instead of choosing great riches or power or status, Solomon asks God for wisdom: "So give your servant a discerning heart to govern your people and to distinguish between right and wrong" (v. 9). God is so pleased with Solomon's answer that He not only grants Solomon's wish, but he throws in wealth and honor on top of it.

This brings us to the third and final element of wisdom: **humility**. Proverbs 9:10 tells us that "the fear of the Lord is the beginning of wisdom." This is what truly set apart Solomon's wisdom from the rest of the world's—it came directly from the true *source* of wisdom. Humility not only admits the need to do better, but it acknowledges our inability to know everything or to always act in the best way. True wisdom only comes from humbly accepting our own mental limitations in the face of an all-knowing, benevolent God.

On the football field, knowledge and discipline gave Stover everything he needed for success. He didn't necessarily need humility or reliance on God to make those field goals and to help us win football games. But that's the thing about peak performance—it expands well beyond the field.

On top of being one of the greatest kickers in NFL history, Matt Stover was a man of God. He had the humility to understand Proverbs 16:9: "In their hearts humans plan their course, but the Lord establishes their steps." Before anything else in his journal, Stover's first two goals were: 1) to glorify God and 2) for God to be great through him. Yes, he had plans to make field goals and win Super Bowls, but in that, he made room for God's sovereignty. If Stover accomplished nothing else—even if he didn't "stay down" or "want the kick"—he was going to glorify God with his actions.

> **True wisdom only comes from humbly accepting our own mental limitations in the face of an all-knowing, benevolent God.**

In fact, Matt was instrumental in my own journey of faith. When we worked together in Baltimore, I was fairly new to my faith, and as I wrestled through questions common to seekers, Matt guided me through my confusion. Using the apologetics (reasoned arguments defending Christian beliefs) he'd studied, he addressed my doubts and helped me understand the wisdom that comes from God. Matt planted the seed and provided a model for a godly man in the locker room, and God did the rest.

We all have a thousand schemes and arrangements in our hearts that we may earnestly wish God to fulfill. Our worldly desires, however, may neither be for our good, nor God's glory. "For the wisdom of this world is foolishness in God's sight" (1 Corinthians 3:19). Without humility, we significantly limit our potential for wisdom and along with it, the entire mental building block. Without God—even with our education, self-talk and positive emotion—we ultimately have nothing more than "foolishness."

Here's the good news: God *wants* to give us wisdom. According to James 1, all we need to do is ask: "If any of you lacks wisdom, you should ask God, who gives generously to all without finding fault, and it will be given to you" (v.5). As followers of Jesus, we don't have to aimlessly search in the dark, hoping to find answers. God is ready to give us what we need if we just have the humility to seek Him and the courage to trust Him.

Coach's Corner

In the 1990s and early 2000s, coaching in the NFL provided numerous perks. We had access to a car or a stipend to pay for a car. Free meals were provided at the team complex. Some teams had special access to concert or other professional sports tickets. It was also common practice for staff to barter tickets to games for other perks or services in real life. For example, I traded my game tickets for airline tickets, handy man services and even carpet cleaning.

> **Without God—even with our education, self-talk and positive emotion—we ultimately have nothing more than "foolishness."**

Like most of my colleagues, I would trade with almost anyone who was willing to make a deal. There was, though, no more valuable perk (and bargaining chip) than access to highly coveted Super Bowl tickets.

Every January, whether we were playing in the game or not, NFL coaches and players were given the opportunity to purchase two Super Bowl tickets at face value. For coaches and players whose teams weren't in the game, this was easy money. Depending on seat location, these tickets could be sold for two to four times their value, without much effort at all. When we went to the Super Bowl after the 2000 season, the average face value of those tickets was $325…but they were being sold for *$1,000-$1,500 each.*

As the years passed, the value of these tickets—and their accompanying black-market value—increased proportionately. And extra cash, especially right after the holidays, was always an attractive offer. There was just one catch—ticket scalping was illegal. The League even sent us coaches a letter stating that exact fact. Still, despite the warning, ticket scalping continued in NFL circles. When individuals could rake in several thousand dollars per ticket, it honestly came as no surprise that coaches turned a blind eye. My first year in Baltimore, I was one of them.

As I spent more time seeking God and understanding who He is and why I needed Him, my perspective began to change. Matt Stover led me by example in this area. He patiently answered my questions. He never cursed. He took time to build into others personally and professionally. Another one of my co-workers, my assistant, Chip Morton, played a similar role in my life at that time. In 1999, when almost everyone else (including myself) scalped their Super Bowl tickets, Chip intentionally chose to abstain. From the locker room to interactions with staff and players, both Matt and Chip were the consummate pros. They were living testimonies of their faith, and in following their example, God began to transform my heart and my mind.

The following year, as Super Bowl season approached, a fellow coach called to let me know he was rounding up tickets to sell. Per usual, it was easy money—hand over the tickets and take your cash. As I was about to pull the trigger, I suddenly felt conflicted. I thought of Chip and the example he'd set. The temptation of gaining an easy profit hit on one of my greatest strongholds (money), but this time around, I knew in my heart that God would not approve. My conscience was clear, and I made up my mind. I was not going to sell out my tickets illegally again.

Without that third element of wisdom (humility), I had no incentive not to sell those Super Bowl tickets. Based on my knowledge and discipline alone, selling tickets for an easy profit with essentially no effort on my part seemed "wise." But because of the journey of faith I'd begun, I realized that true wisdom comes from God. I had two paths in front of me—the wicked (Proverbs 4:14-17) and the righteous (Proverbs 4:18). By God's grace, led by wisdom of His Holy Spirit, I chose the righteous path, and in doing so, I not only avoided a potential problem for myself—several coaches were eventually fined for scalping Super Bowl tickets—but I had peace in my heart. Wisdom from God isn't just about following rules—it's truly about the wisest and best way to live.

In our modern age of information, knowledge is bountiful, but wisdom is scarce. We live in the most technologically advanced culture in history, and because of that, we thrive more on activities that provide immediate gratification and less on those that require patience and preparation. As a result, we end up less committed, more directionless and ultimately, stagnant. We have more information at our fingertips than ever before, yet, also more than ever, we lack the discipline to turn general knowledge into wise action. And often, because the Internet makes everything so accessible, we often feel we don't need anyone else to survive and thrive. Thus, we neglect two critical elements of wisdom: discipline and humility.

My dad, a former high school teacher of 40-plus years, once gave me a great piece of wisdom: "when the student is ready, the teacher will appear." In other words, to gain knowledge, we must be willing and open to receive it. Because of this truth, I try to carve out time each day to pause, listen to God and talk with Him. I affectionately call it my "quiet time." Over the years, God had used this time to speak to me through Scripture, prayer and daily devotionals.

Wisdom from God isn't just about following rules—it's truly about the wisest and best way to live.

Although I haven't always stayed consistent with my quiet time—life is hectic, and the devil works overtime to keep us busy—God has this uncanny ability to meet us where we are, if we just give Him space to speak. This is why, more often than not, I hear His word through a podcast, book, article, song or even radio broadcast. When I do hear something beneficial, I take notes or record it on my phone. This helps me retain the information and gain knowledge. I'm notorious for typing away on my smartphone in the dark auditorium of our church. It drives my wife crazy, but I know God gets it! I then refer back to my notes to spark ideas of my own, apply this new knowledge to my life and use it to help others.

For instance, the day after a game, as I took one Bengals' player through a workout, I noticed he was unusually distracted. As we talked, he shared his disappointment in his performance from the prior day's game. He couldn't seem to get his mistakes out of his head, so I pulled out my phone and opened up my notes.

The thought I was looking for was from a sermon entitled, "Search for Significance," which talks about the importance of failure in the journey of life. Without repeated failure, we can never come to success. When God moved the Israelites from Egypt to the Promised Land, the trek, which should've only taken six weeks, took *40 years.* Why? God wanted His people to see their own hearts and recognize their depravity and sin. He uses pain and failure in our lives as a megaphone.[8]

As I shared that message with this player, I encouraged him that failure is not always bad. It can humble us, help us grow and make us better in the future. Failures will happen to all of us who attempt anything of worth, and character and success result from how we respond to those failures. Although I don't know what was in that player's heart, my words seemed to bring him some comfort. Without the *knowledge* of the sermon, the *discipline* to take notes and the *humility* to seek God with my free time, this teaching moment may never have happened.

> **Ultimately, the more aligned we are with the wisdom of God, the better equipped we'll be to fulfill our potential and achieve peak performance.**

Education, self-talk and emotion all help us build our mental block. All three are essential to fully maximizing our intake of knowledge. But without God, we'll never have true wisdom. Wisdom ties our knowledge together, infuses action through discipline and humbly accepts leading and guidance from God. By its nature, wisdom informs and is informed *by* each of the other three building blocks—and wisdom is evidence of why we need the fourth and final block: spiritual. We filter every conscious decision we make through our wisdom. And ultimately, the more aligned we are with the wisdom of God, the better equipped we'll be to fulfill our potential and achieve peak performance.

Foundation Building Tip

There are three key elements that make up wisdom: knowledge, discipline and humility. The wisest people in the world (think King Solomon) not only *knew* more than most people, but they also *acted* on it. The third aspect of wisdom (humility) brings God into the equation. Think of the formula in this way: **Knowledge + discipline + God = wisdom.** If we align ourselves to these three components, we give ourselves a reliable framework for decision-making and ultimately set ourselves up for success.

Consider these statistics from the American Society of Training and Development:

- **Success is a 10 percent probability** by just thinking about it.
- **Success is a 25 percent probability** by committing to it.
- **Success is a 65 percent probability** by sharing it with people who mean the most to you.

• **Success is a 95 percent probability** by putting an action plan in place and being held accountable.

Knowledge and experience give us a baseline to set goals and grow. Discipline puts that baseline knowledge into action through goal setting. Humility informs the quality and ultimate health of the goals themselves. Don't be like the sluggard in Proverbs 6. Use discipline and humility to create your game plan.

Your Workout

1. How do you evaluate your performance or progress? Write down an example of when you performed poorly (or successfully) and were able to pinpoint the cause.

2. When you hear something that stimulates your thinking or inspires you to act or feel differently, what method do you use to retain and recall the information? If you don't have one, try taking notes, creating an audio recording or processing through the information with a friend afterwards.

3. Provide one example of how you acquired knowledge to either help yourself or help someone else. How could you repeat and/or repurpose this moving forward?

4. The book of Proverbs is 31 chapters. Challenge yourself this month (or the start of next month) to read one chapter every day for the whole month. (If it happens to be a short month, read two chapters on the last day).

Extra Workout Challenge

1. Think of something with which you struggle (i.e., finances, quick to anger, comparing yourself to others, etc).

2. Search the Bible to find Scripture relating to this area.

3. Write down the Scripture and journal about what you feel God is sharing with you.

4. Set a goal of meditating on the Scripture. You could choose five minutes every day or 10 minutes three times a week. Remember, the focus is not on adhering to a strict routine to check off a box (the "outcome"). Rather, it's to be grateful for the work being done to refine you.

5. During your meditation time, ask God to reveal wisdom to guide you forward.

BUILDING BLOCK 3

S

SOCIAL

SECTION 3: SOCIAL BUILDING BLOCK

We were born for relationships. Although the physical and mental building blocks are both critical components of *individual* development, they stop short of addressing how we interact with other people. Ironically, interpersonal relationships are essential to success in both the physical and mental (and spiritual) areas of life. Without our friends, family and community to encourage, challenge, support and love us, we can only go so far.

In the opening book of the Bible, one of the first things God notices about human beings is that "it is not good for man to be alone" (Genesis 2:18). We need other people—not only to push us toward peak performance, but also to provide purpose to our lives. The need for meaningful, authentic social interaction is hardwired into our DNA, and it's why God sent His Son to the earth: to pursue a relationship with us. We grow and develop socially through:

- **Chapter 9: Character** - the full menu of the traits that form the individual nature of a person—the good, bad and the ugly.

- **Chapter 10: Relationships** - the mutual bonds we share with other people built through positive character (trust, empathy, respect, loyalty and love).

- **Chapter 11: Community** - a group of people, or relationships, united by a common bond or goal.

- **Chapter 12: Love** - the underlying, action-based character trait that motivates authentic, uplifting relationship and community.

The social building block is about learning how to both develop and experience deep personal relationships with other people—both for support in achieving our own potential *and* for opportunity to fulfill our purpose to serve others. Character focuses on the individual components necessary to healthily interact with others. Relationships and community are the stages on which those character traits are utilized and acted upon. Love is the foundation of every successful social interaction.

Social health and development empower us to meet our physical and health goals (through accountability and encouragement), grow mentally and intellectually (through exposure to other wisdom and ideas), and deepen our faith and trust in God (through support and community). Relationships and social interaction enable us to do so much more than we could alone. Peak performance is impossible without other people.

With enough time, we become like the people with whom we surround ourselves. Whether or not we're developing physically, mentally and spiritually, the crowd we choose will either pull us down or push us up. Regardless, they're an essential determining factor of our ultimate trajectory in life.

CHAPTER 9: CHARACTER

"Not only so, but we also glory in our sufferings, because we know that suffering produces perseverance; perseverance, character; and character, hope. And hope does not put us to shame, because God's love has been poured out into our hearts through the Holy Spirit, who has been given to us" (Romans 5:3-5)

As a TV reporter asked him questions in a post-game interview, Trent Dilfer's eyes swelled with tears. After overcoming several challenges in his NFL career—he'd just been cut from the Tampa Bay Buccaneers after a five-year run as their starting quarterback—Dilfer, who now led our Ravens, finally had something go *right*.

"All of it was worth it," Dilfer told reporters in Adelphia Coliseum in Nashville, Tennessee. "All of what I've been through. All the mistakes and successes, the adversity, the grind, the humiliation, prepared me for this."[1]

All of his emotions seem to hit him at once—relief, joy, excitement, pride—and rightly so. Just hours before, in a game that served as a microcosm of Dilfer's career to that point, he'd led us to the biggest win of our season.

It was 2000, Week 11 on the road against the AFC Central Division-leading Tennessee Titans. Dilfer was only two games into his starting quarterback role in Baltimore—but he was catching on quickly. We were coming off a much-needed 27-7 win over the Bengals—pushing our less-than-stellar record to 6-4—but the Titans were a different challenge entirely. Led by All-Pro quarterback Steve McNair and All-Pro running back Eddie George, the Titans were 8-1, had won eight games in a row and rode a 12-game home winning streak coming into the Week 11 matchup.[2]

Surprisingly, we jumped out to an early 14-0 lead, but unsurprisingly, the favored Titans clawed back, tying the game at 17 with a 23-yard field goal halfway through the fourth quarter. After unsuccessful drives from both sides, Dilfer and our offense got the ball back on the Titans' 22-yard-line with just over four minutes left in the game—an ideal set-up for a game-winning drive. All we needed to do was run down the clock and kick a short field goal.

After two short runs from running back Jamal Lewis, we faced a third-and-seven, just inside the red zone. Standing on the sideline as a young coach, I was tense, but excited. Even if we didn't convert the first down, we'd have a great chance at the lead with less than three minutes remaining. The odds of victory leaned heavily in our favor. I was hopeful—that is, until the play started. With the roar of the deafening crowd, Dilfer took the snap, dropped back and threw what he would later call an "idiot pass"—an interception into the hands of Titans' safety Perry Phenix. In despair, I stood motionless, hands on top of my head, as Phenix returned the ball 87 yards to the house. They missed the extra point, but the defensive touchdown gave Tennessee a late 23-17 lead.

With just two-and-a-half minutes remaining, we only had one opportunity left. To capitalize on it, Dilfer needed a short memory. Just minutes after watching his crucial mistake lead to a six-point deficit, he had to lead our offense 70 yards to seven points.

After a slow start to the drive, we faced a third-and-five on our own 35-yard line. A minute had already run off the clock, and we'd used one of our three remaining timeouts. Our backs were against the wall—but that's when Dilfer took over. As his career had shown to that point, adversity is where Dilfer thrived.

"He could have went in the tank when he threw that last pick," Ravens right guard Mike Flynn said. "But instead, he is in the huddle and telling us it's not over. He is a vocal guy and brings a certain confidence."[3]

After breaking the huddle, Dilfer delivered a 36-yard dart, under pressure, to tight end Shannon Sharpe. Four plays later, a defensive pass interference call moved the ball down to the Titans' two-yard-line. The enthusiasm on our sideline grew with Dilfer's confidence. Two plays later, with 29 seconds left, Dilfer finished the drive with a two-yard touchdown pass. Matt Stover made *his* extra point, and we became the first team to beat the Titans in the newly built Adelphia Coliseum.[4]

As we celebrated in the locker room, Coach Billick pulled out the *Sports Illustrated* issue released earlier that week entitled, "Remember the Titans: Eddie George & Co. have quietly become the NFL's best team." The cover featured Eddie George, alluding to the movie, *Remember the Titans*, which had been released a few months earlier.[5] Billick held up the magazine and said, "Here it is guys, the NFL's best team."

He looked around at our players and continued.

"Well, maybe they *are...*"

Then he paused. Everyone watched him in silence, waiting.

"BUT NOT TODAY!"

The locker room erupted into cheers and hugs and celebration. That comeback victory and accompanying post-game speech were defining moments for our team. With a new rush of confidence from the players and coaching staff, we knew we weren't going to be beat again—and the prophecy came true. Relying on the formula of a dominant defense and a strong running game, we won our remaining five regular season games (by an average of three touchdowns) and four playoff games to earn the Super Bowl XXXV title in Tampa. And in the middle of it all was Dilfer, one of the unlikeliest of heroes.

After getting cut from the Buccaneers after the 1999 season, Dilfer signed a one-year, minimum salary contract with the Ravens as a back-up to starter Tony Banks. Eight games into the season, after going five games without scoring a touchdown with Banks at the helm, Coach Billick made the switch. And it paid off. Though we leaned heavily on our defense (Ray Lewis) and our running game (Jamal Lewis), Dilfer was a clear difference-maker. As a starter, he lost only one game that season—a 6-9 loss to Pittsburgh in his first start—ending on a (combined regular season and playoff) 11-game win streak. Dilfer may not have been our biggest offensive weapon, but he prioritized the team's goals over his individual success. He put his own desires for personal success, statistics and recognition aside, and he turned our season around. That Week 11 game in Tennessee was the turning point.

"I lost us the game," Dilfer said, recalling that matchup with the Titans. "We were moving the ball, and all we [had] to do is not turn the ball over, and we kick the game-winning field goal. I threw an 87-yard pick-six. We get the ball back with 2:30 left on the clock, and we get in the huddle, and every guy looked at me and said, 'OK, now you get to be the hero.' And we went down, and I threw a touchdown...to win. I think you truly have to be at the bottom and pull yourself out. I always say confidence isn't previous success, confidence is overcoming the tough stuff. If you can overcome tough stuff, you're going to have confidence in a lot of different situations.[6]

> **Character isn't defined by what you say, project or post on social media; it's defined by consistency in action.**

"It, to me, was six years of mental, emotional maturity coming out in a matter of three-and-a-half minutes," Dilfer continued. "When I got on my knees and thanked God for it, it wasn't 'God, thank you for the win.' It was 'God, thank you that you put me through the fire for six years so that when this moment came, you had developed enough in me to overcome it."[7]

This was Dilfer's M.O. to that point. He wasn't a spectacular athlete—his numbers didn't jump off the stat sheet—but he knew how to lead a football team. He knew because he'd faced suffering and adversity and come out stronger on the other side. In the words of Billick, "Chemistry and character [are] part of what [Dilfer] has brought to us."[8]

Character is the full menu of the traits that form the individual nature of a person. It's "the outward reflection of the inner man."[9] Your character is who you are on and off the field—it can't be hidden because it's at the very core of your identity. Character isn't defined by what you say, project or post on social media; it's defined by consistency in action. What you do over and over—regardless of circumstances—is the most authentic reflection of your character. And as you probably know well, character isn't *just* the positive—it's the good, the bad and the ugly.

Good character traits include positivity, honesty, accountability, reliability, self-restraint, concern for others, humility and sincerity.

Good character is demonstrated not only by what we do, but also by what we *don't* do. It is not quick-tempered, violent, dishonest or selfish. By no means does having good character imply one does not have faults. There is no one righteous man, not even one! We want to do the right thing, but often are unable to do it (Romans 7:19). Living out good character requires effort and self-discipline. Perhaps more than anything, character development results from response.

Every positive character trait has an equally effective opposite. An evil twin, of sorts. In other words, character can swing one of two ways—genuine vs. hypocritical, loving vs. selfish, humble vs. prideful, grateful vs. entitled—and much of it has to do with how we respond to adversity and suffering in our lives. Although some clearly face more hardships than others, none of us are exempt from difficulty in life. Jesus promised us that in the book of John: "In this world you will have trouble" (John 16:33). So, it's not avoiding adversity that leads to good character; it's responding well.

Look at Dilfer's career for an example. He had been permanently benched, suffered season-ending injuries and watched his team in the playoffs from the sideline, but he used all of that for his growth and development. Because Dilfer had been through the ringer, in a sense, he knew how to rally his team and push them toward success. Dilfer's struggles and failures—his benching and eventual release from Tampa—led him to develop gratitude, determination, consistency and leadership. Because of the humility he learned after losing his starting job, Dilfer took his role in Baltimore—rely on the running game and defense, not the passing game—in stride. And the team benefitted because of it. Although Dilfer did have his less-than-proud moments—in 1995, he became the first NFL quarterback to be ejected from a game after throwing a punch at, funny enough, Vikings' John Randle[10]—his character grounded and guided him.

> *It's not avoiding adversity that leads to good character; it's responding well.*

"We've allowed adversity to sharpen us, to make us stronger, and to make us better football players," Dilfer said. "More important than that…it's made [me] a better person. I'm also going to use football because it's a great opportunity to develop character traits and life skills that will be priceless when I'm done with this game."[11]

Dilfer's character, in turn, earned him the respect and loyalty of his teammates. That's why character is such a vital component of the social building block. Our interaction with others starts with ourselves, our character and our corresponding reputation. And while it may be possible to fabricate a positive reputation while having negative character, this isn't sustainable—especially if you develop true, genuine, intimate relationships with others. Eventually, if you don't live out the positive qualities in which you believe, your reputation will suffer. And while we can't be perfect, that's not what it's about. It's about pursuing a high level of character and being consistent. Character lived out consistently creates a good reputation. A good reputation helps build a strong social foundation.

On the other hand, when we slip up—when we misbehave, sin or fall below certain standards—it has a ripple effect that impacts our relationships with others. The essence of sin is selfishness.[12] When we think too much of ourselves, someone is usually forgotten. When we try to puff ourselves up, someone is usually shoved down. When we paint a false picture of ourselves, others will be tempted to do the same. When character is compromised, someone else will always be affected.

> *That's the thing about character—when it's present, it breeds other character traits of its same nature. If left unchecked, negative character will quickly spiral out of our control.*

Even with a Super Bowl ring on his hand after the 2000 season, more adversity loomed on the horizon for Dilfer. Despite his leadership and success the previous year, the Ravens moved on from Dilfer as their quarterback. Instead of re-signing him at the end of his one-year contract, the Ravens turned over the offense to free agent Pro Bowl quarterback, Elvis Grbac.

Just six weeks after Dilfer led Baltimore to the championship, he was back in the unemployment line. Dilfer became the first quarterback in NFL history to win the Super Bowl and lose his job before the next season.[13] He was not only hurt by the decision that denied him the opportunity to return as champions with his teammates, Dilfer was also wounded by the manner in which the process was carried out. He felt disrespected when Coach Billick didn't contact him personally to tell him he was being released.[14]

In the past, similar bouts with adversity had led only, it seemed, to positive character development for Dilfer—but this time was different. After leaving Baltimore, Dilfer played six more seasons in the NFL with various teams.[15] For much of those six seasons, he remained angry and bitter. He held a grudge against Billick. Despite playing against the Ravens several times after his reluctant departure from Baltimore, Dilfer wouldn't speak to Billick. He wasn't shy about expressing how he felt over the years, either:

- **2003**: "I deeply, deeply respect 90 percent of that [Ravens] organization, and I don't want to cheapen that aspect of it for the 10 percent that I think is ridiculous...The myth is that they are playing the type of football that we played when we won the Super bowl. The people that matter to me know we had a special gig there, and that it was kind of taken away from us."[16]

- **2005**: "I think Brian Billick's a really good football coach. Obviously, Brian and I disagree on some things."[17]

- **2006**: "[Billick] grossly misunderstood the talent of that football team, myself specifically, I totally agree with so many of the things he did. But to this day, I am so sad I didn't have the chance to face the challenge of repeating."[18]

Dilfer's unexpected release from Baltimore looked similar to his departure from Tampa Bay, but his response differed. Dilfer fell into a trap we all face on a regular basis: the snare of bitterness. Bitterness is a feeling of deep-seated anger and resentment toward someone or something, usually initiated by a past event. It arises from a sense of entitlement—gratitude's evil twin—and activates when something to which we feel entitled is taken away. Bitterness eats away at the mind like a poison; it makes us hold on to anger and quick to take offense. When people respond to trials with bitterness, they lose their spirit of reconciliation and instead come off as harsh, hostile and explosive. That's the thing about character—when it's present, it breeds other character traits of its same nature. If left unchecked, negative character will quickly spiral out of our control. Developing positive character, therefore, is not only responding well to trials; it's recognizing and rooting out the negative.

Seven years removed from his championship season with the Ravens, Dilfer finally buried his bitterness. Tired of carrying the heavy weight of his grudge against Billick, Dilfer found closure in the organization's decision to not renew his contract. Realizing the negative character his actions had rooted in his heart, Dilfer started a four-step process to re-establish his own character:[19]

1. Confession

Confession is a brief description of one's offense and admitting fault. To fully learn from a mistake, you first need to confess it. You need to bring it to the surface, into the light, and identify the wrong behavior to be rejected, not repeated. After seven years, Dilfer owned up to his shortcomings without making excuses. He took full responsibility for his actions:

> "I've been the childish one and I want to end that right now," Dilfer told reporters in 2007. "I strongly disagree with it, but there's a difference in disagreeing with a decision and letting that decision bring bitterness in somebody."[20]

Dilfer added, "I regret many of the things I said…What I do stand by is the fact that I'm heartbroken that I didn't get the chance to repeat and go through the struggles of what that entails. Where I've been wrong…I haven't been able to let it go."[21]

2. Restitution

Restitution moves beyond confession to action, to making things right. It's the outward evidence of inward heart change. For instance, if you steal something from someone, confession is, "I stole this from you. I was wrong. I take full responsibility for my actions." Restitution takes it a step further: "Not only was I wrong, but I want to make things right by returning or replacing what I stole from you." Restitution eases the pain you've caused and allows the receiving person to be in a better position to offer forgiveness. Restitution shows the other person you're taking your past mistakes seriously.

Dilfer's time for restitution came in 2007. Prior to playing against the Ravens as the starting quarterback for the San Francisco 49ers, Dilfer made a public apology on a conference call with the media:

> *"I want to take this opportunity to publicly apologize to Brian [Billick] for that bitterness," Dilfer told reporters. "I'm going to make a point to see him on Sunday. He's been the man in this deal, and I haven't. He's been the adult."* [22]

True to his word, Dilfer sought out Billick moments before the game and told him face-to-face that he regretted the harshness of his remarks. Dilfer also apologized for his refusal to speak with him after Billick had sought to repair their relationship. [23]

3. Ask for forgiveness

Forgiveness is critical to restoring relationships. Asking for forgiveness is an act of humility. It takes vulnerability to admit your wrongdoing and put your fate in the hands of someone you've hurt, not knowing what will happen. Forgiveness starts with the offender (Dilfer) confessing, offering restitution and asking for forgiveness from the offended (Billick). Forgiveness on Billick's part buries the offense.

God wants us to live in love, peace, joy and holiness. To do so, we must "love each other deeply, because love covers over a multitude of sins" (1 Peter 4:8). In Proverbs 10:12, King Solomon observes, "Hatred stirs up conflict, but love covers all things." Hatred spurs the desire for revenge, leaving people who despise each other unable to connect. By contrast, God's way of love covers, or forgives, all wrongs. Forgiveness doesn't mean ignoring the wrongdoing committed against us. In fact, forgiveness recognizes the wrong and decides to no longer allow that wrong to be a barrier to relationship. It cancels the debt owed. This doesn't mean we overlook offenses or enable a wrongdoer. We do, however, need to release resentment toward others when they are truly remorseful. Forgiveness opens the doors for relationships to be rebuilt.

4. Reconfirm the standard

Reconfirming the standard is changing your behavior so that the error doesn't happen again. It's consistently re-aligning yourself with the positive standards instilled in us as human beings—love, equality, forgiveness, etc. Everybody makes mistakes—and anybody can ask for forgiveness—but when we repeatedly rise to the positive standard of how we should behave, we allow positive character to flow back into our lives.

"I think I've grown up as a man," Dilfer said after reconciling with Billick. "You're always trying to get better. Here I am six years later, and I wasn't letting something go. This is as much a stretch to me as a human being and not be hypocritical in my parenting.[24]

"I feel very hypocritical because I'm dealing with my sixth grader every day and talking to her about relationships and how to handle [them], and yet I'm a 35-year-old man and I can't let something go [from] the past."[25]

When we show those whom we wrong—and others watching us—that we've truly changed course and learned from our mistakes, we rebuild trust. We re-establish our own credibility and give others a reason to count on us once again. Trust is the foundation of all healthy relationships, and without it, our interactions with others will remain surface-level and empty. Until someone can truly trust you, they'll never be vulnerable and truly authentic—seriously preventing relational intimacy. Thankfully, this four-step process gives us the opportunity to rebuild positive character and, in turn, trust.

> **We'll always have another chance to start becoming a better person and, in turn, build trust in our relationships with others.**

+·+·+

At the end of the day, our character—who we are, what we do consistently—is dynamic. It has the potential to ebb and flow. We aren't born hardwired with certain character traits—even if we may be predisposed *toward* some. That's the beauty of character development. Even if we consider ourselves to be a "naturally angry person," we'll always have opportunities to consistently respond differently. We'll always have another chance to start becoming a better person and, in turn, build trust in our relationships with others.

It takes both self-discipline and courage to attain a high level of character—courage to go against the grain, admit your mistakes and pursue what is right. It takes effort to remove qualities that hinder us like pride, selfishness, laziness or a lack of self-control. In light of that, keep your eyes open. Don't shy away from trials or hardships; embrace them. Accept them for what they are—God-given opportunities to grow. As Dilfer once said:

> *"You can't go running from adversity. You have to let it hit you straight in the face. You have to allow God to build character."* [26]

Coach's Corner

As I mentioned in Chapter 5, I went through a turbulent time during my tenure as head strength coach with the Ravens. We were coming off a disappointing 6-10 season, and certain players had decided to forgo my off-season training program and hire an outside personal trainer. The grumblings from these players eventually reached Coach Billick, and he asked me to give a presentation to our coaching staff on our training program to get everyone on the same page. The pressure I felt from both players and coaches landed me at a crossroads.

With the strength and conditioning program under scrutiny, and my credibility in question, I searched for answers. I knew one of the players was using a brand of supplements provided to him by the outside trainer, so I decided to do some digging. I went to the player's locker and wrote down the brand names of the supplements I saw. NFL rules seriously restrict coaches in what supplements we can give players, so my hope was to glean insight as to what advantage this player may be receiving from what I was not able to provide him myself.

Soon after my investigation, I learned one of my staff members had told the player I'd looked in his locker without permission. I felt violated and betrayed. At the time, I thought I'd done nothing wrong. I was simply gathering information to help me better understand what competitive edge the player was seeking.

Once I knew the player heard of my actions, I felt awkward and uncomfortable. As I worried about my reputation of trustworthiness, God convicted my heart. He showed me that my defensiveness had arisen from a place of guilt for what I'd done. Lockers are a personal space—much like a desk in an office. Even though my intent was to better understand how I could help the players, I had overstepped my boundaries. Absorbed by my own insecurities of not measuring up as a coach and feeling like I was on the hot seat with the coaching staff, I lost sight of the potential unintended consequences of breaching locker room protocol.

> **Character, ultimately, is about integrity and morality—about doing the right *thing, even when no one is watching.***

My conscience spoke to me loud and clear. I knew I had to make it right, so I called a meeting with the player to confess what I had done. I told him my heart was not to incriminate him, but to learn about the supplements he was taking. I even provided him with a printout of the research I had done. I made restitution by apologizing for my action. More importantly, I reconfirmed the standard for myself by committing not to put my integrity at risk by succumbing to outside pressures. We left the meeting on amicable terms.

Character, ultimately, is about integrity and morality—about doing the *right* thing, even when no one is watching. It's upholding a certain standard. That's why making things right and rebuilding trust involves reconfirming that standard. So, when it comes to establishing good, upstanding character, it's really about aligning ourselves with what is right and good. But if we only believe in the material world, where can we find this standard? Society? That varies from culture to culture. The government? Ourselves? How do we know that it's better to be honest, selfless, forgiving and loving?

In his book, *Mere Christianity*, C.S. Lewis outlines what he calls the "law of human nature," It's our innate sense of right and wrong—how we know that only helping ourselves is "bad" and helping others is "good." In the first paragraph of the book, Lewis lays it out like this:

> *"Everyone has heard people quarrelling. Sometimes it sounds funny and sometimes it sounds merely unpleasant; but however it sounds, I believe we can learn something very important from listening to the kind of things they say. They say things like this: 'How'd you like it if anyone did the same to you?'—'That's my seat, I was there first'—'Leave him alone, he isn't doing you any harm'—'Why should you shove in first?'—'Give me a bit*

of your orange, I gave you a bit of mine'—'Come on, you prom-
ised'...Now what interests me about all these remarks is that
the man who makes them is not merely saying that the other
man's behavior does not happen to please him. He is appealing
to some kind of standard of behavior which he expects the other
man to know about. And the other man very seldom replies:
"To hell with your standard." Nearly always he tries to make
out that what he has been doing does not really go against the
standard, or that if it does there is some special excuse...It looks,
in fact, very much as if both parties had in mind some kind
of Law or Rule of fair play or decent behavior or morality or
whatever you like to call it, about which they really agreed.
And they have...Quarrelling means trying to show that the
other man is in the wrong. And there would be no sense in
trying to do that unless you and he had some sort of agreement
as to what Right and Wrong are."[27]

Essentially, there's a standard of right and wrong embedded within every human being from birth—across national, societal, cultural and historical lines. According to the Bible, that standard is given to us by God...The problem is, as Lewis points out, despite our knowledge of the Law of Human Nature, we all consistently break it. As Romans points out, when we sin, we all "fall short": "For all have sinned and fall short of the glory of God" (Romans 3:23). This is the problem of humanity: we're all born knowing how we *ought* to behave, yet we all consistently fall short of it.

That passage doesn't end at the problem, however. Before he even concludes the sentence, Paul points to the hope we have in Christ: "For all have sinned and fall short of the glory of God, and *all are justified freely* by his grace through the redemption that came by Christ Jesus" (Romans 3:23-24, emphasis mine). Because of Jesus' work on the cross, we don't have to justify ourselves—we don't have to earn our salvation. And that's good news, because we *can't*. The beauty of the gospel, though, is that this isn't just a future promise—it's a present reality. When we trust in Jesus, He gives us His Holy Spirit to dwell within us. When that happens, the Spirit empowers us to do what we couldn't do before—to rise up and meet the standard.

All positive character traits for which we can strive result not from our own willpower or effort, but from the work of the Holy Spirit. When we lean into and rely on the Spirit, the Bible says we produce fruit: "But the fruit of the Spirit is love, joy, peace, forbearance, kindness, goodness, faithfulness, gentleness and self-control. Against such things there is no law" (Galatians 5:22-23).

Because of Christ's work on the cross and the Holy Spirit's work within us, God has given us a supernatural power to overcome evil and produce good character. If we're constantly looking to ourselves alone to produce humility, love and kindness, we'll eventually come up empty. To produce lasting, deeply rooted fruit, we need to turn to the Source, to "remain in the vine" (John 15:1-4).

This is what it means to be a person of character. It's knowing the truth and, through the Holy Spirit, having the discipline and intentionality to follow it. It's, like Dilfer, using trials and adversity and opportunities to learn, grow and develop positive character traits.

Because of the hope we have in Jesus, adversity is opportunity—so much so that we can "glory (or rejoice) in our sufferings" (Romans 5:3). Through the Holy Spirit, problems in life actually *build* perseverance, which, in turn, develops character, deepens our trust in God and gives us greater confidence about the future (Romans 5:3-5). When you find yourself tested on a daily basis, you can *thank* God—not only because they're opportunities to grow, but also because He's equipped you to face them in His strength.

> **Because of Christ's work on the cross and the Holy Spirit's work within us, God has given us a supernatural power to overcome evil and produce good character.**

It's not clear what the motives were of my colleague who told that player I'd looked through his locker. The fleshly desire for approval and acceptance tempts us all on a daily basis. One thing I do know: What man intends for harm, God can use for good (Genesis 50:20)! Had the player never been informed of what I had done, I may have never had the opportunity to cleanse my heart, seek restitution and re-establish my character. It took humility to admit the fear that had dictated my behavior and courage to confront the player. This lesson has stuck with me to this day.

Foundation Building Tip

In the end, our character is *who we are*. It's not what we say, what we strive for or even necessarily what we believe—it's what we consistently do. When no one is watching, when it's not beneficial to him or her, a person of character still rises up to meet the standard. Character builds trust and intimacy in relationships (social), enables learning and mental growth (mental) and empowers physical development (physical). All of this is accomplished through reliance on the work of Jesus in our lives and the presence of the Holy Spirit (spiritual).

No one is perfect. We all make mistakes. We all face obstacles. We "all fall short." The point of growth is not to avoid trials and never make mistakes, but to learn and grow in the midst of adversity. Admitting wrongdoing is often too hard for our egos to take. If we don't, however, we'll never learn from our past mistakes. Even worse, the negative character will only lead to more of the same. As a good friend of mine always says, "When you mess up, fess up!"[28] Take full responsibility for your actions. Admit your mistakes, apologize to the person you offended and change your behavior so that it doesn't happen again. This process will re-establish your character and set you up for success in all facets of your life.

Your Workout

1. Think through how you've responded to adversity in the past. Have trials led to positive or negative character development in your past? Write down 3-5 examples of trials you've faced in life and how you've changed—positively or negatively—as a result.

2. For the positive change, what did you do to respond well? What factors influenced your productive response? For the negative responses, what could you have done differently?

3. Self-assessment—especially when it comes to character—can often be difficult. Ask two to three of your close friends and/or family members to give you honest feedback about your character. What positive traits stand out? And, if they're willing, what negative traits could you address?

4. Dilfer apologized not only because his grudge had negatively affected him, but also because he wasn't upholding a standard he set for his children. Choose three character traits you want your family (and yourself) to stand by and post them somewhere visible in your household.

Extra Workout Challenge

1. Character development does not occur from a single event but over a period of time. Ask the same two to three people you trust (see Question 3 of "Your Workout") to assess your progress on a scale of one (beginner) to ten (flawless) with regard to the following character qualities. Ask the Holy Spirit to help you develop those areas of which you are on the lower end of the scale.

__ Punctuality (promptness, on-time)
__ Tactfulness (what is fit, proper or right; skill in avoiding offending)
__ Courage (willingness to say and do the right things)
__ Loyalty (strong feeling of support or allegiance)
__ Honesty (truthfulness, freedom from deceit)
__ Attitude (positive state of mind, without grumbling or questioning)
__ Perseverance (steady persistence despite difficulty)
__ Diligence (attentive care)
__ Integrity (act according to values, beliefs, and principles)
__ Compassion (desire to alleviate suffering or concern for other's misfortunes)
__ Patience (willingness to endure)

2. Is there someone you have not forgiven for a wrong they committed against you? Write down their name and reflect on how they wronged you. Through prayer, ask the Holy Spirit to cleanse your heart and give you the power to forgive them for their actions. When you are able to do so, write the word "forgiven" next to their name.

CHAPTER 10: RELATIONSHIPS

"Though one may be overpowered, two can defend themselves. A cord of three strands is not quickly broken." (Ecclesiastes 4:12)

On Thanksgiving Day 1998, Randy Moss had a chip on his shoulder. Inside of Texas Stadium, in just his 12th game as an NFL wide receiver, Moss matched up against the team he viewed as his biggest rivals—the Dallas Cowboys. The Cowboys weren't *our* (the Vikings') rivals, per se—they weren't even in our division—Moss's vendetta was personal. On November 26, 1998—the first of many matchups with Dallas in his career—the 21-year-old rookie was poised to gain the upper hand.

And he only needed three catches to do it.

Catch one came on the game's opening drive. Just four plays in, we were on our own 49-yard line, first-and-10. With Moss by himself at the bottom of the field, Cunningham dropped back and handed the ball off to running back Robert Smith. Smith ran a couple steps before stopping, turning around and tossing it *back* to Cunningham—a flea flicker. The misdirection gave Moss just enough time to break free downfield, and Cunningham made the throw. Moss skipped into the endzone untouched. Fifty-one yards and six points.

Catch two came just before the end of the first quarter. We'd scored touchdowns on our first two drives and started this possession on our own 44-yard line. On the first play—again, with Moss alone at the bottom—Cunningham dropped back and launched the ball in Moss's direction down the field. Despite a Cowboys' cornerback grabbing his arms to slow him down, Moss caught it in stride and fell into the endzone for his second touchdown of the game. Two catches, two touchdowns, 107 yards.

Catch three came late in the third quarter, with us leading, 32-22. And, you guessed it, it was another 50-plus-yard touchdown. I can still picture it to this day. On the drive's third play, again, from our 44-yard line, Cunningham gave Moss one final chance to show off in front of Cowboys' owner, Jerry Jones. This time, his speed was on display. After taking the snap, Cunningham got the ball out quickly, connecting with Moss just four yards down the field. After shaking a tackle from his first defender, Moss simply started sprinting. I'll let iconic commentator Pat Summerall take it from here:

> *"Randy Moss breaks a tackle, and Randy Moss races down the sideline, and Randy Moss just outruns everybody into the endzone. He is incredible."* [1]

Three targets, three catches, three touchdowns, 163 yards. On Thanksgiving Day, Moss singlehandedly dismantled "America's Team." As he feasted on his celebratory post-game turkey leg on the sideline, Jerry Jones and the Cowboys thought back to the moment that could've prevented it all.

Moss's beef with the Cowboys went back to April 18, 1998—the first round of the '98 NFL Draft. In the weeks leading up to the draft, rumors circled they were interested in taking Moss with their eighth overall pick. They'd even brought Moss into Dallas for a pre-draft visit. He was the second-best offensive player—behind quarterback Peyton Manning—and the Cowboys needed a top-tier wide receiver. But when their time came, Dallas passed. [2]

Moss was, without question, the best receiver in the draft, but the Cowboys didn't pass on him because of lack of talent. They were concerned about Moss's character issues off the field—and rightly so. Moss had earned a scholarship to play for Notre Dame, but after three days in jail following a fight, the Fighting Irish withdrew their offer. A year later, Moss was dismissed from his next school, Florida State, after testing positive for marijuana. Even after becoming an All-American and Heisman Trophy finalist at Marshall University—amassing more than 3,500 yards and 54 touchdowns in two seasons—questions about Moss's character still lingered.[3]

With several other teams just as uneasy about his troubled past, Moss slid into the sights of the Vikings, owner of the 21st pick. Our coaches wanted Moss and also had concern about his off-the-field issues, but we had a secret weapon: Cris Carter. One of our scouts who made a final push for Moss felt Moss could succeed if he had a relationship with Carter. Carter was an aging, but perennial Pro Bowler who had overcome his own off-the-field issues—the perfect mentor candidate for a young receiver like Moss.

> *"If you listen to me and do everything I say, I'll also make you two promises. First, in about three to four years, you'll be the best receiver in football. And second, all that money you just lost in the draft? I'll make sure you make it back."*

Before the pick, Coach Dennis Green called Carter and told him, "We're going to get this kid." He then asked, "Will you take care of him?"[4]

"Of course I will," Carter replied. "I just need to know all the issues up front. I need to know what I'm dealing with. If there are any issues with his personality, I have to know about it before we get started."[5]

Before the end of the first round, Carter's phone rang again. This time it was Moss.

"Mr. Carter," he said. "I want to work with you and learn from you. I really want to be good."[6]

Carter could've viewed Moss as a threat, but instead, he welcomed the relationship. He invested his time, knowledge and experience into Moss. Rather than protect his own standing as the top receiver on the team, Carter demonstrated humility. He let Randy know he was serious about helping him achieve his potential as an NFL receiver. He told him, "If you listen to me and do everything I say, I'll also make you two promises. First, in about three to four years, you'll be the best receiver in football. And second, all that money you just lost in the draft? I'll make sure you make it back."[7]

The Vikings understood the importance and power of relationships—not only when it comes to personal development, but also achieving peak performance. Relationships usually stem from some commonality (family, work, school, proximity, common interests, etc.), and their success or failure is largely based on the character of those involved. For example, in order for a relationship to succeed, a certain baseline of positive character traits is required—things like trust, empathy and loyalty. The minute these qualities start to disappear, the relationship begins to deteriorate.

Moss and Carter's relationship started that 1998 off-season when Randy worked out with Carter near his home in Boca Raton, Florida. Carter's bigger goal, aside from the fieldwork, weightlifting and speed training, was to build a solid relationship with Moss. Their common bond was clear: football. They played the same position on the same team. They practiced together, worked out together and enjoyed spending time together. After their training sessions, Moss would hang out with the Carter family—playing basketball and video games, sharing home-cooked meals, and fishing. Carter even bought a boat so he and Moss could cast their lines on the lakes around Minneapolis.[8]

On a deeper level, Carter and Moss shared similar backgrounds with drugs and alcohol. Because Carter had dealt with character issues of his own—failing three drug tests during a three-year period while with the Eagles—he was one of the few people who could truly meet Moss where he stood.[9] The duo also had similar goals on the horizon—to win a Super Bowl and become Hall-of-Fame receivers along the way. Now, they could help each other get there.

As you've probably experienced, a common bond or goal only gets you so far in a relationship. I'm sure you've met people—I know I have—either similar to you (e.g., family) or with similar goals (e.g., "to be great in your field") that you've *not* clicked with relationally. That's why character is so crucial to relationship development.

Moss and Carter's relationship started with that phone call on draft night. From the beginning, they knew they came from similar places. Carter could see his young self in Moss, and he *empathized* with the rookie. Empathy is the ability to know how another person feels—and it leads to compassion. Carter knew what it felt like to have people underestimate you based on your past mistakes. He experienced that when he was cut from Philadelphia in 1990, and the most important thing he wanted Moss to know was that he was giving him a clean slate.

From there, Moss began to *trust* Carter—the second key characteristic of a successful relationship. As I talked about last chapter, trust results from feeling safe and understood. When another person shows us genuine care, along with reliability and integrity of their own, the leap of faith that it takes to trust someone else grows smaller and smaller. Author and management consultant Gary Hamel put it like this:

> *"Trust is not simply a matter of truthfulness, or even constancy. It is also a matter of amity and goodwill. We trust those who have our best interests at heart, and mistrust those who seem deaf to our concerns."* [10]

This is evidence of why "The Golden Rule"—treat others the way you want to be treated—is a self-fulfilling prophecy. When we have empathy for others and treat them with care, love and understanding, odds are they will, in turn, trust us and treat us with those same qualities. Moss trusted Carter enough to fly his remarkable talent under Carter's wing. He listened to what Carter said. That trust led to mutual respect in their relationship, which opened the door for mutual benefit. Respect acknowledges another person's value; it lets others know they're important, that they count for something. [11] Moss and Carter could now stand on that foundation of trust and respect and begin to *challenge* and *encourage* each other. Both pushed the other to be better—and we (the Vikings) reaped the benefits on the field.

As we witnessed firsthand in Dallas, Moss benefitted from Carter's mentorship. Through Carter's guidance, Randy channeled his raw talent and set receiving records for rookies that still stand to this day. He finished his rookie season with 69 catches for 1,313 yards and a League-leading 17 touchdowns. He was voted Rookie of the Year and was a pivotal factor in our franchise-best 15-1 record and NFC Championship berth. [12]

> **When another person shows us genuine care, along with reliability and integrity of their own, the leap of faith that it takes to trust someone else grows smaller and smaller.**

True to Carter's word, Moss made up his draft position. Moss became one of the best receivers in football, making the NFL 2000s All-Decade Team on his way to a remarkable 14-year career. After his fourth season, Moss became the highest-paid wide receiver by signing an eight-year, $75 million contract extension. In 2018, he was elected into the Pro Football Hall of Fame.[13]

"There are two objectives for building relationships: Find your commonality and add value to the other person."

What did Moss do for Carter? He returned the favor. Because of Randy's eye-popping speed and raw talent, other teams had to game plan and strategize around him. Consequently, this created more opportunities for Carter and other teammates to catch the ball. Just his mere presence on the field helped boost the career of an aging veteran like Carter.

A colleague of mine once said, "There are two objectives for building relationships: Find your commonality and add value to the other person."[14] Carter provided value through his experience and knowledge. In return, Moss provided opportunity and encouragement. Both parties benefitted each other.

Beyond empathy, trust, respect, encouragement and value added, there's one more quality that separates the "good" relationships from the "great" ones—the ones that last from the ones that eventually fade. It's *loyalty*. Loyalty is the greatest evidence and true test of genuine friendship because it keeps the relationship alive even when it stops being easy, fun and mutually beneficial. Loyalty takes sacrifice. It means being available to help in times of distress or personal struggles. It means continuing to follow up and encourage, even when the other person stops deserving your love and respect. Too many people are fair-weather friends. They stick around when the friendship helps them and leave when they're not getting anything out of the relationship. Loyalty fights against that.

After our loss to the Falcons in the '98 NFC Championship game (see "Chapter 6: Self-Talk), Carter was devastated. At age 33 and in his 12th NFL season, he realized he missed his best opportunity to reach a Super Bowl. There were no guarantees he'd ever have another shot. As Carter sat by his locker amid his own sadness and frustration, Moss came and sat beside him.

After a few seconds of silence, Moss said, "Thanks, dawg. Thanks for everything that you did for me."[15]

That exchange shifted Carter's thinking. It helped him to view the season not in terms of falling short of their ultimate goal, but how he helped a friend and teammate grow. Even in that tough loss, there was still a "win" that resulted.

That's the beauty of relationships. Yes, they're based on common interest or goals, and they end up adding value to our lives, but the end goal is *not* that added value. The ultimate reward of being in relationship is *being in relationship.* Yes, in the process, we can spur each other on to better things, but along the way, we gain a friend. It's why we were created—to have relationship with God and with others.

In the book of Genesis, after God creates Adam, He sees that "it is not good for man to be alone" (Genesis 2:18), so He creates Eve to be a partner for Adam. From the beginning of human existence, our need for love and relationship has been clear. Studies have shown us the evidence of this. Single men are jailed more often, earn less, have more illnesses and die at a younger age than married men. Married men with cancer live 20 percent longer than single men with the *same* cancer.[16] Another study conducted over two decades, involving more than 37,000 people, shows that social isolation—the sense that you don't have anyone with whom you can share your private feelings or have close contact—doubles the chances of sickness or death.[17]

In psychologist Abraham Maslow's "Hierarchy of Needs," our needs for love and belonging land just above physiological and safety needs, and just below esteem and self-actualization. In other words, in order to pursue our innate needs of recognition, status, freedom and become the best person we can be—or, achieve peak performance—we need our relationship needs met first. They're a foundation on which we can begin to take steps toward personal peak performance.

The ultimate reward of being in relationship is being in relationship.

But, as you know, relationships alone won't satisfy those needs or achieve that mutual benefit I mentioned above. It's about the people with whom we choose to surround ourselves. The Bible—Proverbs, in particular—is filled with wisdom about our companions in life. Proverbs 13:20 says, "Walk with the wise and become wise, for a companion of fools suffers harm." Proverbs 18:24 says, "One who has unreliable friends soon comes to ruin, but there is a friend who sticks closer than a brother."

"I'm thankful that Cris Carter was really put in my life early in my career because I think not having a veteran in my life, I don't know really what direction I would have been in. Would I have won rookie of the year? Would I have scored 17 touchdowns? Would we have gone to the NFC Championship? I really don't know."

As humans, we want to assume that we're individual beings—self-made men and women—arriving at our own conclusions and values based solely on our intuition and judgment. That's just not true. Like anyone else in this world, we are a compilation of different influences, which, in large part, are the people around us on a regular basis. In other words—or, probably the words of your parents, coaches and/or teachers at some point in your life—"show me your friends, and I'll show you your future." Surround yourself with lazy, unmotivated, selfish people, and eventually, you'll become indistinguishable from the crowd. Build relationships with hard-working, dedicated, selfless people, and you'll see yourself rise to those standards. We affect those with whom we spend time, and they affect us.

In the commentary of the Life Application Study Bible for Proverbs 13:20, it says:

> *"Be careful whom you choose as your closest friends. Spend time with people you want to be like—because you and your friends will surely grow to resemble each other. When most people need advice, they go to their friends first because friends accept them and usually agree with them. But that is why they may not be able to help them with difficult problems. Our friends are so much like us that they may not have any answers we haven't already heard."* [18]

Seek out friendships with those who will understand you, empathize with you and remain loyal to you, but also those who will encourage you and challenge you to grow and develop.

Carter and Moss were teammates for four years, and to this day, Moss credits Carter for helping him launch the beginning of his Hall-of-Fame career. "I'm thankful that Cris Carter was really put in my life early in my career because I think not having a veteran in my life, I don't know really what direction I would have been in. Would I have won rookie of the year? Would I have scored 17 touchdowns? Would we have gone to the NFC Championship? I really don't know."[19]

Coach's Corner

Growing up, different kids take pride in different things when it comes to athletics. For a softball player, it might be the speed of her fastball. For a track athlete, it might be his vertical leap. For me, on my sixth-grade basketball team, it was my decision-making ability. Maybe I wasn't the fastest or the most athletic, but in my mind, I could make quick, sound judgments at critical points in the game—or, at least, my coach must've thought so because that's the role he assigned me. So, at the end of the game, when we needed to execute our in-bounds play to set-up a game-winning shot, I wanted to be the one on the sideline with the ball in my hands.

There's one game, in particular, that I remember. It was the last play of the game, and I was in my preferred spot under my own basket during our drawn-up in-bounds play. The referee handed me the ball and blew his whistle. But this time, I made a mistake. At the most critical point of the game, I turned the ball over, and we lost the game. We lost because of my mistake.

For an 11-year-old kid—and for anyone, really—that's an especially hard pill to swallow. I was already pretty down on myself, but my coach *let me have it* on the sideline—so much so that I still remember it to this day. With the game slipped out of our hands, he made it very clear what my "good decision-making skills" had done for the team. I didn't need the lecture on my mistakes—I'd already relived them over and over in my head.

My dad, though, took a different approach. He didn't yell at me or criticize me. Instead, he empathized and encouraged. "Mistakes happen," he would say. "There's no need to knock people down for them." He and my mom were always in the stands, supporting me—and for that, I'm incredibly grateful—and after my dad watched the grilling I'd received, unbeknownst to me, he took it upon himself to have a conversation with my coach. Sure enough, next practice, Coach showed a bit more empathy and encouragement himself.

> **No man is an island. Of all the topics we've discussed to this point—fitness, nutrition, practice habits, rest, education, self-talk, emotion, wisdom, character—none of them are possible without relationships.**

I know different techniques motivate different people—and maybe some people need to be yelled at—but for me, my dad's approach was instrumental. Too many young men and women grow up without a father, so I know how blessed I am to have that relationship in my life—still to this day. In its own way, my relationship with my dad was a mentor-mentee relationship, like Moss's and Carter's. He knew what I was going through, he cared for me, and he set a positive example to follow. His marriage to my mom and his role as a dad laid the groundwork for the man, husband and father I am today.

Maybe you didn't have a father—or a great relationship with your father—but we all need those positive influences in our life, whether it be a coach, older sibling, teacher or someone else. We need mentors and positive role models in our lives. We need those relationships.

No man is an island. Of all the topics we've discussed to this point—fitness, nutrition, practice habits, rest, education, self-talk, emotion, wisdom, character—none of them are possible without relationships. To achieve our peak potential in the weight room, we need others pushing us along. To channel positive emotions, we need encouragement and positive reinforcement from others. That's God's design. He made us for those relationships.

As the story of Adam and Eve shows, as humans, we are *designed* for relationship with others. Look at the two main commandments of Scripture:

1. "Love the Lord your God with all your heart and with all your soul and with all your mind" (Matthew 22:37).

2. "Love your neighbor as yourself" (v. 39).

Of these two commands on which Jesus said, "all the Law and the Prophets hang," the first is about relationship with God, and the second covers relationships with others. If that's not evidence enough, check out at the story of the gospel as summed up in John 3:16:

> "For God so loved the world that he gave his one and only Son, that whoever believes in him shall not perish but have eternal life" (John 3:16).

God wanted relationship with us *so badly* that He sent Jesus, His only son, to die for us. That's the good news we have as followers of Jesus. Because of our relationship with Jesus—built on trust in His character, Word and promises—we have freedom from our sin, brokenness and bondage. We have a new identity and inheritance through Christ. Because of God's love for us, we now have both the power to love others and an example to follow as we do it.

As Christians, this is our common bond, our shared interest. Christ is the glue that unites all Christ-followers in relationship. Ecclesiastes 4:12 says, "Though one may be overpowered, two can defend themselves. A cord of three strands is not quickly broken." God is the third member of the cord in our relationships with others. If our relationships are united on Christ—not each other—we set ourselves up for success. Instead of relying on another human being to satisfy our deep needs for love, belonging and companionship—and inevitably be disappointed—we can turn to Jesus, who will never let us down. And as we find our satisfaction in Jesus, we're then free to love, empathize and encourage others without fear or expectation.

If our relationships are united on Christ–not each other–we set ourselves up for success.

When we lose sight of Christ as our center—and let sin and brokenness creep in—that's when we see relationships deteriorate. Sin—which can simply be defined as "rebellion from God" or, as I mentioned last chapter, selfishness—creates a wedge both in our relationship with God and our relationships with others. That's why Jesus needed to come to earth in the first place—because of the gap our sin created between us and God. In the same way, selfishness, pride and broken trust—all of which usually stem from fear—destroy relationships. When we look inward, we lose empathy for others. When we lose empathy, we stop caring. When we stop caring, we break trust. When we break trust, relationships fall apart.

So, what's the biblical alternative and the key to healthy relationships? It's already in the verses I mentioned: love. *Love* the Lord your God. *Love* your neighbor as yourself. Love—which is perfected in God, who *is* love—is both the antithesis and antidote to fear. While fear focuses inward, loves looks outward. While fear protects us, love looks to the interests of others. As 1 John 4:18 says, "Perfect love drives out fear."

I'll dive deeper into love in Chapter 12, but it can be summed up in the character traits already mentioned in this chapter: empathy, understanding, trust, respect, encouragement, loyalty. All of those characteristics come down to one simple command: love.

Foundation Building Tip

God put us on this earth to serve others, not ourselves. He made us for relationships, and those relationships are built through empathy, trust, respect, encouragement, loyalty and love. Whether we try to or not, eventually, we become like the people with whom we surround ourselves, so be careful to build relationships with those who share goals and character traits that reflect our own values and ideals. To help you hone your focus, identify three essential people you must have in your life at all times if you want to be truly great:[20]

1. **A mentor.** Typically, someone older, more experienced and wiser than yourself.

2. **A companion.** Someone who is equal (in wisdom and experience) with whom you can exchange ideas.

3. **A mentee.** Typically, someone younger, whom you can mentor to keep you energized and engaged.

Your Workout

1. It was important to Carter that Moss understand he was giving him a "clean slate." So often, we are tempted to judge someone based on their past, whether it was something directly related to us or not. God commands us to love our neighbor and forgive those who have sinned against us, yet it can be much easier to ask someone else to offer us grace than it is for us to offer it to another person. Has anyone ever given you a clean slate? If so, how did it feel?

2. Think of a time you gave someone a clean slate. Was it hard to do? Did the relationship benefit both parties? Would you do it again?

3. List three of your most significant relationships. Tell them something you've noticed about them that is uplifting and positive.
   a.
   b.
   c.

4. Unhealthy relationships can erode our integrity and belief system. Which relationships, professional or personal, are hindering you? Sometimes, you need to let go of these types of relationships. What can you do to build the relationship? Is the relationship worth building or do you need to let go?

Extra Workout Challenge

1. Who's on your list? Write down those who influence you in a positive way.
   a. My mentee is
   b. My mentor is
   c. My equal is

2. Spend quality time with those on your list. Invite the individuals to grab a cup of coffee, have lunch, go for a walk

or just hang out. The investment in quality time will pay dividends not only in your life, but in theirs as well. When you touch the heart, you touch the person!

CHAPTER 11: COMMUNITY

"Just as a body, though one, has many parts, but all its many parts form one body, so it is with Christ." (1 Corinthians 12:12)

Despite being 35 degrees, rainy and a Tuesday morning in January, Baltimore residents packed the streets on January 30, 2001. More than 200,000 Ravens fans congregated for a parade through downtown Baltimore, ending at a rally in front of city hall to celebrate our Super Bowl XXXV victory over the New York Giants.[1]

It was all sort of a whirlwind. We'd won the Super Bowl just hours before, and now Baltimore natives of every shape and size swarmed the streets around us like sardines, climbing up trees and on top of cars—anything to get a better look at the team that had brought home the Vince Lombardi trophy to their city. I'd never seen anything like it. Among all of the vehicles that made up the caravan of players, coaches and staff members, defensive coordinator Marvin Lewis and I were assigned to the same Humvee. From our starting point at M&T Bank Stadium to our destination at city hall, fans around our Humvee shouted the same thing:

"Marvin, don't leave us!"

"Marvin, please stay!"

Now, as another coach sitting next to Lewis, I might've taken this personally, but I knew my role as a strength coach was less prominent than a coordinator. I also knew the fans had a point. Having orchestrated, alongside head coach Brian Billick, one of the best defenses in NFL history, Lewis was all-but-certain to leave Baltimore for a head coaching position. Our Lewis-led 2000 defense shattered the single-season NFL record for fewest points allowed with 165, beating the previous record (187, held by the 1986 Chicago Bears) by a whopping 22 points. Not only that, but the defense set an NFL record for fewest total rushing yards allowed (970).[2] We held Pro Bowl running back Corey Dillon, All-Pro running back Eddie George and Hall-of-Fame running back Jerome Bettis to a combined 137 rushing yards over the course of *six games* (less than 23 yards/game).[3] Coach Lewis' defense was historically great, and they had carried us to that Super Bowl victory.

The year before, in 1999, our defense was good, but not great. We held our opponents to 277 points—good enough for sixth in the League that year—and just 4,222 yards (second), but we still only finished with a .500 record.[4] Following that season, Billick issued a challenge to our defense. He knew these players were a talented group—the local media had even made a point to talk about their potential to be great—but they needed motivation to *achieve* their potential. After talking it over with Coach Lewis, Billick addressed the defense directly one morning in our team meeting:

> *"You all can keep sending four or five guys to the Pro Bowl every year, and we can keep winning six, seven, eight games a season," Billick told them. "Or you all can figure it out and be special."*[5]

The defense grew up right there in that moment. They decided to be special, and that mindset carried us into the 2000 season.

From the start of training camp, everyone on the roster—from the linebackers to the quarterback—knew that our defense defined that 2000 Ravens team. Behind tackle Sam Adams, safety Rod Woodson and Hall-of-Fame linebacker Ray Lewis, our defensive unit tallied shutouts in a quarter of our games that season—falling just one game short of the 1976 Steelers historic feat of five shutouts. During a five-game stretch in October where our offense failed to score a single touchdown, our defense still managed to muscle out two wins—holding our opponents to an average of 8.6 points per game.[6] Though our offense started clicking by the end of the season—and tallied 20 of our 34 points in the Super Bowl—the theme of that season was clear: "defense wins championships."

Shannon Sharpe had this to say about the offense: "We know where our bread is buttered. We're not going to try to fool anybody, and everybody knows it. Our job is not to lose it for those guys. We're going to play true to form. We're going to take care of the football. And if we get an opportunity to make some plays, we're going to make them. If not, we're going to live to see another day and punt the ball away."[7]

Throughout that year—especially during the offensive drought and three-game losing streak—a less unified team might've divided into "offense vs. defense." Coach Lewis' group definitely had a right to be frustrated, but across the board, they continued to support each other. We didn't look like a playoff team in October, but because of our tight-knit cohesiveness, to the credit of the players and coaches, we fought our way out of it. We became a better team on the other side of that adversity.

We had a secret that season— one that allowed our defense and entire team to rise up to the

> *Our secret was that we worked as a unit. Even more than wearing the same colors on gameday, we operated as a community.*

coaches' preseason challenge. It wasn't that we had a bunch of individually talented players—we knew that already, and that was true of almost any NFL team. Our secret was that we worked as a unit. Even more than wearing the same colors on gameday, we operated as a *community*.

A community is a group of people united by a common bond or goal. It's more than just a group of friends. As author and professor Sherry Turkle defined it, "Communities are constituted by physical proximity, shared concerns, real consequences, and common responsibilities."[8] In a strong community, members have a sense of responsibility to the whole group and a specific role which allows both the individuals and the overall unit to function properly and efficiently. In other words, individuals operate on behalf of the collective, and in the end, they not only make the community better, but they see themselves grow in the process.

In a sense, communities are like a mirror: they show us a reflection of ourselves—they expose both the very best and the very worst in us. Take marriage, for example—the first and most central community in most people's lives. If you were to ask married people, including myself, about what surprised them in the early parts of marriage, most will tell you the same thing: "I had no idea I was this (fill in the blank) until I got married." Put simply, when we live alongside other people, we become exposed to the truest form of ourselves.

Although that vulnerability might be scary for some, studies show that it's unavoidable if we want to achieve peak performance. Like relationships, we *need* community—it's not an option. We need other people to survive. After a 2017 report that discovered more than 9 million people (14 percent of the population) in Britain often or always feel lonely, the prime minister appointed a minister for loneliness to address this very issue. The study also found that loneliness often negatively affects health, especially in older people. Those who live in isolation are more likely to experience impaired sleep, depression and decreased overall health.[9]

> **In a sense, communities are like a mirror: they show us a reflection of ourselves–they expose both the very best and the very worst in us.**

Naturally, communities make us better. If they're healthy, communities take a group of unlike individuals who could accomplish a decent amount on their own and turn them into a well-oiled, cohesive machine—capable of significantly more than the individual parts. As Helen Keller said, "Alone, we can do so little; together, we can do so much."[10] The end goal of a community—or, in our case, a football team—is empowering its members to flourish and thrive. Members make each other better and build a strong unit. But this doesn't happen automatically when a bunch of individuals with some commonality group together. It takes intentionality and effort from each person.

On one hand, communities are made up of a handful of individual connections, so the key aspects of a healthy relationship (empathy, trust, respect, etc.) from last chapter apply here as well. But communities also have a unique secondary relationship to them: the individual's relationship *to the community* as a whole. For example, in our first and foremost community, the family, we have individual *relationships* (with our mother, our father, our siblings, etc.), but we also have a specific role within the whole unit. In order for the whole family to function properly and efficiently, we need to not only maintain our individual relationships, but also keep up with our responsibilities to the community. This might be household chores like mowing the lawn or vacuuming, maintaining a certain level of communication, or even providing emotional support to other members when they're unable to do it themselves. While relationships have their own criteria for vitality, so do communities—three, in particular.

If they're healthy, communities take a group of unlike individuals who could accomplish a decent amount on their own and turn them into a well-oiled, cohesive machine—capable of significantly more than the individual parts.

The first, as I mentioned before, is a **common goal or bond**—and the respect for the authority of that common goal and/or the person enforcing it. Without this critical element, and without the leadership to implement it, a community is directionless and destined to fail from the start. The second key is **humility**—viewing others higher than yourself. When we see everyone in our community as valuable, we're more likely and willing to put their needs above our own. This helps inform and motivate the final element of a healthy community: **sacrifice**—a willingness to give of yourself for the betterment of others in your community. When we choose selflessness and sacrifice instead of self-assertion and self-indulgence, we end up strengthening the entire unit and accomplishing more collectively than we ever could individually. These essential ingredients helped that 2000 Ravens defense transform a group of widely divergent individual personalities into a unified team—and ultimately, take the Lombardi Trophy back to those fans in Baltimore.

A defense like that 2000 team requires all eleven players on the field to work as one unit. If a team member doesn't fulfill their role, the team will be less effective. If one player doesn't do their job, the defense won't function properly. Each team member is important and adds unique value to the whole. Each one of the defensive players on our roster that year had varying egos, motivations, personalities, self-interests, economic circumstances and talent levels that Lewis and Billick had to manage and utilize to benefit the entire team. Each member brought unique skills and abilities, and because every person sacrificed for the guy next to him, they made each other better. They succeeded because they were a community.

First, each player bought into their individual role within the larger game plan—**the common bond**. They respected the authority of Billick and Lewis, united around their leadership and strategy, and moved forward in a clear direction. In short, everyone *did their job*. It was the coaches' job to put athletes in a position to succeed—through practice, preparation and game planning—and it was the players' job to respect that and execute accordingly.

For example, Tony Siragusa—"Goose," as he was known in the locker room and around the League—would often occupy two offensive linemen at the line of scrimmage. Although this mostly (but not always) neutralized his individual effort to make tackles or pressure the quarterback, it was all according to the plan. When Goose drew a double-team, it kept the offensive linemen away from middle linebacker Ray Lewis, freeing him up to attack the QB or stuff the run. Linebacker Jamie Sharper took a similarly collaborative role with Ray. Instead of angling his attack toward the middle of the line to try to make a play, he held the edge—incapacitating the outside lineman and forcing the play right into Lewis' awaiting arms.

This selflessness from Goose and Sharper not only showed their loyalty to the coaches and the game plan; it also reflected their **humility**. In a profession where personal accomplishments are often elevated above a team's achievement, each of these players put aside their need for the spotlight and instead sought to shine it on their teammates. That humility allowed them to respect the coaches and work for their fellow players—it empowered them to be a part of something bigger than themselves. When this is practiced effectively in a community, a beautiful thing happens. While each person tries to point the spotlight on the guy next to him, he actually often ends up in the spotlight himself. His humility and commitment to the unit lead to team success, and that success, in turn, provides that recognition for which he may have been looking in the first place.

A great example of this is marriage. If, as a husband, I try to put my own interests above Jen's or the health of our marriage, she ends up feeling unimportant and unloved. This might lead to an argument, and pretty soon, I'm feeling unloved because my needs aren't being listened to or met. My selfishness leads to unhappiness on both sides. However, if I choose to love Jen by putting her needs first, that love she feels may actually motivate her to *love me* in new ways. In the end, one spouse's selflessness leads to both partners feeling loved, and in the end, the marriage is stronger. Individual humility and selflessness strengthen communities.

The humility of the players—combined with their commitment to the game plan and the unit as a whole—naturally led them to **sacrifice** for one another. They fought against the temptations of pride, jealousy and individual achievement—which, as you might imagine, are very prevalent in professional sports—for the sake of the success of the entire unit.

There's a team meeting from Baltimore I remember vividly in which Coach Billick emphasized this point—do your job, sacrifice individual glory for the sake of the team. He gave the example of pass rushers like Michael McCrary and Rob Burnett who were often assigned to hold the edge of the line. If they decided to disregard the game plan and go for a sack—which could mean a place in the highlight reel and extra money in their pockets—they'd leave the defense vulnerable to giving up a big gain. But because of their selflessness and commitment to the unit, they did their jobs and opened doors for their teammates to do theirs—and the whole team succeeded as a result. Their sacrifice made the unit stronger.

Rod Woodson put it like this, "I really didn't know how good we could be. I knew we had talent, but talent doesn't always win football games…We made a pact as a defense at the beginning of the year: we're all going to run to the ball for our other brothers. Not for us, but for our other brothers. And we kept getting better and better and better. We kept believing in each other."[11]

While everyone on our defense had a unique role to play, so did the man at the helm. Coach Lewis led and directed the community, but he was also an essential part *of it*. Whether it's a family, a church or a team, every community needs a leader to provide order, direction and authority. Someone on the inside, getting everyone to execute their specific role in a way that supports the whole group. Someone who's leadership and vision are absolutely crucial to the community's success. The humility, selflessness and willingness to sacrifice might all be there, but without a dedicated leader to provide order, direction and a common goal, a community has nothing to move toward. For our defense, that was Marvin Lewis.

From the challenge he issued before the 2000 season to every time he said, "Do your job," on the practice field, Coach Lewis built and orchestrated a world championship-level defense. He understood the goal, assigned roles accordingly and held people responsible to those roles. Each one of these aspects was crucial to the team's success. On his grease board in Cincinnati, where he later became head coach, Lewis wrote the word, "Jenga," to remind him of this process. Like the popular Hasbro® game, if you keep "pulling blocks" (sacrificing team goals for individual ones), eventually, the whole structure collapses. Don't pull blocks. Do your job.

The humility, selflessness and willingness to sacrifice might all be there, but without a dedicated leader to provide order, direction and a common goal, a community has nothing to move toward.

Coach Lewis was one of the biggest reasons why he and I rode side-by-side in that caravan of Humvees from M&T Bank Stadium toward Baltimore City Hall. Along with Coach Billick, he kept every cog in order and working properly. He prioritized respect, humility and sacrifice, and he held his players accountable to that standard. He knew what our team needed to foster a successful unit, a healthy community, and he provided the leadership to make it happen. The cries from the crowd that cold and rainy morning—"Marvin, don't leave us!"—were justified.

Although the stakes might not be as high and the roles might not be as clear, this is what community is. It's a group of people coming together and putting aside their selfish ambitions for the sake of seeing one another succeed. And, in the end, healthy communities empower each individual person—as well as the unit—to flourish and thrive. That's what happened in 2000 with our defense—and really, with our entire team. Our offense supported our defense, and the defense made the offense better. All of these factors came together, and we reaped the rewards on Super Bowl Sunday. And it wasn't a single person that caravanned from the stadium to city hall two days later. It wasn't just Ray Lewis or Tony Siragusa or Trent Dilfer or Shannon Sharpe. We moved as a unit.

Coach's Corner

February 2019 was the end of an era. After 16 seasons and a franchise-record 131 wins with Marvin Lewis as the head coach of the Cincinnati Bengals,[12] Coach Lewis was fired. He was released on what's known in the NFL as "Black Monday"—the first weekday after the end of the regular season and, for underperforming teams, typically the last day of employment for coaches and general managers. After finishing last in the AFC North with a 6-10 record and missing the playoffs for three straight seasons, our run under Coach Lewis was over. A few weeks later, the rest of us coaches joined Lewis on the chopping block.

Working a job in professional sports, we knew this moment was bound to happen—it had happened 10 years earlier with the Ravens, too—but in a sense, getting fired from the Bengals (and the Ravens) was like a death, of sorts. I was being torn from a community I'd dedicated my time and effort to for the last decade. I'd invested myself into making the players, coaches and organization better—and they'd invested in me. Almost immediately, I felt a tangible loss—the daily interactions, the friendships, the journey, the unity, the successes and the failures. I'd given so much of myself for the sake of the unit, and now it was all gone. That part hurt. There's a sense of inevitable loneliness that comes after an event like this. My community was gone. But God had a plan.

Within a week of being released by the Bengals, I had the opportunity to meet with the Christian sports organization, Athletes in Action (AIA), whose U.S. headquarters was located just 30 miles from our house. Even before the meeting—based on an email I'd received earlier that day—I could already sense the synergy in this potential relationship. I felt God preparing me to connect with them. We both needed each other. They needed me because of my expertise, marketability and credibility. I needed them as an avenue to utilize my gifts and talents. That meeting reinforced God's control over my life. He had a path for me. He had a plan for me. He was going to use me. He gave me hope.

I left that meeting so excited and energized about this new community God had so quickly placed in my path. AIA gave me a new perspective. They encouraged me to think bigger: "Yes, God wanted to use Jeff Friday in the weight room., but what could God do *for the world* through *Jeff Friday?*"

Out of our conversation and this new relationship, AIA gave me a platform to workshop and refine the material I wanted to turn into a book—the book you're reading now—and I helped them develop their sports performance institute. That spring, I volunteered with the AIA sports performance team to help architect and develop an athletic development program at a local high school in Lebanon, Ohio. This new community—including the athletes and coaches at the school—made me feel valued for the wisdom and experience I shared. I utilized my spiritual gifts and, in return, received the fruits of the Spirit such as love, joy and peace.

In 1 Corinthians 12, Paul compares a community (the body of Christ) to a human body: "Just as a body, though one, has many parts, but all its many parts form one body, so it is with Christ. For we were all baptized by one Spirit so as to form one body—whether Jews or Gentiles, slave or free—and we were all given the one Spirit to drink. Even so the body is not made up of one part but of many" (v. 12-14). Each part of the body, each member of a community—as Paul goes on to say—has a specific function that's different from others, but essential to the whole. If any part is taken away, the whole body loses its effectiveness. We are better together.

Take Jesus' disciples, for example. The 12 men Jesus chose came from a variety of differing backgrounds and life experiences. Some were working men from strong Jewish backgrounds. Others, like Matthew, the tax collector, were "sinners"—or Jewish people who had betrayed their heritage to serve the Roman government. Simon the Zealot was on the opposite end of the political spectrum. He used any means necessary, even violence, to remove Roman rule from Jewish territory. The disciples weren't, by nature, a unified group. Jesus brought each person in for their individual gifts and potential to contribute to the community. Although their differences probably made it difficult to get along with each other, those same differences increased their perspective and ability to make real change. Over time, the 12 learned to understand, love and believe in each other. Acts 2 tells us they sacrificed for one another. Like the 2000 Ravens defense, this group of unlikely companions became a flourishing community, a healthy body, because of the one thing they did have in common: their leader.

Like any team or community, the body needs a head—and that head is Jesus. At the center of every healthy, thriving Christian community is a common faith and trust in Christ. This is what unifies believers from across the globe. When we enter relationship with Jesus, we also become part of a new community, a body of believers. In Christ, our strengths and gifts are no longer for our own self-promotion, pride and personal desires, they are for the good of the body. This is how God designed the Church. This is how Jesus could transform a bunch of incompatible individuals into a cohesive team. This is why, despite our differences, we can sacrifice for our brothers and sisters in Christ and put others above ourselves. We're committed to the common bond we have in Christ. As author

Like each of those players, God has given us individual strengths, gifts and abilities to use for the good of the whole unit, not just for ourselves.

and theologian Dallas Willard put it, "The aim of God in history is the creation of an all-inclusive community of loving persons, with Himself included in that community as its prime sustainer and most glorious inhabitant."[13]

Not only did Christ give His disciples a common bond and mission, but He also gave them an example for how to live. When two of the disciples, James and John, asked to be elevated in the Kingdom of God, Jesus called the whole group together and told them, "Whoever wants to become great among you must be your servant, and whoever wants to be first must be slave of all. For even the Son of Man did not come to be served, but to serve, and to give his life as a ransom for many" (Mark 10:43-45). Humility and sacrifice.

As was the case with each member on Coach Lewis' defense, our role when it comes to community should not be a posture of receiving or self-promotion, but of service. Like each of those players, God has given us individual strengths, gifts and abilities to use for the good of the whole unit, not just for ourselves. There's no room for pride in a healthy community.

The beauty of a healthy community, though—especially community in the body of Christ—is that it provides something beyond exposure. It not only reveals the best and worst in ourselves, but it responds to our weaknesses with encouragement. In an unhealthy community,

> **Community is the only way to become like Jesus, which is to achieve peak performance.**

this exposure of flaws, shortcomings and brokenness might lead to division and animosity between members. Seeing the worst in others (and ourselves) naturally causes us to feel insecure and thus pursue our own interests over others'. But when people, despite our flaws, still choose to encourage us, we're given both the opportunity *and* the motivation to grow.

As I've mentioned before, no man is an island. We need people, we need community to follow Jesus and, ultimately, to fulfill our God-given potential. This is non-negotiable. Community is the *only way* to become like Jesus, which is to achieve peak performance. How will we maintain a workout program without others to encourage us, walk alongside us and hold us accountable? How can we gain wisdom without learning from others? How can we develop positive character traits without others telling us where we need to grow? We are both designed for and defined by our communities.

Odds are, you're probably not a member of an NFL defense, so where is your community? For all of us, it starts in the home—with our spouse, our kids, our siblings, our parents. From there, it branches out to school, to our workplace, to the field, and then on to our broader community at-large. Wherever God has placed you—whatever team He's put you on—you have both a responsibility and an opportunity. If you lead with humility, sacrifice and respect for authority, you can open the door to accomplish much more than you ever could alone.

Foundation Building Tip

God created us to be in relationship with other people. He designed His Church to be a sacrificial, humble, united community. In healthy communities, members selflessly sacrifice and serve one another for the sake of their common bond or goal, with the end goal being a flourishing, thriving unit—capable of much more than the individual parts. Every cog, every Jenga block in the machine of community of essential;

every member is required for the body to function properly and efficiently.

Look around, find your community (or communities) and, as Marvin Lewis said, "do your job." Take care of your responsibilities to the unit and serve your community well. God designed us for this specific purpose.

Your Workout

1. Who is in your community? Take some time this week to assess your spheres of influence and where your communities might currently exist. Remember: a community is more than just a group of friends; it requires physical proximity, shared concerns, real consequences and common responsibilities.

2. What strengths, gifts and perspectives can you bring to your community? If you have multiple, how might your contribution differ from group to group?

3. In what ways in the past have you used your God-given talents and abilities to serve a larger group? Maybe it was a basketball team, a small group or even your immediate family. List two to three examples of how you exercised sacrifice and humility for something larger than yourself.

4. How have your communities supported, encouraged and strengthened you? How have they helped you accomplish more than you could've on your own?

5. In what ways has your own pride inhibited you from serving others? Where did that pride come from? What effect might it have on your community to change that pride to humility for the sake of others?

Extra Workout Challenge

1. Our community starts in the home, branches out into the workplace and extends into our broader community. What is one way you could serve someone (or multiple

people) in each of these communities every day this week?

2. Keep a scorecard for yourself to measure your progress. Write down who you served, what you did and how it affected the other person (or you).

CHAPTER 12: LOVE

"Dear friends, let us love one another, for love comes from God. Everyone who loves has been born of God and knows God. Whoever does not love does not know God, because God is love." (1 John 4:7-8)

The first time I got fired came as somewhat of a shock. I was in Baltimore, with the Ravens. We'd come off a disappointing 5-11 season in 2007, but just a year before that, we'd finished 13-3, tied for the best record in the League, and made the divisional playoffs. Now, after nine seasons, it was just, all over. Baltimore was where it all started—my first head strength coaching job, the Super Bowl win, our first house, the birth of our two kids, the relationships and community we'd developed over nearly a *decade* spent in one location—and just like that, all of it was stripped away. In one day, my life as I knew it was gone.

Sitting in the weight room that afternoon, I flipped—yes, flipped—open my phone. I had a voicemail. It was from one of the pastors at my church, Dave Michener.

I'd known Dave pretty much since I'd arrived in Baltimore in 1999. Jen and I started attending Bridgeway Community Church, where Dave pastored, soon after settling into our new home. During my time with the Ravens, "Pastor Mich" and I developed a friendship. Over the years, we prayed together, worshipped together and fellowshipped in each other's homes together. He even provided wisdom and prayer for me during that tumultuous time in my career when some of my athletes hired their own personal trainer during the off-season (see Chapter 5: Education).

Although Dave's and my relationship benefitted both of us—he prayed for me and guided me spiritually; I hooked him up with training camp and game tickets— it started as somewhat of a one-way street. He often spoke truth, wisdom and encouragement into *my* life, but I rarely, if ever, did that for Dave. And even when he did help me in my spiritual growth, it was usually solicited by me in the first place. That cold February day in Baltimore, though, that all changed.

Back in the weight room, I hit play on my voicemail:

> *"Hey Jeff," Dave said through my phone speaker. "I just felt God compelling me to call you and tell you that I care about you, whether you're a coach in the NFL or not. This might sound crazy, but I had an accountability partner I used to get together with, and that person is no longer in my life. I don't know exactly what it would look like, but if you want to turn it up a notch in our friendship, just think and pray about it. You don't even have to say anything right now."*

After a long day of season-ending meetings and grappling with the reality that I'd no longer be working for the Ravens, Dave's simple message to me provided exactly what I needed. I had a friend out there—and not just a "friend" who wanted the perks of knowing an NFL coach. Dave's voicemail made it clear: he cared enough about me to, in vulnerability, step outside of his comfort zone and invest in my life.

From that phone call, my friendship with Dave deepened to a new level. I sent him a book, which we read together and discussed. That led to another book study, which led to prayer time together, conversations over coffee, and time together in community and with each other's families. In those following months and years, we realized we now had that "ride or die" type of relationship. It was this sense of, "OK, we're in life together now."

Our friendship became a two-way street—not simply a pastor-congregant relationship. While Dave continued to mentor me and disciple me when I transitioned to the United Football League in Orlando, started my own sports training business and eventually moved to Cincinnati with the Bengals, I also started to speak into and invest in *Dave's* life. When he called me the day I got fired from the Ravens, he was in the middle of a difficult season of ministry. Although I didn't know it at the time, Dave was trying to decide whether or not to leave full-time pastoral work, and I provided the stability and friendship he needed.

When you say "yes" to a friendship like that, you don't know where it's going to go or where the road will lead you each individually. In almost every sense, our lives developed in different directions, but because of the decision Dave and I made and the time we invested into each other's lives, our friendship only deepened. It continued to grow because, at the foundation of our relationship, we loved each other.

What *is* love? While it's one of the most talked-about and utilized themes, in Western society in particular, love is also one of the most complex topics of our world. Definitions of love range from "affection" and "desire" to "sacrifice" and "commitment," and depending on the context in which you grow up and live, that definition could vary drastically from the next person. All of us can connect, in some way, with the ideas and themes around love, but the only thing we seem to agree on about its objective meaning is that 1) it's important and 2) everyone needs it. Or, in the words of John Lennon and Paul McCartney, "All you need is love. Love is all you need."

We were created to love. There's a reason a vast majority of movies and TV shows have some sort of romantic element (if not main theme) to them. Love is universal. Sigmund Freud said, "Love and work are the cornerstones of our humanness." "Love and belonging" rank third on Maslow's Hierarchy of Needs. Love seems to be one of the few things our Western culture can agree on—the idea that love, whatever it is, is something we need and desperately desire. Not only that, but love is something we're

> *In almost every sense, our lives developed in different directions, but because of the decision Dave and I made and the time we invested into each other's lives, our friendship only deepened.*

supposed to show other people—hence, Jesus' words in Matthew 22: "Love your neighbor as yourself." Regardless of upbringing, political standing or belief, most of us would admit that love is something in which we'd like to participate—we just haven't exactly settled on what it is.

The first—and maybe most accepted—definition of love is something along the lines of romantic affection, attraction or a deep, emotional longing to be with another person. We see this in almost every fictional (and often non-fictional) story. In popular culture, love is portrayed as this powerful, unavoidable force that binds us together with other people. Primarily, this kind of love manifests itself as a feeling inside of us. "I'm in love with you," then, essentially means that "I am feeling and experiencing this inescapable sense of love toward you." To love is to feel affection for another person.

A second definition of love is one that's been popularized by Western culture. According to this idea, love is essentially "live and let live"— do whatever you want and let everyone else do the same, so long as it doesn't hurt anyone else. Since our culture has largely accepted the idea that truth is relative, love in this context is up for each individual to determine for themselves. And on a universal level, we can best love other people by accepting—or, at least, tolerating—their beliefs without imposing any of our own onto them. To love is to wholeheartedly accept someone for exactly who they are.

One final definition—and this list is by no means exhaustive—is based not on feelings, but actions. This kind of love is rooted primarily in two things: commitment and sacrifice. Someone who loves in this way might say, "Regardless of how I feel about you on any given day, I will *choose* to love you." In this sense, it's opposite to the first definition—instead of love being an unavoidable, mysterious force that sweeps us up when we least expect it, love is something we voluntarily decide to give. When we choose this love, we also choose to put another person's needs above our own. You might see this played out in a war setting—when one soldier chooses to jump in a front of a bullet, sacrificing himself for his fellow man. To love is to choose someone else over yourself.

All three of these examples make legitimate points, but they also all have problems. Yes, love has an emotional element to it—I have felt and continue to feel that with my wife and kids on a regular basis—but it's also more than that. In order for love to last, it needs some sort of action or commitment independent of our emotions. Otherwise, I'd only love my family when I felt like it. On the other hand, it's not only based on our choice to act. There's also a mysterious, emotional side to love that makes it easier to sacrifice and commit to other people. One side initiates and fuels the loving action, and the other sustains and produces loving feelings. A true,

> *In order to truly love another person, we have to give him or her our authentic, transparent selves.*

full sense of love, in my opinion, takes elements from all of these definitions. Given that, let's look at three things love *is* and three things love is *not*. First, what it is:

- **Love IS both a choice and an attitude that reveals itself in action.** This is why the phrases, "I am in love with you," and "I love you by..." can both be equally true. We give up time, money, effort and energy (sacrificial acts) to those we love, and we also love those people *by* giving up those things. In my relationship with Dave, we both chose to love the other person and took action to invest time into each other's lives, which is probably the most precious commodity we have as human beings. Sacrificial actions are both ways to love and evidence of love.

- **Love IS a belief in the best in another person.** In his book, *The Meaning of Marriage*, pastor Tim Keller put it like this: "Falling in love in a Christian way is to say, 'I am excited about your future and I want to be part of getting you there. I'm signing up for the journey with you. Would you sign up for the journey to my true self with me? It's going to be hard, but I want to get there."[1] In marriage, love means maintaining that belief in your spouse you had at the altar on your wedding day. That's why love can grow and deepens as marriage goes on—you get to know the other person that much more, and you choose to still love and believe in them. Even in sin and brokenness, love recognizes what God's doing in another person and partners with God in that process.

- **To love IS to be vulnerable.** This one comes from C.S. Lewis and his book, *The Four Loves*: "To love at all is to be vulnerable. Love anything and your heart will be wrung and possibly broken. If you want to make sure of keeping it intact you must give it to no one, not even an animal. Wrap it carefully round with hobbies and little luxuries; avoid all entanglements. Lock it up safe in the casket or coffin of your selfishness. But in that casket, safe, dark, motionless, airless, it will change. It will not be broken; it will become unbreakable, impenetrable, irredeemable. To love is to be vulnerable."[2] In order to truly love another person, we have to give him or her our authentic, transparent selves. In my relationship with Dave, I don't think there's a subject about which we haven't talked. Because of the love and trust we have for one another, we're freed to be vulnerable and real, no matter our emotions or circumstances.

Now, three things love is *not*:

- **Love is NOT just equivalent with enjoyment or desire.** On top of the nuanced definitions of love throughout culture, the uses of the word make understanding true love even more complex. For example, we're quick to throw around phrases like, "I love this burger" or "I love this song," as if love is nothing more than another way to say you enjoy someone or something. If that were the case, then love would fluctuate from day to day, depending on how the person giving love (Person A) happened to be feeling. If, all of a sudden, Person B is no longer enjoyable to Person A—say, when they disagree—then their love would last only as long their cravings for lunch that particular day.

- **Love is NOT based only on feelings and physical at-**

traction. Like enjoyment or desire, feelings and attraction might spur on love or *make it easier* to love, but by themselves, they don't encompass all of what love is. Emotions fluctuate and attractiveness fades, but love remains constant. This is how love empowers us to sacrificial action.

• **Love is NOT self-serving.** A common, and often detrimental, misconception about marriage is that your spouse is there to meet *your* needs—to completely satisfy your deep, innate desire for intimacy, love and relationship that you've waited for your entire life. The harsh reality is—as any married person will tell you—this just simply isn't true. Marriage is two broken people merging their lives together, committing to love each other daily while, unavoidably, letting each other down. If you expect your spouse to fully meet your needs, you'll only end up frustrated, disappointed and probably with a broken marriage. Love is about sacrifice and commitment—dedicating your life to serving another person and putting their interests above your own, expecting nothing in return. Love is about what we *give*, not what we get back. That's why we can love people who don't (or can't) give us anything in return. John 15:13 says, "Greater love has no one than this: to lay down one's life for one's friends."

When we understand what love means and how it's lived out, we give ourselves a framework not only to love others, but to *receive* love ourselves. Here's an excerpt from a sermon entitled, "The Inner Ache of Loneliness," which, referencing C.S. Lewis' *The Four Loves*, talks about this distinction between "need love" and "gift love":

> *"There are basically two kinds of love which we as human beings well understand because we see it. The first is 'need love.' It is a love that says, 'I want to belong. I want to be cared for. I want somebody to take my hand. I want somebody to put their arm around me. I want somebody to come give me that hug.' We all understand it. Psychologists tell us babies roll to the*

edge of a crib because they want that contact. They want that warmth. We all have 'need love.'"

The second is what we call a 'gift love.' A 'gift love' is that we give of ourselves to somebody else. If you look at a Mother Teresa pouring her life and affection to the destitute of the streets of Calcutta, it is a gift love. It's giving love to the destitute and dying. Everyone who is a parent knows. We understand 'gift love.' It's a love that gives of itself."[3]

Giving and receiving love are inseparably linked together. If we've never given love, we can't truly receive it. If we don't receive love, we won't have the capacity to give it. Look at the example of two of Jesus' disciples in John 13:18-38. In this passage, Jesus predicts two things: His betrayal (by Judas) and His denial (by Peter). Though He knew both things would happen and that both His trusted friends would turn against Him, He didn't try to stop the situation, nor did He stop *loving* Judas or Peter. He knew exactly what Peter and Judas would do, yet He chose to still love them unconditionally—expecting nothing in return, ready to offer forgiveness. He still wrapped a towel around his waist and washed the dust off their feet—the lowly job customarily carried out by a household servant after guests arrived, and the ultimate act of humble, sacrificial love. Jesus loved both disciples in the same way, yet their lives ended in drastically opposite ways. In his guilt, Judas took his own life. In repentance, Peter ran back to Jesus.

> **Giving and receiving love are inseparably linked together. If we've never given love, we can't truly receive it. If we don't receive love, we won't have the capacity to give it.**

The difference between Judas and Peter was *not* Jesus' gift of love, but their response. Jesus offered both disciples the same gift—unconditional love and forgiveness—but only one accepted it. Only Peter received Jesus' love. Because Peter did this, despite his brokenness, the Holy Spirit empowered him to demonstrate the love of Christ to thousands of people as he helped start the early Church. Because Judas couldn't receive Jesus' love, he was left only with his own shortcomings—a reality he unfortunately wasn't equipped to face.

From the moment we're born, we crave love and relational intimacy.

That's why those early years are so foundational from a developmental psychology perspective. If our parents address and meet our early needs for love and belonging, our brains are freed up to develop healthily.

If those needs *aren't* met, however, our brains need to work extra hard to protect ourselves from hurt and neglect again, so they develop coping mechanisms—protecting us from pain, but ultimately, like Lewis said, making our hearts "unbreakable, impenetrable, irredeemable." Those wounds and traumatic experiences inhibit us from receiving love as adults; they make us fearful of relationship.[4]

> *That's the beautiful thing about love—when those needs for love, security and belonging within relationship are met, we're then freed up to share that love with other people.*

The only way to heal those relational wounds, however, is through relationship. In order to overcome those unhealthy coping mechanisms, we need to experience that real love that was lacking early on in life. As Tim Keller puts it, we need to be "fully known and truly loved":

> *"To be loved but not known is comforting but superficial. To be known and not loved is our greatest fear. But to be fully known and truly loved is, well, a lot like being loved by God. It is what we need more than anything. It liberates us from pretense, humbles us out of our self-righteousness, and fortifies us for any difficulty life can throw at us."[5]*

That's the beautiful thing about love—when those needs for love, security and belonging within relationship are met, we're then freed up to share that love with other people. We're no longer focused on those internal fears and relational wounds in ourselves; instead, we're empowered to love others in new ways.

When Dave called me that day I was released from the Ravens, he took a risk. He chose to be vulnerable, to put himself out there, ultimately, out of love for me. And at a uniquely vulnerable point in *my* career, I chose to trust and love him—even though our relationship hadn't developed to that level yet. At a time when my identity as a strength coach and confidence as a husband, father and man *could've* taken a blow, the love Dave showed me—the love of God—provided the antidote I needed. And as that relationship developed, I learned, in new ways, what love looked like.

We spent time together; we shared experiences together. I'd have a meal at his table with his family, and he'd have one with mine. We pushed each other and encouraged the other to be better—to fulfill our God-given potential. When Dave struggled with health issues surrounding his weight, I got in the gym with him. I helped him diet and taught him principles of healthy living. When I started writing and speaking more often, Dave provided both encouragement and helpful criticism. We sacrificed for each other. Because of that mutual love, we were willing to do just about anything—however irrational or inconvenient—for the good of the other person.

That's why love is so critical to the social building block—it informs and supports all of the other elements. It's perhaps the most important character trait we can develop. It's an essential ingredient to a healthy relationship. And it's a critical motivating factor for members of a community to execute their individual roles and benefit the whole group. It's the underlying, essential component of the entire section, and it's the reason why there *is* a fourth building block (spiritual) at all.

After my mom died in 2016, we held her funeral service in my hometown of Milwaukee. It was a beautiful service and tribute to my mom, and so many people showed up to tell our family how much my mom meant to them. While I stood there and greeted people coming down the receiving line—which, because of my mom, was remarkably long—my son, Aidan, saw Pastor Dave waiting his turn. He hadn't told me he was coming—and I didn't expect him to, given the distance—yet there he was, ready to be there for me in another uniquely vulnerable time in my life.

In its purest, most ideal form, love is never-ending.

After the service ended and most people had left, Dave, another one of my best friends and I sat ("eating fatty meats and cheese," as Dave remembers) and just shared a few extra moments together. I'd just finished speaking at the funeral and saying goodbye to my mother for the last time, and in that emotional, transparent space, these friends were there for me. Dave was there for me, and the full extent of our love for each other—vulnerability, sacrifice, commitment, authenticity—was on display. It's a moment I'll never forget.

Despite the new jobs, despite the miles between us, despite the different directions in which our lives have progressed, Dave and I still have a deep, loving friendship. To this day—although it can be awkward at times—we're never shy or afraid to tell each other, "I love you." That, I think, is the final and most-telling characteristic of love: it lasts. In its purest, most ideal form, love is never-ending. From the moment he called me on the cold February afternoon, even in the middle of his own difficult season, Dave was empowered to love me. He loved me because someone else—someone eternal—loved him first.

Coach's Corner

On May 24, 1997, Jennifer and I stood in front of my uncle, Joe Campagna, and a crowd of some 100 people in Saint Patrick's Church in Milwaukee, Wisconsin, ready to make our wedding vows to each other. I'd played touch football with my groomsmen that morning, but now was the real "game time." To this day, I still remember choking up at how beautiful Jen looked walking down the aisle. This was the woman I would love for the rest of my life. Before we said, "I do," though, Uncle Joe read a passage of Scripture from 1 Corinthians 13—one you've probably heard at weddings before:

> *"Love is patient, love is kind. It does not envy, it does not boast, it is not proud. It does not dishonor others, it is not self-seeking, it is not easily angered, it keeps no record of wrongs. Love does not delight in evil but rejoices with the truth. It always protects, always trusts, always hopes, always perseveres" (1 Corinthians 13:4-7).*

For all of the nuanced, complex, convoluted definitions of love, this verse from Paul's letters to the church in Corinth lays it out clearly—this is how love should be manifested toward others. Standing up at the altar on that spring afternoon, I knew this was my standard, my compass, when it came to loving my new bride. It's the standard I still do my best to emulate today.

Of all the different stances on "what love is"—from Christians to skeptics to agnostics—not many people can argue with Paul's definition. It's probably why this passage is read at such a large majority of weddings—Christian and non-Christian. The natural follow-up to that is: Why? If we have so much trouble defining what love *truly is* on a universal level, why are these 15 characteristics so widely accepted?

> **When we learn how to receive love—both from God and other people—it counteracts those internal fears we all experience that "I'm not good enough" or "I'm a terrible person."**

I have a working theory: maybe, just maybe, it's because the Creator of the universe (and of every human being) instilled that idea and standard of love in us from the moment we were born.

According to Scripture, God gives us the comprehensive picture, in Himself, when it comes to true, authentic, lasting love. He does this in three ways: He is love; He loves us (and thus, empowers us to love others); and He gives us the ultimate example of *how* to love.

First, His character. The verses at the beginning of this chapter come from 1 John 4: "Dear friends, let us love one another, for love comes from God. Everyone who loves has been born of God and knows God. Whoever does not love does not know God, because God is love" (1 John 4:7-8).

God not only *tells* us what love is; He *shows* us. He shows us because He Himself is the standard of love. Because God created love and perfectly exemplifies love through His character, He's incapable of *not* loving. God is love, so if we're looking for a true definition of love, we need look no further.

Second, His love for us. Verse 19 of 1 John 4 sums this point up well: "We love because he first loved us." Before we loved Him—before we even had the capacity to love at all—God first loved us. And not for anything we did. He didn't love us for anything we accomplished or anything we could give Him in return; He loved us, simply, because He loved us.

The book of Genesis tells us that, in the beginning, God created us in His image. Although everything else in creation was also declared "good" by God, human beings were the only thing made in God's image. And because of that, we have inherent value—regardless of what we do with it. Regardless of how many times we may fail or fall short,

God still loves us, perfectly and completely.

Because God loves us—in a more fulfilling and complete way than any human can—our need for love is satisfied. This love gives us the ability to love others without fear of not receiving anything in return. When we learn how to receive love—both from God and other people—it counteracts those internal fears we all experience that "I'm not good enough" or "I'm a terrible person." 1 John 4:18 says, "Perfect love drives out fear." Fear and love are opposites—they can't coexist. If you're acting out of fear, you can't act out of love, and vice versa. Think about how this plays out in parenting. If my son or daughter started to develop some concerning habits, and I let the fear of who they're becoming take over, I'll start acting on that fear alone. I might tighten my grip on their privileges, give harsher punishments and get angry more often. Over time, as I try to gain more control, I'll develop more negative emotions because I'm afraid of how my kids will turn out and what that would mean for me as a father. I'm afraid of those internal messages ("I'm not a good enough dad. I'm a terrible parent."). In that moment, I've stopped actively loving my children. If, on the other hand, I receive God's love and acceptance of me, despite my flaws, that fear, is "driven out," and I can now choose to actively love my kids for who they are and who God made them to be.

Third, His example for how to love. As a father, when I tell and show my kids that I love them, I'm not just trying make them feel loved. Although I do, at the core of my being, want to show them my love, I'm also trying to set an example of *how* to love. That's why I'll often tell them, "I did this because I love you."

> *Despite what we deserve, despite what other people have done (or not done) to us, despite everything broken about our human understanding of love, God offers His perfect love to every human being, expecting nothing in return.*

Although I often fall short in modeling love to my kids, God gives us the perfect example to follow. Let's go back to 1 John:

> *"This is how God showed his love among us: He sent his one*

*and only Son into the world that we might live through him.
This is love: not that we loved God, but that he loved us and
sent his Son as an atoning sacrifice for our sins" (v. 9-10).*

Earlier in the New Testament, the same author (John) writes this in
his Gospel: "For God so loved the world that he gave his one and only
Son, that whoever believes in him shall not perish but have eternal life"
(John 3:16).

Everything I've talked about to this point, everything true about
love, everything evident about God's love—it can all be summed up in
Jesus. Because of His love for us, God sent His only Son, Jesus, down
to earth to die a sacrificial death for us. In love, Jesus—fully man, fully
God—took the penalty for our sin, what we deserved, and in return,
offered us eternal life, joy and hope. "While we were still sinners, Christ
died for us" (Romans 5:8). This is the beautiful, remarkable, transformational gospel message. This is the "good news" for all people. One
more insight from Keller:

*"The gospel is this: We are more sinful and flawed in ourselves
than we ever dared believe, yet at the very same time we are
more loved and accepted in Jesus Christ than we ever dared
hope."* [6]

Despite what we deserve, despite what other people have done (or
not done) to us, despite everything broken about our human understanding of love, God offers His perfect love to every human being,
expecting nothing in return. No one can earn God's love, yet He offers
it as a gift to all, which makes it all the more beautiful.

God made us in His image, and while this does mean we're inher-
ently valuable and born into God's love, it *also* means that we were
created *to* love. He *is* love, and we are His representatives to the world.
Therefore, we're called to love others. When Jesus was asked by the
religious leaders about the "greatest commandment in the Law," Jesus
said this:

*"'Love the Lord your God with all your heart and with all
your soul and with all your mind.' This is the first and greatest
commandment. And the second is like it: 'Love your neighbor*

as yourself.' All the Law and the Prophets hang on these two commandments" (Matthew 22:37-40).

As followers of Jesus, our mission is to love others. Since God created us both with the capacity to *feel* love and to *communicate* love to others, this mission is two-fold: a command and sign to others. John gives us another insight into this when he quotes Jesus in his Gospel: "A new command I give you: Love one another. As I have loved you, so you must love one another. By this everyone will know that you are my disciples, if you love one another" (John 13:34-35).

In his book, *Loveology*, John Mark Comer writes this:

> *"We were set up to love. To absorb the love of God into our bloodstream and then to share it with another human being."* [7]

Love satisfies us. Love gives us mission. Love gives us purpose. Because of God's love, Dave could still call me and choose to love me despite going through a difficult season of his own. That unconditional, beautiful, divine love provided all Dave needed, and it equipped him to share that love with others, with me. When we ask ourselves the question, "How can I love others?", we're really just asking, "What would Jesus do?" As a coach, as a player, as a parent, as a teacher, as a spouse, as a friend—what would Jesus do? How would He show love to these people in my life? And if we need a more tangible, descriptive picture than that, John helps us out in 1 Corinthians:

> *"Love is patient, love is kind. It does not envy, it does not boast, it is not proud. It does not dishonor others, it is not self-seeking, it is not easily angered, it keeps no record of wrongs. Love does not delight in evil but rejoices with the truth. It always protects, always trusts, always hopes, always perseveres" (1 Corinthians 13:4-7).*

This is love. Not desire or enjoyment or just a feeling of general affection for someone, but selfless, unexpecting, action-based sacrifice for another person. And it's a love offered to you—no matter who you are, no matter where you come from, no matter what you've done or will do. All you need to do is receive it. And Paul's next words in 1

Corinthians 13:8 tell us exactly why it will be worth it:

"Love never fails."

Foundation Building Tip

We were created to both give and receive love. Love establishes our relationships with both God and men. Once we understand and accept God's love, we can extend it to our family, friends and communities. We can all be better spouses, siblings, coaches, friends and co-workers when we choose to view others through the lens of love. Maybe it's simply giving tough advice or not dodging around the truth. The real test of our love is how we treat the people right in front of us. Love the people in your life.

Your Workout

1. Who, in your life, has modeled the love of Christ to you? What did he or she do that reflected the elements of true love that Paul outlines in 1 Corinthians? What response did that love invoke in you?

2. Who can you love in your circle of influence? Family members? Friends? Neighbors? Write down three to five names of people in your life whom you can show love on a consistent basis.

3. Love is an attitude revealed through action, not simply a feeling, and it requires sacrifice. What are some specific ways that you can love the people you mentioned above this week? What sacrifices can you make to show your love for them?

4. Looking at the example of Judas and Peter, we're reminded that love is just as much about receiving as giving. Have you received God's love in your life, or do you have trouble accepting it? Ask God to help you understand and accept His love, that you might rest in it and share that love with others.

Extra Workout Challenge

1. Read each of the characteristics from 1 Corinthians 13:4-8. From that list, do your best to write down your strengths and weaknesses when it comes to loving others. Choose one of your "weaknesses" and write it down. Then write down one action you can take this week to practice this quality in your relationships.

   a. The characteristic of love that I will work on this week is:

   b. The action I will take to demonstrate this quality is:

BUILDING BLOCK 4

S
SPIRITUAL

SECTION 4: SPIRITUAL BUILDING BLOCK

I dropped the first down chains on the field and took the phone from Bill Connelly's hand. When the operations manager of an NFL club walks on the practice field to bring you the phone, the call is never good news. Jen spoke to me from the other end.

"Your sister just called to let us know your mom is in the hospital with pneumonia. She was rushed to the ICU because her blood pressure plummeted. The doctors are concerned your mom may not be able to hold on much longer. You need to call the hospital as soon as possible to say good-bye."

My mother had a very weak heart, and her health had been in question for some time, but this was the first time I had to truly face the reality of her passing. I immediately left the practice field to call my dad.

My dad explained that Mom was unconscious. I asked if he thought she'd be able to hear me if I spoke to her. "I'm not sure," he said. "I'll put the phone to her ear, and you can talk to her."

"I love you mom," I said. "You are a good mom. You are a wonderful grandmother. I'm so thankful for all you have done for our family."

After I hung up, I wondered if I'd just spoken to my mom for the last time. Heading home, my spirit was unsettled. My mind raced. *Should I drive the seven hours to the hospital? Would I get there in time? Would it be too late?*

When I got home, I went upstairs to the study in my bedroom, sat in my favorite chair and prayed. *I kept wondering: if my mom passed, would I see her in heaven?* I honestly didn't know the answer. After all, my mom loved people, treated everyone with grace, attended church avidly throughout my childhood and was referred to as a "saint" by family members. Still, I had my doubts. I needed reassurance my mother had a relationship with Jesus. I needed to know if I had done everything I could to get my mom into heaven. Isn't that what all of us want for our loved ones?

God was presenting me with a life-changing decision: I could be silent and never truly know my mother's eternal destiny, or I could step out in faith and confront my mom directly. God challenged me to communicate the good news.

I called the hospital again. My dad answered.

"Dad, this is Jeff. I need to know if mom is going to heaven."

"Yes, I think mother is going to heaven for sure. She is a good mother, grandmother and wife. She serves her community and—" I cut him off.

"Dad, the Bible says you need to know Jesus in order to get to heaven. I want to make sure Mom knows Jesus."

By the grace of God, as my dad and I were talking, my mom woke up from her unconscious state.

"You can ask her yourself," Dad said. He put my mom on the phone.

"Mom, I want to see you in heaven, and the way to heaven is through a relationship with Jesus Christ. Do you know Jesus? Have you accepted Him as your Savior?"

"I did," she replied. God gave me the peace for which I was searching.

+++

The day I got the call on the practice field, the doctors predicted my mother would only live an hour or two after I spoke to her on the phone, but Mom was a fighter. She eventually moved from the hospital to hospice care. God blessed me with one more opportunity to see her in Milwaukee where she lived.

On the return trip home to Ohio, the emotional toll of what was happening hit me hard. As I was driving, my eyes started to well up with tears. I was focusing on the negative prospect of her death instead of the positive aspects of our time together. The next week, I listened to a sermon that gave me strength through my suffering.

"When we look at this world, we often get confused," the speaker said. "We think that this world is permanent, it will be here forever, and we're here just temporarily. But actually, what the Bible teaches is the opposite of that. It teaches that you and I are eternal, we will live forever, and this world is temporary."[1]

I've spent my entire life learning that the real issues in life are spiritual. Beneath everything else—the physical, mental and social—at the very core of our being, the spiritual determines the very purpose and meaning of our existence. It is the most important of the building blocks and the foundation on which all other growth is built. Spiritual issues examine the deep, underlying questions of life: *Where did I come from? What gives life meaning? How do I determine right from wrong? Where do we go when we die?*[2] Our spiritual growth determines our direction not only in this life, but also beyond.

The spiritual building block refers to our relationship with God—how we communicate with Him, how He reveals Himself to us, and how He uses different means to lead, guide and direct us. Without the spiritual, all of our aims and pursuits in life will ultimately be meaningless and aimless. Without connection to God's deeper, greater plan for our lives, we will never achieve peak performance. We grow and develop spiritually through:

- **Chapter 13: The Bible** - a collection of 66 individual books, written by many authors over hundreds of years, that tell a collective story of God's plan of love and redemption for humankind; the Word of God.

- **Chapter 14: Prayer** - our ultimate communication with God, either through spoken words or internal thoughts.

- **Chapter 15: Church** - the body of Christ; our family of believers—both locally and globally.

- **Chapter 16: Purpose** - our identity, our ultimate goal in life and the answer to the question, "Why am I here on this planet?"

The spiritual building block is about communicating and connecting with God, about trusting Him and committing to His purposes for our lives. The Bible gives us a map for who God is and how to live according to His will. Prayer gives us direct access to God and teaches us to truly, constantly depend on Him. Church is the intersection point of our spiritual life with that of other believers, and Purpose gives us an end goal with which to align everything we think, say and do.

When we invest in our spiritual life, we naturally invest in each of the other building blocks as well. If we listen to God and submit to His will, He will show us opportunities to grow physically, mentally and socially—not just for our own benefit, but ultimately, for His glory and the good of others. Outside of relationship with God, it is impossible to achieve peak performance. Without Him, we'll never know or comprehend the path that will lead us to the deepest, fullest life on this earth (and beyond).

SPIRITUAL

CHAPTER 13: THE BIBLE

"For the word of God is living and active…discerning the thoughts and intentions of the heart." (Hebrews 4:12)

Linebacker Vincent Rey finished the 2014 NFL season with 121 total tackles. In a 10-week span (Weeks 7-16), Rey notched six double-digit tackling performances (10, 10, 11, 12, 15, 16) for the Bengals,[1] and after the regular season, he led our team in tackles (by 26) and came in 12th in the League as a whole.[2] Looking at that 2014 season alone, it would've been easy for someone to assume Vinny's past—elite high school recruit, top-five college football school, first-round draft pick—but that wasn't the case. What most people didn't know was that Vinny wasn't supposed to be there.

Just four years earlier, in 2010, Vinny was sitting in a room with me and seven other players on the Bengals' practice squad—the unit designed to develop players and emulate future opponents in practice—where he stayed for the majority of that season. Coming out of Duke University (a lower-echelon Power-5 school for football), Vinny was undersized and, according to the National Football Post, "[wasn't] a physical tackler in any area of the game." In their draft profile of Rey in 2010, the online news source claimed he "didn't have what it [took] to find a spot on an NFL defense."[3] After going undrafted in 2010, the Bengals signed him to a two-year contract, waived him, then re-signed him to the practice squad the very next day. Rey had barely squeaked by, but his NFL dream stayed alive.

During his time spent on the practice squad, Vinny took nothing for granted. He knew no one expected him to succeed—except himself. From the start of that 2010 season, Vinny went to work. He ran a diagnostic test on each of the four building blocks and responded accordingly. **Physically**, Rey took advantage of his unique role as a member of the practice squad. Since he couldn't play in the games, he used his extra time to run and lift. **Mentally**, Rey spent more time in the film room and around the veteran players—soaking in knowledge and experience in order to understand the game better and play faster, without hesitation, on the field. **Socially**, beyond the interaction with the veterans, Vinny immersed himself in the Bengals' linebacker group. On top of time together on the practice field and in the weight room, Vinny made an intentional effort to grow those relationships off the field—at the movies, bowling, playing video games—so that when gameday rolled around, the interpersonal trust within that group was even stronger.

> *By incorporating a spiritual element to his training, Rey created a comprehensive plan for achieving peak performance. And it all started with a book, Vinny's secret weapon: the Bible.*

Each of these three key areas was essential to Rey's growth as a player and as a man, but plenty of his teammates followed in his footsteps physically, mentally and socially—even on the practice squad. What really set Rey apart early on was the fourth and final building block. By incorporating a **spiritual** element to his training, Rey created a comprehensive plan for achieving peak performance. And it all started with a book, Vinny's secret weapon: the Bible.

Rey began seriously reading the Bible at age 15. He'd grown up in the church—his parents were volunteer youth leaders—and he'd always known the Bible was the Word of God, but it didn't really hit home until Vinny was introduced to a group of Christian rappers, about 10 years older than he was. Growing up in Queens, New York, in the 80s, Vinny loved rap, so he instantly connected with these men of character and integrity. Comparing their lyrics to some of the other hip-hop artists he was listening to at the time, he noticed something unique:

"The words they were saying were uplifting. In 'normal' rap, you have some words that are uplifting, some that are degrading, but this was just all uplifting. All positive words of affirmation. Seeing those men inspired me to want to learn more about the Bible. I saw myself in them."

From that point on, Vinny read the Bible virtually every day of his life. He began to memorize a variety of Bible verses to better equip himself to handle life's daily challenges. Before he left for college, Vinny's father encouraged him to continue reading his Bible every day, if he could. Vinny was on his own now, and he'd need Scripture to light the path forward—so that's what he did. Every night at Duke, Vinny read one chapter—seven chapters each week. To help himself retain the information, he read every word out loud, incorporating his eyes, mouth and ears to create a multi-level sensory memory. For Rey, it was about building up an arsenal: "I start to remember the words and meaning so that when I'm in that particular situation, it will come to life. The more [Scripture] you read, the more [truths] you gather, the more readily you can retrieve those truths to help you gain a better understanding of situations."[4]

The Bible (or, "Scripture") is a collection of 66 individual books, written by many authors over hundreds of years, that tell a collective story of God's plan of love and redemption for humankind. To those who believe it, Scripture is the written Word of God. Although it was crafted and recorded by human authors, ultimately, the Bible is divinely inspired. As Paul says in his letter to Timothy, his disciple, "All Scripture is God-breathed and is useful for teaching, rebuking, correcting and training in righteousness, so that the servant of God may be thoroughly equipped for every good work" (2 Timothy 3:16-17).

> **"The more [Scripture] you read, the more [truths] you gather, the more readily you can retrieve those truths to help you gain a better understanding of situations."**

The Bible begins with, well, "the beginning"—the beginning of time, space and all of Creation. From the first human beings (Adam and Eve), Scripture tells the story of a partnership between God and man gone wrong (because of man's sin and failure to uphold God's holy standard) and God's corresponding plan to save humanity through the sacrificial love of His only Son, Jesus. The incredible thing about Scripture, though—as Paul mentions in 2 Timothy—is that it's more than a story. It's more than a history book to help us learn about the past. It has a specific purpose: to help us *live better lives.* In his book, *The Seven Laws of the Learner,* author Bruce Wilkinson addresses the two-fold intention of Scripture: "God gave the Bible to accomplish two goals: change in character (who I am) and change in conduct (what I do)."[5]

> *As Vinny recognized, not only does Scripture tell us how to think and act in essentially every situation, but it also equips us to do so.*

Because of its comprehensive nature, the Bible offers wisdom for nearly every situation we might face in life—if not specifically, then indirectly. Whether it's through direct commands (Ten Commandments in Exodus), words of wisdom (Proverbs), teachings of Jesus (the four Gospels), lessons from stories (Genesis) or instructions from an early church leader to a new church (Paul's letters), Scripture provides a roadmap with which to navigate life.

The Bible is more than a story, but it's also more than a rulebook. Through the teachings, stories and wisdom of the Bible, God wants to change our actions by first changing *our hearts.* As Vinny recognized, not only does Scripture tell us how to think and act in essentially every situation, but it also *equips* us to do so. As we read, learn and experience the love of Jesus through the biblical story—with the help of the Holy Spirit living inside of us—God empowers us to love and serve Him and others. So, when situations come around where biblical principles can be applied, we not only have the guidebook that outlines the necessary steps, we also have the proper resources to execute them. True change doesn't come from blind obligation; it comes from an authentic change of heart.

After college, as he began his NFL career, Vinny upped his intake of biblical truth. By the time he was in the weight room with me, he was reading three to four chapters a day—sometimes topping 25 chapters in any given week. Eventually, he read through the entire Bible—multiple times. Rey's foundation in and renewed emphasis on Scripture and his spiritual life boosted his performance. Through His Word, God began to change both what Vinny did and who he was.

First, his **conduct**. During games and practices, Vinny would turn to particularly impactful verses in his life to remind him of God's truth, hold him to a higher standard and bring out the best in himself. In this sense, Scripture served as Vinny's self-talk. In any scenario—on or off the field—that Vinny needed encouragement, accountability or just authentic truth, he could turn to the well of Bible verses he'd built up in his mind to re-align his perspective and push him toward his full potential.

For example, one of Vinny's go-to verses was 1 Corinthians 10:31: "So whether you eat or drink or whatever you do, do it all for the glory of God." In Vinny's rookie year, as was fairly common, some of the veteran players didn't do all the drills during training camp. Their age and experience allowed them to pass some of their reps onto other players, and since Vinny sat at the bottom of the totem pole as a rookie, often he was that "other player." So, on multiple hot, summer days in Cincinnati, Vinny ended up doing his reps *and* their reps. Initially, Vinny was tempted to complain, to tell his coaches why this wasn't fair, but then he remembered 1 Corinthians 10:31—"do it all for the glory of the God." In light of that biblical command, "fair" or "not fair" became a much smaller issue to Vinny. He had no control over that. He was there—

In any scenario—on or off the field—that Vinny needed encouragement, accountability or just authentic truth, he could turn to the well of Bible verses he'd built up in his mind to re-align his perspective and push him toward his full potential.

on the practice field, in the weight room, on game day—to bring glory to God. While Vinny remained aware of and concerned about his personal rights, his main goal was giving glory to God.

Although, off the field, Rey was quieter and more reserved, he had a commanding presence and loud voice in games and on the practice field. This new persona might've gone against his nature or his instincts, but Rey saw it as an opportunity to follow Paul's example in honoring God: "I take my job seriously. This is important to me. I feel this is how I honor God. It's very important to me. I'm not just working for [my head coach] or [defensive coordinator] or [linebacker coach]; I'm working for God, so I want to make sure everything is done with excellence."[6]

Every snap, every rep, every play, Vinny viewed as a privilege—not a right. Through the lens of Scripture, Vinny actively reminded himself of this. According to the Bible, God, the Creator of the world, became man in order to live the life we should've lived and die the death we deserved. Because of that incredible work of mercy and grace, God offers us forgiveness and freedom from all our sins, and on top of that, eternal life. Vinny knew he didn't deserve to be right with God, yet because of Jesus, he was. Everything on top of that in life was an absolute privilege—not a right. When he applied that mindset to his NFL career, it motivated him to push himself even further. He wasn't entitled to anything, so he came on-time and prepared to every meeting. He sprinted every rep. "Yes, Coach." "No, Coach." He did his job to the best of his ability—all for the glory of God—and it ultimately led to success on and off the field.

While Vinny did everything he could to take advantage of his privilege of playing in the NFL, he saw other players slip in this area. In training camp, players often "cut themselves," Vinny would say, because they showed up late to meetings, didn't get enough sleep, didn't hydrate or eat good meals, etc. Even though other players might've had more talent than Vinny, he pushed himself farther and higher because of his biblical perspective of gratitude. While the average NFL career at the time lasted about three years, Vinny ended up playing *nine*.

Beyond Vinny's conduct on the field, the Scripture Vinny stored and utilized (his "self-talk") changed *his identity*. One example of this comes from 2 Corinthians 12:9, where Paul recalls a message he received from God: "But he said to me, 'My grace is sufficient for you, for my power is made perfect in weakness.'"

In context, God essentially tells Paul, "You don't need to have it all together. You don't need to be strong all the time. Because of me, even your weakest moments can be times of strength." This is the truth of God's power. Despite our shortcomings, despite our flaws, despite our limitations, God wants to step in and work through us—if only we'd let him.

Rey knew his talents and abilities were limited—he was undersized, undrafted and hadn't established credibility as a reliable NFL linebacker—yet through the Holy Spirit's power, he believed God enabled him to make plays on the football field. Although Rey knew God didn't owe him anything—and God could take away his NFL career at any time—Rey attributed his on-field success to his faith. He believed that, if God felt it was best, He would give Vinny the energy, effort and talent necessary to succeed. And because of where he started, Vinny's success put God's strength and power on display all the more.

Another theme across Scripture is gratitude. Again, throughout Paul's letters, he repeatedly instructs his fellow believers to practice thankfulness toward God: "give thanks in all circumstances" (1 Thess 5:18), "[give] thanks to God through [Jesus]" (Col 3:17) and "[give] thanks to God…for everything" (Eph 5:20).

From a young age, Rey learned to adopt a similar mindset. As these memorized passages of Scripture flowed through his mind, he began to fundamentally change. He viewed life as a gift of grace and credited God in all of his circumstances—trying to be as specific as possible. On the field, he'd often pray, "I am so thankful you put me on this team. I am so thankful you put me at 'will' (weakside inside) linebacker. I am so thankful to get to defend this zone drop." With hearts full of gratitude, Rey and another practice squad player, Jeromy Miles (who both eventually made the active roster) would often tell each other, "We aren't supposed to be here."

These constant reminders of God's goodness and faithfulness transformed not only Rey's way of thinking, but also his identity. Despite living in a culture that preached independence, self-reliance and entitlement, Vinny lived his life in gratitude and dependence on God. The truths of Scripture replaced the lies that culture told him (or he told himself) about his identity and the world around him, empowering him to love God and other people—and ultimately, this led to success in his NFL career.

At the end of his rookie season, Vinny earned his first minutes on the game field. From there, he worked his way up to becoming a regular contributor, and in 2012, he earned his first NFL start.[7] The next year—in an early-November road game against the Ravens in Baltimore (just his third NFL start)—Vinny notched a season-high *15 tackles* and became the first Bengals player to record three sacks and an interception in the same game.[8] That performance, along with the rest of the 2013 season, earned Rey a new two-year contract in March 2014, and two years later, in March 2016, another three-year deal.

In the end, Rey played five different positions over nine seasons in the NFL. He saw action in all but two games from 2011-2018 and was voted team captain by his teammates four years in a row for his work both on and off the field. In 2014, the Bengals named Rey as their Walter Payton Man of the Year nominee for his work promoting proper education for kids and helping women escape sex trafficking.[9] Physically, mentally, socially and spiritually, little by little, Vinny grew.

"When you do the little things in the building blocks, you may not see the result immediately," Rey said later. "But over time, a lot of little things done well, adds up to something significant or tangible."[10]

Following his retirement from football in 2019, Vinny began to memorize Scripture with family—specifically, his two young daughters. Each week, they'd pick a new verse to learn together, and a couple weeks in, Vinny noticed God speaking to him through one verse, in particular.

Although Vinny understood his identity wasn't in football, it was really the only life he knew since he was six years old. Now, two-and-a-half decades later, as Vinny transitioned into a completely new world, career-wise, he was 10 years behind other professionals his age who hadn't played sports beyond college. He didn't know if he'd be good at anything else. He felt the fear of entering "the real world." That's when God spoke to him again through Scripture.

In the first chapter of Joshua, God addressed Joshua—the successor of Moses and new leader of Israel. As Joshua entered this new season of uncertainty and fear, God spoke over him: "Have I not commanded you? Be strong and courageous. Do not be afraid; do not be discouraged, for the Lord your God will be with you wherever you go" (Joshua 1:9). Although this was new territory for Vinny, he knew his equipment hadn't changed. God and His Word would go with him wherever he ended up.

Like his training, Rey's growth wasn't limited to just one area of his life (football). His development transformed him not only from an undersized, undrafted free agent to a full-time starter and team captain, but it also grew him into a deeper, truer, more committed man of God. He took the one thing to which all of us have access—the "living and active" Word of God (Hebrews 4:12)—and used it to overcome his weaknesses and to glorify his Creator in everything he did.

Coach's Corner

The road home after an away game is a *long* one. Yes, it's true that any loss in the NFL is tough to swallow—after home losses, I often refuse to watch football for the rest of the day—but there's something unique about losing on the road. You don't have those regular processes in place like you do at your home stadium. Instead of packing up your stuff, meeting your family, heading home and starting to move on, you load onto a bus, take a long, slow ride to the airport, then board a plane for another long, slow flight home. All the while, the game from earlier in the day replays over and over in your mind.

The sting of that loss hits you immediately after the final whistle... then it lingers. It marinates. This happens after home losses too, but on the road, you don't have anything to distract you—you can't move past it—giving you no other option than to just sit with it.

Emotionally, the NFL is a "mountains and valleys" type of profession—euphoric highs and devastating lows without much in between. Those road trips home after a loss are some of the most brutal memories I have as a professional strength coach. In those moments, in particular, the Holy Spirit would turn my mind to a specific verse I'd memorized:

"Shall we accept good from God, and not trouble?" (Job 2:10)

If I could stand on that field with the Ravens on January 28, 2001, celebrating our Super Bowl victory, why couldn't I swallow those tough losses? How could I accept a Super Bowl ring when I couldn't accept defeat? Could I only receive the good of life, not the bad? Was I depending on God to keep my life comfortable and successful, or did my faith run deeper than that? Amid the devastation of loss, that truth and perspective from Scripture have soothed me. Life isn't always going to be painful, but it will certainly have its fair share of disappointments. Yet, in every situation, we're called to gratitude for what we have, contentment in what Jesus has done and hope in what God will continue to do.

Throughout my life, that's been a consistent theme: in the midst of an often-turbulent career field, the Bible has helped me regroup and reground myself in truth and reality. When I was a new Christian, I received a great gift: a "Read-the-Bible-in-a-Year Guide." Chip Morton, my assistant strength coach at the time and one of my spiritual mentors in Baltimore, bought me a yearly subscription for Christmas, and each month, I received a little booklet with a reading plan, insights and comments for that month. As that year progressed, I began to establish a habit of reading the Bible on a consistent basis. Unfortunately, because of the program's fast-paced schedule, I wasn't able to absorb a lot of the content. So, after the year ended, I went back through all 66 books at my own pace—absorbing the content, letting it marinate in my soul. From that point on, like Rey, Scripture has served as a roadmap for all areas of my life.

Today, I use what the Bible says as a reference point for important everyday elements of life such as: love (1 Corinthians 13:4-8), character (Galatians 5:22-23), finances (1 Timothy 6:17; Matthew 6:21; Haggai 2:8), parenting (Hebrews 12:7-11) and marriage (among many other things). With the help of tools like podcasts, sermons, commentaries and Study Bibles, I can better understand each verse, chapter and book and utilize the corresponding wisdom and truth in my own life.

Throughout my life, that's been a consistent theme: in the midst of an often-turbulent career field, the Bible has helped me regroup and reground myself in truth and reality.

Like Rey, the Bible has changed both what I do and who I am—it has structured my thinking and guided my conduct. For me, the most important part of Scripture is that it helps me to know God. The Word shapes how I live because it communicates God's omnipotent, benevolent character and his unique, personal love for me. It not only tells us the story of who God is and what He's done, but it also provides a framework for how to pursue a deeper, more intimate relationship with Him.

In Hebrews 4, referencing God's Word, the author says this: "For the word of God is living and active, sharper than any two-edged sword, piercing to the division of soul and of spirit, of joints and of marrow, and discerning the thoughts and intentions of the heart." That's incredible. While we might be tempted to believe the Bible is stagnant, outdated and washed-up, Hebrews 4 refutes this claim entirely. Yes, the Bible is consistent, but it's not stagnant—it's *living* and *active*. The truth remains the same, but as we develop into different contexts and stages of life, the Scripture, without compromising its character, morphs and adapts with us. When we're blind to thoughts, fear and emotions running wild in our minds, God's Word discerns "the thoughts and intentions of the heart." The Bible is more than a book—it plays an *active* role in our discipleship to Jesus. That's why the great preacher Charles Spurgeon said, "Nobody ever outgrows Scripture; the book widens and deepens with our years."[11]

> **"Nobody ever outgrows Scripture; the book widens and deepens with our years."**

Consider sin, for example. We all sin, and it's only when we *recognize* our sinfulness that true life change can begin. This is where Scripture can take a living and active role in our lives. Through the Holy Spirit, the Bible connects with our souls to reveal truths about who we are—and sometimes, it's like getting hit with a bucket of cold water. One of my favorite passages of Scripture is Matthew 7:3: "Why do you look at the speck of sawdust in your brother's eye and pay no attention to the plank in your own eye?" Although our insecurities might tell us to be quick to judge, God's Word hits us with reality: while we're busy pushing others down, we're almost always blind to our own faults. When the piercing light of Scripture shines on our lives, we're gently reminded that "we all sin and fall short of the glory of God" (Romans 3:23). Thankfully for us, if we acknowledge this, God is ready to offer grace, forgiveness and healing—empowering us to offer the same to others.

The Bible convicts, but it also *equips*. Studying and memorizing Scripture is critical to preparing for those circumstances you can't predict or expect. Although He was all-knowing, Jesus' life provides a perfect example of this truth played out.

In Matthew 4, before Jesus begins His public ministry, He "was led by the Holy Spirit into the wilderness to be tempted by the devil" (v.1). Talk about hitting the ground running. Naturally, Jesus starts this time away with fasting…for "40 days and 40 nights" (v.2). Assuming this could be a weak point for Jesus, the devil steps in, first targeting his physical needs:

> *"The tempter came to him and said, 'If you are the Son of God, tell these stones to become bread' (v.3).*

Without missing a beat, Jesus replies:

> *"It is written: 'Man shall not live on bread alone, but on every word that comes from the mouth of God'" (v.4).*

To rebuke the devil, Jesus turns to His strongest weapon: the "sword of the Spirit" (Ephesians 6:17). He quotes Deuteronomy 8:3 back to Satan, shutting down his attack. When Satan tries to use Jesus' tactic against him—quoting Psalm 91 and telling him to throw himself down from the highest point of the temple because God would save him—Jesus is ready again with Deuteronomy 6:16: "It is also written: 'Do not put the Lord your God to the test.'" After the devil pulls out his final trick—offering Jesus "all the kingdoms of the world in their splendor" in exchange for Jesus' worship—the reader can see the writing on the wall. Jesus says, "Away from me, Satan! For it is written: 'Worship the Lord your God, and serve him only'" (Deuteronomy 6:13).

The more time you spend meditating over Scripture, the more deeply engrained and readily accessible it will become to equip you in all of life's circumstances.

While most of us have never fasted for 40 days, we certainly can relate to feeling weak and vulnerable under pressure. In each situation, Jesus was challenged to put his Father's laws above his fleshly desires. Jesus had the same needs and temptations we all have. He was tempted with the physical need for nourishment, emotional need for protection and psychological need for power. Yet, in all three rounds, Jesus won. What was his game changer? The Word of God.

Just as an athlete needs to go through a progression in order to achieve mastery, you too, need to approach your spiritual growth in this way. First, you "practice" by reading and studying Scripture. Then, to awaken its power, you need to remember it amid escalating levels of pressure with an opponent competing against you—not the person in front of you or the one in the mirror, but the "rulers, authorities, powers and spiritual forces of evil" (Ephesians 6:12). Your ability to live according to God's word comes with practice and more practice. The more time you spend meditating over Scripture, the more deeply engrained and readily accessible it will become to equip you in all of life's circumstances.

The Bible provides the foundation for every element of every building block—physical, mental, social and spiritual—because it undergirds every situation we might face with truth, power and authority. Just look at the verses that preface each chapter. Physically, the Bible tells us our bodies are "temples of the Holy Spirit" (1 Corinthians 6:19). Mentally, Scripture teaches us to think about whatever is "true, noble, right, pure, lovely, excellent and praiseworthy" (Philippians 4:8). Socially, we're called to "love one another, for love comes from God" (1 John 4:7), and spiritually, I wouldn't have any other chapters to write (prayer, church, purpose) if not for the Bible.

In fact, as I talked about in the introduction, this entire book is built around one specific verse from the book of Luke: "And Jesus grew in wisdom and stature, and in favor with God and man" (Luke 2:52). The power of these 14 words has led me to invest years of money, time and effort to dive deeper into making this verse "living and active" for other people, like it has been for me.

Foundation Building Tip

God communicates with us through Scripture. It is the Word of God, the divinely inspired roadmap for navigating life. This is why Bible study is imperative for spiritual growth—it provides a way to understand ourselves, know God better and learn how to pursue a relationship with Him. Read the Bible as part of your personal growth plan to build a strong spiritual foundation. Read it out loud. Memorize it. Soak in its wisdom, truth and authority. Use it as a vehicle to connect with God. Allow Him to change both who you are and what you do through Scripture—just as Rey did.

Your Workout

1. How has the Bible influenced your thinking and/or guided your conduct? List (at least) one way and the corresponding verse.

2. In what areas of your life can the Bible strengthen you? Circle one, then write a sentence or two on why you answered as you did.
   a. Increase joy and contentment
   b. Increase peace
   c. Increase strength
   d. Increase hope
   e. Increase awareness of God's presence

3. Set a Scripture reading goal for the week. Start small—if you're just starting, maybe one chapter per week—and make sure your goal is reasonable, attainable and measurable. Track your progress and, as you meet your goals, increase them.

4. Set a Scripture *memorizing* goal for the week. Again, start small. Try writing the verse down somewhere you'll regularly see it. Whenever you think of it, read it out loud to engage as many senses as possible.

Extra Workout Challenge

1. There are two books in the middle of the Bible, Psalms and Proverbs, that have provided me with incredible perspective and wisdom. Psalms helps us understand our relationship with God. Proverbs helps us interact with the people around us. Use these two books to help you navigate through everyday life situations. There are 31 chapters in Proverbs. By reading a chapter each day, you can complete the entire book in one month. You can do this with Psalms at five chapters/day. To engrain the Scriptures in your heart, repeat your monthly readings for a year. By the end, you'll have read both books twelve times.

2. Take time to meditate over the verse you chose in "Your Workout" (#4) and ask God to reveal the depth of His truths to you. There is a difference between "reading the Bible" and fully grasping and applying its meaning. To truly absorb God's word, we must ponder it.

CHAPTER 14: PRAYER

"This is the confidence we have in approaching God: that if we ask anything according to his will, he hears us." (1 John 5:14)

J ust three days after Christmas 2015, we (the Bengals) were in Denver for a Week 16 road matchup with the Broncos. As was customary, at the pregame two-minute warning, Coach Lewis gathered the players in the locker room for his final encouragement. I needed to go to the bathroom, and since I'd be busy with coaching responsibilities as soon as the players hit the field, I knew my window to do so was closing. As soon as Coach Lewis finished, I took my opportunity.

Walking through the coaches' locker room, I made my way to the coaches' designated restroom. Given how close we were to kickoff, I assumed I'd have the place to myself, but as I crossed from the carpet to the tile, I noticed something that took me by surprise. Near the sinks, on the cold, hard bathroom floor, one of our coaches was kneeling in prayer. As I continued around the corner, sure enough, next to the stalls was another prominent member of our coaching staff—eyes closed, on his knees. In separate parts of the coaches-only restroom, in their own individual worlds, two different coaches—who'd I'd never really seen pray on their own—were silently crying out to God on their knees. In 20 years of coaching, I'd never seen anything like it.

Given the context of the situation, I didn't have to think too hard to understand why those coaches might appeal to a higher power. It was arguably the biggest game of our season. We had a good team that year—we'd started out the season 8-0 and entered that Denver game at 11-3. The Broncos had also started hot, with seven straight wins, but came into that Monday night, nationally televised matchup on a two-game slide with a 10-4 overall record. Given our standings atop the AFC, both teams were fighting for a top-2 seed in the upcoming postseason. A top-2 seed not only meant home field advantage for (at least) the first game, but also a coveted playoff *bye week*—a free pass into the divisional round. At that point in the season—after a grueling five-plus months of games every week—any advantage you can get is extremely important, and both sides knew it. Whoever won the Monday night matchup would essentially lock up the tiebreaker for the playoff bye.

> **It was a big game for us, and in the face of something significant, beyond their own power, these coaches sought something greater than themselves.**

So, although it took me by surprise, I could relate with these two grown men on their knees on a bathroom floor. As they humbled themselves in vulnerability, completely out of their own volition, I could understand why. It was a *big* game for us, and in the face of something significant, beyond their own power, these coaches sought something greater than themselves.

Unlike possibly any other professional sport, prayer is woven into the culture of football. Looking back at my professional coaching career, I can see evidence of prayer all around me—in the locker room, during pregame warm-ups, in the shower, at midfield postgame, everywhere. In fact, during that weekly pregame speech from Coach Lewis—the time I took to use the bathroom—Lewis always started by leading the team in the "Lord's Prayer." I'm sure many of you have probably recited it. It's a prayer of adoration, provision, forgiveness and protection. Together, the coaches, players and staff took a knee, held hands and recited Jesus' words to His disciples from Matthew 6:9-13, and we'd do it again after the final whistle—win or loss:

"Our Father in heaven
(Holy and loving God),
hallowed be your name
(we honor and respect Your holy name),
your kingdom come
(bring Your spiritual reign),
your will be done
(and accomplish Your perfect purpose),
on earth as it is in heaven
(right here, like it's already happening in heaven).
Give us today our daily bread
(We trust You to daily provide what we need).
And forgive us our debts
(Give us mercy and forgiveness for our sins),
as we also have forgiven our debtors
(and we will follow Your example to offer mercy and forgive-
ness to others).
And lead us not into temptation
(You allow us to be tested, but You don't tempt us),
but deliver us from the evil one
(give us strength to overcome the temptation from the devil)."

This emphasis on prayer wasn't unique to the Bengals, either. In Baltimore (and Cincinnati), during pregame, the players would gather in the shower—the only space big enough to accommodate a prayer circle of 50-plus players—to read a Bible verse and say a quick prayer. For Matt Stover, this shower prayer (or some version of it) happened in every location he played (New York Giants, Cleveland Browns, Ravens, Indianapolis Colts) during his 20-year NFL career. But why? How does so much prayer and spiritual influence work its way into the world of professional football?

First, the danger, the risk factor. Football is a game defined by constant adversity. Of 250 of the most perilous occupations in the U.S., professional football ranked the sixth-most hazardous and the fifth-most stressful.[1] One in *five* players, at some point, suffer an injury that shortens—if not completely ends—their playing career.[2] Every season, every game, every play has the potential to have significant implications for the health, future and overall livelihoods of players, coaches and staff members. One wrong move—a fumbled snap, a dropped pass, a missed practice or meeting—could mean the difference between a job (and the accompanying NFL salary) and a total career transition. With the high incidence of injury and the physiological demands and stresses of the sport, players naturally turn to God for supernatural power and protection. In a profession revolving around pride, they turn to humility. In an absence of power and control, they turn to prayer.

As God's creation, prayer is our ultimate communication with our Creator. Whether through spoken words or internal thoughts, prayer provides a means of conscious, back-and-forth interaction between us and God. As Deuteronomy 4:7 says, God is near to us when we pray to Him—when we authentically and *humbly* present ourselves before Him. Prayer allows us to practically show our humility before God as we acknowledge everything that's outside of our control and beyond our power as finite, limited human beings. Psalm 147:11 tells us that God "delights" in this dependence on Him—not out of pride, but because in our weakness, He makes us strong (2 Corinthians 12:9).

> **With the high incidence of injury and the physiological demands and stresses of the sport, players naturally turn to God for supernatural power and protection. In a profession revolving around pride, they turn to humility. In an absence of power and control, they turn to prayer.**

As humans, when we want something that's outside of our own power—like safety, security or success—we have this natural sense to look outside of ourselves, to appeal to a higher power. This has been true throughout human history, especially in war, natural disasters and other life-threatening situations. Hardwired within our DNA is a tendency to, in the face of difficult circumstances, recognize our own humanity, and prayer is our method of humbly acting upon it. In his book, *Prayer: Experiencing Awe and Intimacy with God*, Tim Keller says, "To pray is to accept that we are, and always will be, wholly dependent on God for everything."[3]

Like an NFL player who protects himself with a helmet and pads, prayer is the believer's way of "putting on the armor of God" (Ephesians 6:10-18). As Paul talks about in Ephesians 6, the armor of God consists of the belt of truth, the breastplate of righteousness, the shield of faith and the helmet of salvation. Truth, righteousness, faith and salvation—all of which we can access through prayer—protect us from attacks from the enemy. Just like an opponent on the field, the devil is a fierce attacker. To withstand the attacks of our enemies, we need to rely on God's strength and every piece of his armor through prayer. Football pads provide *physical* protection; the armor of God shields us from *spiritual* attacks.

Prayer also provides a way to build and develop a *relationship* with God. As followers of Jesus, God calls us into an authentic, two-way relationship. Like any relationship, our relationship with God is developed through time spent together in communication. Prayer not only opens the doors for us to present our requests to God, but it gives Him space to speak truth, wisdom and instruction into our lives. Prayer is the vehicle that calms storms (Mathew 8:26), moves mountains (Mark 11:23-24) and heals the sick (James 4:14-15). When you set aside time to *listen* to God through prayer, you'll find He'll provide the energy, strength, peace and power you need to face every day and every circumstance. When those coaches got on their knees in the visitors' locker room in Denver, they weren't doing so in vain—they were, in humility, gaining access to true, divine power.

When NFL players kneel and lock arms with each other–regardless of which teams they're playing for–they're entering into communion with God together.

The power and benefits of prayer aren't just supernatural and mystical, either. A *Newsweek* article from 2003 entitled, "Faith & Healing," notes that meditative prayer can "change brain activity and immune response" and, in some cases, "lower heart rate and blood pressure, both of which reduce the body's stress response."[4] On top of that, praying with others in community—like, say, in the pregame locker room or at midfield afterwards—provides both tangible encouragement and new perspective on God and His character. When NFL players kneel and lock arms with each other—regardless of which teams they're playing for—they're entering into communion with God together.

In my NFL coaching career, my interactions with prayer weren't limited to the locker room—or our sideline, for that matter. On several occasions, I witnessed opposing teams and players pray on the field during the game. One example of this was Hall-of-Fame Pittsburgh Steelers safety, Troy Polamalu—the "Tasmanian Devil." Both in Cincinnati and Baltimore, we played the Steelers twice every season, and during one of those matchups, watching Polamalu on defense, I noticed something interesting. After every play, he made the sign of the cross. As I would later learn, Polamalu would accompany the gesture with a short prayer, on every play.[5] In an average NFL game, that's roughly 65 prayers each game!

Polamalu understood one of the critical ingredients to a vibrant, sustainable prayer life: consistency. In Ephesians 6:18, Paul ends his description of the armor of God by telling the church in Ephesus to "pray in the Spirit *on all occasions* with all kinds of prayers and requests. With this in mind, be alert and always keep on praying for all the saints." Or, as other translations of this verse say, "pray *continually*." Just as our cell phones need a daily power source, our prayer life can be viewed the same way. If we don't charge up regularly, we quickly lose power.

"It got to a point in high school where I was almost constantly in prayer," Polamalu said in an interview with GQ. "Praying through the whole football game, praying through the meetings, praying as I'm driving—this constant conversation with God. Football was not, and is not, a sport to me. It's a spiritual battle. So it wasn't like after a play I would go 'God! Why did I miss that tackle?' It was more like 'Okay, God, you've blessed me, and this is play, but I want to thank you so much for giving me the opportunity to play this beautiful sport.'"[6]

Often, the most difficult thing can often just be finding time *to* pray. A problem many of us (including myself) often face with prayer is, "I don't talk to God *enough*." The devil will do all he can to keep us away from prayer, and in my life, he does this through busyness. We live in a culture and era where we're all "busy" and rarely find quiet times to fit prayer into our schedules. Thankfully, Jesus gives us a perfect example for how to act in these situations.

It's estimated Jesus' ministry lasted three to three and a half years. In this time, Jesus traveled to approximately 15 cities—some of them multiple times—and walked an estimated 3,125 miles. An average of 20 miles per day on all of his journeys would mean he would have spent

1,076 days and nights on the road.[7] Nearly every day of his ministry, Jesus was traveling. He travelled with his disciples from town to town preaching, teaching and performing miracles. It was exhausting work, both mentally and physically, from sunrise to sunset. If anyone had a "busy" schedule, it was Jesus. Yet, despite the tremendous demands on his time and energy, Jesus found time to be alone with God and pray. In Mark 1, after one of the busiest days of Jesus' ministry, verse 35 tells us that "Very early in the morning, while it was still dark, Jesus got up, left the house and went off to a solitary place, where he prayed." In possibly the only time Jesus had for solitude, He used it to pray, to be in His Father's presence and seek wisdom and direction from the Holy Spirit.

God wants to speak to us! We just need to open the door and let Him in.

God is a prayer-hearing and a prayer-answering God.[8] To hear from God, you must make yourself accessible to Him. Often, we don't hear from God because we don't take time to listen. We spend time with things that take energy away from us, rather than taking time to do things that bring us life! The first step is to seek God. Give him your time. Instead of starting your day on your social media feed, start it by building a relationship with your heavenly Father.

When you pray constantly, when you turn your communication with God into a habitual response to every situation, "you can make prayer your life and your life your prayer while living in a world that needs God's powerful influence."[9] And these don't have to be elaborate, Psalm-esque prayers. Praying continually can be as simple as using short, brief statements throughout your day. In Matthew 14:30, Peter's prayer was "Lord, save me." On the cross, Jesus prayed, "Lord, forgive them, for they do not know what they're doing" (Luke 23:34). During games, Bengals running back and special teams ace Cedric Peerman would pray, "Lord help me to do my job." Bengals linebacker Emmanual Lamur, often repeated, "I can do all things through Christ who strengthens me" (Philippians 4:13).

When we give Him the space and the opportunity, God speaks to us in a number of ways. Like I talked about last chapter, it might be through His Word or through a devotional. As we learned in the Social Building Block, God also speaks into our lives through other people.

Finally, as you might've already experienced, God speaks through the Holy Spirit, through impressions on our hearts. God wants to speak to us! We just need to open the door and let Him in.

When we do, the Bible tells us we can have confidence that God hears our prayers when we ask for things according to His will (1 John 5:14). Jesus said the Father knows our needs even before we ask (Matthew 6:32) and wants to give us good gifts (Matthew 7:11). So why, then, don't we pray more often?

Beyond busyness, for many of us, we rely too much on our own power. We don't have enough of those "finitude of humanity" moments in which we cry out to God. We get so caught up in our day-to-day activities that we forget to make space for God through prayer. If we're only praying in the heat of the moment, before the big game when we have "nowhere else to turn," how often will we actually be in communication with God? Probably very little, if ever. And when we fail to pray continually and consistently, we begin to convince ourselves that anything and everything is within our control, which leads to even *less* prayer. God becomes only our last resort (if that), and we begin to lose our sense of His nearness and power.

> **To pray is to be humble, and true humility means complete surrender and dependence on God.**

True dependence on God (and true prayer) is consistent communication with Him, independent of circumstances. It's prayer in the good, bad and in-between. That's why Paul calls us to "pray continually," not just "pray when you need it the most." To pray is to be humble, and true humility means *complete* surrender and dependence on God.

In that humility, another potential problem arises—one that you might've faced when trying to surrender to God through prayer: *What happens when God doesn't answer my prayer? What if God doesn't say "yes" to what I need?* That brings me back to our matchup with the Broncos on that Monday December night in Denver. You might be wondering, "Were the prayers of those two coaches answered?" We may never know.

Despite jumping out to an early 14-point lead after our first two offensive drives, we lost a thriller in overtime. We lost out on the playoff bye week, and our season ended in the Wild Card round of the playoffs, in a heartbreaking loss to the rival Steelers at home. The Broncos, meanwhile, used that Week 16 win to propel them to a first-round bye and ultimately, the franchise's third Super Bowl championship.

God may not always answer our prayers how we want Him to— sometimes it's "no"; sometimes it's "not yet"—but that doesn't mean that He isn't listening or doesn't care. It may just mean that He has a better, broader perspective. It may mean He has something even better and more beneficial for us. And in that truth is the essence of prayer. When we pray, we humble ourselves to not only say, "God, you know more than me," but also, as Jesus said in the Lord's Prayer, "Your will be done." Prayer isn't about getting exactly what we want; it's about the overwhelming peace available to us knowing His plans are far greater, bringing glory to the One who deserves it all. The important thing is to not lose faith or cease praying, even when we don't get the answer we expected.

The Bible tells us that if we have faith, prayer has the power to move mountains (Matthew 17:20)! The first step is to ask. This is why praying continually is so vital to a vibrant life. Remember, God is everywhere, so pray anywhere. Ask, and trust that—despite what it looks like from your limited perspective—He has your best interest and ultimate good in mind. As Matthew 7:9-11 says, "Which of you, if your son asks for bread, will give him a stone? Or if he asks for a fish, will give him a snake? If you, then, though you are evil, know how to give good gifts to your children, how much more will your Father in heaven give good gifts to those who ask him!"

Coach's Corner

In 1 Chronicles 4, we read about a man named Jabez. From the context, all we really know about Jabez is that he was an "honorable" man from the tribe of Judah. In verse 10, he offers this prayer to God: "Oh, that you would bless me and enlarge my territory! Let your hand be with me, and keep me from harm so that I will be free from pain." The next sentence simply says, "And God granted his request."

Jabez's prayer isn't complicated or complex. He doesn't dedicate an exorbitant amount of time crying out to God. Yet, he gives God an opportunity. He opens the door for God's power to bless him, enlarge his territory, be with him and keep him from evil and harm. And God responded! For someone in leadership—a coach, for example—this is an encouraging example of the power of prayer, and on several occasions, I've prayed specifically about Jabez's second point ("enlarge my territory"). While I was with the Bengals, I prayed this exact prayer.

At the time, having been in Cincinnati for nearly a decade, I was enjoying my role with the organization. I'd developed strong relationships, the team had seen success on the field (five consecutive playoff appearances), and I felt like I was accomplishing my role effectively. But, like Jabez, I wondered if God had more for me to give—if He wanted to "enlarge my territory"—so I asked.

After that prayer, I started creating videos, developing different messaging and investing in projects outside of my typical workflow (like this book). Eighteen months later, I was released from the Cincinnati Bengals organization.

Well, I thought to myself, *that backfired.* I asked God to *expand* my territory, not take it away! In my limited perspective, it seemed like God didn't hear my prayer. Little did I know just how "limited" my view actually was.

Being away from the NFL gave me a *new* capacity to invest in those projects I'd started in Cincinnati, in my community (see Chapter 11: Community) and in other avenues I'd put on the backburner. Not only that, but a few months after the Bengals let me go as their *assistant* strength coach, I was hired as the *head* strength and conditioning coach for the D.C. Defenders in the XFL. Although I thought and prayed through the decision, hesitation began to grow in me during the five months between signing the contract and reporting to camp. I knew my decision made sense and God would be with me, but I still felt unsettled. I'd asked God to open a door, not realizing I wasn't even ready to walk through it! But after talking to friends, family and spiritual mentors, I moved forward in faith and discovered that, as often is the case, the other side was far more fulfilling than I'd expected. I refined my coaching techniques and had the joy of creating my own weight room culture. I learned to adapt to a fast-paced, unpredictable environment and had the incredible opportunity to connect with the lives of many XFL coaches and players at a crossroads in their careers. God had responded all along! I prayed for God to work, questioned it, then watched as He did something greater than I'd imagined. I had expectations attached to my request, but God had something bigger. I just needed to wait on Him, His plan and His timing.

Sometimes God doesn't answer our prayers how we want (an immediate "yes") because doing so may lessen His glory. We might not always see it right away (or in our lifetime), but if we feel like God didn't hear our prayer, it's probably because He has something greater, something bigger in store. Instead of expanding my territory with the Bengals, God said, "wait," and gave me an even greater opportunity to grow in leadership as a head strength coach in a start-up league. Just because God doesn't respond how we want doesn't mean He isn't listening.

Still, other times, God *does* answer how we want and when we want. Those are rare moments when we get to see the powerful, transformational and *immediate* impact of prayer.

> **We might not always see it right away (or in our lifetime), but if we feel like God didn't hear our prayer, it's probably because He has something greater, something bigger in store.**

Many years earlier, after the birth of our daughter, God gave me and Jen the desire for a second child—to "enlarge the territory" of our family. Although we didn't really have to "try" with our daughter, now, as we thought about a second child, we had extreme difficulty conceiving. We consulted a fertility specialist and spent several months going through various tests and procedures. After a somewhat "easy" first pregnancy, now, all of a sudden, we had to rely on powers outside of ourselves. It was a difficult concept to grasp, but Jen and I were in prayer about it throughout the whole process. I prayed individually, she prayed individually, and we prayed together. In fact, right before the actual procedure, Jen prayed one last time—again, opening the door for God to work.

A short time later, we received a letter in the mail from the fertility specialist, telling us we had a 5 percent chance to get pregnant. That same day, Jen's pregnancy test came back positive. Our son, Aidan, was on the way. God had heard our prayer, loud and clear, and gave us the gift of an immediate "yes."

Whether He answers our prayers how we expect or not, the point is the same: God knows *best*. He has the broader perspective, the larger plan, the greater glory in mind. Unlike ourselves, He *knows* what we really need. If He says "no" or "not yet," it's not because He isn't listening or doesn't care. As Tim Keller put it, "In short, God will either give us what we ask or give us what we would have asked if we knew everything he knew."[10]

Despite its power and potential to impact change, prayer isn't complicated. God makes it simple for us: let Him in and trust that He knows what He's doing. Again, prayer isn't necessarily about the amount of time or the way in which we pray, it's about dependence on God. It's about humility, surrender and allowing him to work. It's about providing God the opportunity to address our concerns, speak into our lives and show us His presence. I don't often spend large chunks of time in prayer, but like Ephesians 6 says, I try to "pray continually"—walking, driving in my car, cutting my grass, sitting on my deck. Like Polamalu, these prayers are often quick and simple—"Thank you, Lord" or "You are my God"—but they create in me an attitude of constant dependence and reliance on God. In some ways, I view prayer like self-talk—except more effective, because it taps into the Holy Spirit's power. Through short, quick phrases, it helps me conquer my own insecurities and lack of self-confidence.

Anytime I enter a situation with uncertainty or anxiety, I'll often pray, "Lord, be with me" to give God the opportunity to work through me in His power and through the Holy Spirit. On the flip side, when I don't understand what's going on or what I'm doing with my life, I might ask God, "What am I doing?" But even in those moments of doubt, God quickly reminds me of His control and purpose for my life. Philippians 4:6-7 says, "Do not be anxious about anything, but in every situation, by prayer and petition, with thanksgiving, present your requests to God. And the peace of God, which transcends all understanding, will guard your hearts and your minds in Christ Jesus." Regarding those verses, my Study Bible says, "True peace is not found in positive thinking, in absence of conflict, or in good feelings, it comes from knowing God is in control."[11] Prayer = peace.

> "True peace is not found in positive thinking, in absence of conflict, or in good feelings, it comes from knowing God is in control."

The power of prayer is found in complete dependence on and trust in God. When we give Him opportunity, He removes our fear and works through us. God gives us access to immense, transformational spiritual resources that empower us in all other facets of peak performance. The question isn't whether or not God is willing and able to help us, it's whether or not we'll give Him the chance.

Foundation Building Tip

God invites you into relationship, communication and partnership with Him through prayer. A regular time of prayer and devotion will strengthen your spiritual life and give you access into all God has for you and your life. Every day, we face our own personal battlefield in which prayer can be our ally—and it doesn't have to be complicated. Here's a simple template I sometimes follow for prayer:

1. Thanksgiving: "Thank you Lord for …"
2. Confession: "Forgive me father, I …"
3. Ask: "Lord, I pray that you grant me …"
4. Praise: "Lord, you are the almighty, maker of heaven and earth …"

Whatever the method of prayer, be in constant communication with God. Remember, God is everywhere, so pray anywhere. Make space for God, and He will invite you into something incredible.

Your Workout

1. How do you feel about asking God for help? Explain your answer.

2. What keeps you from praying? Fear? Busyness? Your schedule?

3. In what areas do you have the most difficulty surrendering to God's plan and will for your life? Where are you afraid to hand over control and power to your Creator? Write them down and make a note to pray for those areas on a regular basis.

4. Where in your life have you seen God work through prayer? What did you learn about His character through that experience?

5. Has God spoken to you through his Word, other people and/or an impression on your heart? If so, share an example and explain how you responded.

Extra Workout Challenge

1. Set aside a time to pray daily. It can be the first thing you do when you wake up or the last thing you do before going to sleep—just be sure to do it! You may find it easier to pray when you have it scheduled. I get an alert from my daily devotional application ("Jesuit Prayer") to remind me to reflect and pray. Many people also set an alarm on their phone. Do what works for you.

2. Keep a prayer journal to jot down answered prayers. Use a paper journal or your phone, whatever works best. Just be sure to write them down. As you do, you will begin to learn who God is. He is a gracious and loving Father who delights in giving us good and perfect gifts! As you watch how God is working in your life, your faith will deepen. Too often, we are quick to remember the challenge in front of us and forget the grace God has already given.

3. Give each person in your family a notecard. Ask them to write down a prayer request. Pray for each person and add their answered prayers to your prayer journal.

CHAPTER 15: CHURCH

"For where two or three gather in my name, there am I with them."
(Matthew 18:20)

When it comes to Sunday church, NFL players and coaches aren't necessarily set up for success. Excluding the Bye Week, for four to five months out of the year, our professional careers revolve around Sunday mornings.

Maybe you've even experienced this as an NFL *fan*. See if you can relate to this scenario. You're at church on a Sunday morning, and the pastor is "going a bit long." You keep pulling out your phone to check the time—calculating how long it will take you to get in your car, drive home, get the snacks ready and turn on the TV. As the pastor wraps up his message, you run through your team's keys to victory in your head. Your anxiety grows as you get closer and closer to kickoff.

For NFL personnel, take that mental investment, multiply it by 100, and add commitment, accountability and job security. On any given Sunday—after a full week of practices, meetings and walk-throughs—players and coaches are expected to arrive at the stadium typically no later than 10-10:30 a.m. for a 1 p.m. kickoff. Factoring in time to wake up, get ready and mentally prepare for gameday, you're pretty much engaged from the moment your alarm goes off. Once at the stadium, it's two hours of stretches, warm-ups and pregame speeches leading up to the coin toss, followed by post-game speeches, showers, interviews and family time—and that's just *home* games. It's no secret there isn't much time to catch a 90-minute worship service in between breakfast and kickoff.

Despite the obstacles to church attendance, though, there was one player, in particular, who still found intentional time for spiritual growth on Sunday mornings. He was the quarterback with whom I worked in Cincinnati for eight years: Andy Dalton.

Dalton began his football career as the QB for the freshman "B" team at Katy High School—a football-crazed community in the suburbs of Houston, Texas. Because of the level of competition, it took Dalton until his *senior year* to finally earn the full-time varsity starting job, but when he got his opportunity, he took advantage. In his only season as starting QB, Dalton led the Katy Tigers to a 14-1 record, their only loss coming in the state championship. The *Houston Chronicle* named Dalton as their 2005 Greater Houston Area Offensive Player of the Year.[1]

In the middle of that senior season, with only three D-I scholarship offers, Dalton committed to Texas Christian University (TCU) in Fort Worth. After redshirting his freshman year, Dalton won the starting job for the Horned Frogs and kept it for all four seasons of his eligibility. In that time, Dalton led TCU to a school-record 42 wins (in 49 games) and three straight top-10 AP Poll finishes (No. 7 in 2008, No. 6 in 2009, No. 2 in 2010)—ending in a perfect 13-0 record and a 21-19 Rose Bowl victory over No. 4 Wisconsin. Along the way, Dalton not only broke every major TCU passing record, but he also won two straight Mountain West Conference Offensive Player of the Year awards.[2]

His success in Fort Worth earned Dalton the Bengals' second-round pick (35th overall) in the 2011 NFL Draft—the fifth of 12 quarterbacks selected.[3] When Dalton joined us in Cincinnati, our incumbent QB, Carson Palmer, was threatening to retire if he wasn't traded. After Palmer failed to report to training camp, Dalton was named our starting QB as a rookie, and again, he took advantage of the opportunity. In that first season, he led us to a playoff berth and did so for the next *four seasons*, earning multiple Pro Bowl nominations in the process.

An outside observer could probably look at Andy's career and successes and come up with a few common themes—hard work, taking advantage of opportunity, leadership, etc.—but what most people *don't* know are the behind-the-scenes factors that influenced Dalton's accomplishments. Although only those closest to him, who interacted with him on a daily basis, regularly saw it, Dalton's keys to success reached far beyond the practice field. Dalton was a devoted man of God—an identity he carried with him wherever he went.

"My talents and abilities are all from Him," Dalton said. "So, when I take the field to play and use those abilities, it is my way of giving thanks to Him for all He has given me."[4]

Not only did Christ give Andy a reason to play the game, but his faith also equipped him with consistent confidence and poise on the field. Dalton's spiritual life and relationship with God gave him practical and tangible tools that proved essential in such an emotionally charged profession.

"His faith plays a major part in his life, and everything he does revolves around it," said Andy's former TCU teammate, Jake Kirkpatrick. "He has views and morals he sticks to. That's why he's such a leader on this team. I think it shows on the field."[5]

Knowing his reputation as a man of faith, one day in the Cincinnati weight room, I asked Andy, "How are you able to connect with God during the busy NFL season?" Given the prominence, pressure and commitment associated with his position (starting NFL QB), I was curious as to how he could still maintain such an emphasis on his spiritual growth.

Andy's answer came quickly.

"Since we don't have time to go to church on Sundays, I'll find time to watch something on the mornings of games. I'll come home pretty early and listen to a podcast."[6]

This might sound simple enough for the average person, but for those in the NFL, they know just how much dedication this actually involves. For Andy to watch a sermon, *at home, prior* to coming to the stadium on game day, this meant stopping at home *after* spending the night at the team hotel. It meant more *discipline* around sleep and prep time, amid the pressures of playing in such a high-stakes profession, to connect with God and His people—on arguably the most important morning of the week for his professional career, nonetheless.

During away games—despite not being able to stop home before reporting to the stadium—Dalton kept his Sunday morning routine.

To stay consistent, he still pulled up a podcast or sermon video before beginning his pregame routine. Beyond that, Andy connected with other believers in chapel (usually the night before game day), team Bible studies and other things like gameday prayer.

"You want to be encouraged, you want to learn, and when you're not able to go to church on Sundays for half the year, you still have to find a way to do it. [Church] is truly a relationship, and I need to keep up with it."[7]

> **The Church is the people of God, the body of Christ, the collective group of believers both locally and globally.**

If you closed your eyes and visualized a church, what would you see? Would it be a small white building with a steeple? Or a cathedral with stained glass windows? A spacious room with rows of benches and Bibles? Think again! Contradictory to popular belief, the Church isn't a building, a specific place or even a set format or routine. The Church is *the people of God*, the body of Christ, the collective group of believers both locally and globally. As Matthew 18:10 says, "For where two or three gather in my name, there I am with them." That's the Church—a group of believers pursuing God together. Here's how Andy put it:

> *"Church is who you surround yourself with, how you interact with people, how your character shows and how you live your life."* [8]

Let's break down that definition. First, **Church is the people with whom you surround yourself**—not a place to gather. You and I are the Church. We are the Church. *Because* the Church is a people, it builds off of what I talked about in Chapter 11 (Community). The Church is actually interwoven with the *entire* social building block (character, relationships, community and love). Like any other community, the Church is a group of people in relationship, united by a common bond. The body of Christ shares all of the same characteristics that defined that 2000 Ravens defense: physical proximity, shared concerns, real consequences and common responsibilities. As each member of our Marvin Lewis-led defense had a unique position to play, so people within the

Christian community also have specific roles that are accountable to the overall body (e.g., "love one another").

Because the Church is the *people* of God, Andy could still "attend Church" on game day by seeking God with other believers—in the locker room, in chapel, in the shower during team prayer. Andy's Church, while also being at home in Cincinnati, traveled with him to away games, wherever the schedule took him. His Church was the people of God with whom he surrounded himself to pursue Christ together. That's what distinguishes the Church from any ordinary community, the common bond that defines it: Christ.

Ephesians 2:20 says the Church is "built on the foundation of the apostles and prophets, with Christ Jesus himself as the chief cornerstone." Later, in chapter 4, Paul says, "From [Christ] the whole body, joined and held together by every supporting ligament, grows and builds itself up in love, as each part does its work" (v.16). Jesus, the Head of the Church, unites us with other believers. On a local and international level, we're brought into the body, the family of Christ because of Jesus' unifying work in all of our lives. It's a common bond that reaches deeper than any other union of this world, and because of that, the Church has a uniquely powerful ability to encourage, strengthen and feed us as followers of Jesus.

It's a common bond that reaches deeper than any other union of this world, and because of that, the Church has a uniquely powerful ability to encourage, strengthen and feed us as followers of Jesus.

When those who believe in God are involved in one another's lives, mutual improvement occurs. This is the second part of Andy's definition: **Church is *how you interact with others.*** Hebrews 10:24-25 says, "And let us consider how we may spur one another on toward love and good deeds, not give up meeting together, as some are in the habit of doing, encouraging one another." Showing a belief or approval in someone may spur them to higher levels of achievement. When we receive words of encouragement from other believers, we feel we're meeting expectations, which, in turn, builds our confidence and lifts our spirits. We're better when we're together.

Just as humans were made for community, believers were made for the Church. As Christians, we need the Church—for encouragement, for community, for connection, for accountability, for building character. The Church gives life to the people within it. Like any other community, it empowers its members to flourish and thrive, and for the body of Christ, this means loving and serving both God and others. As an outgrowth of this love and service, the Church invented public education, founded orphanages and started hospitals.

At TCU, in 2010, God led Andy and a few classmates to bring the people of God together right there on campus in Fort Worth. The goal was to give students a place to worship and interact without the strictness and stuffiness often felt in a traditional church setting. So, alongside ten others, Andy founded a weekly nondenominational faith gathering called "Ignite"—motivated by the desire to "ignite" the TCU campus to live out authentic faith in everyday life. While college is often a time when students who grew up in the church drift away, Andy and those ten others wanted to give students a safe place to rediscover what it really meant to "go to church." With the slogan of "Come as You Are," the student-led ministry brought in a Christian rock band and guest speakers to attract attendees.

The night of Ignite's first gathering, April 5th, also happened to be the same night as the 2010 NCAA Men's National Basketball Championship. Because of that, Andy and the others weren't sure how many people to expect. Before the doors opened that night, Dalton prayed, "Lord, if it's just us in here, that's OK." A few minutes later, the place was packed. On the first night, more than 400 people showed up, and eventually, Ignite grew to an average weekly attendance of more than 700 students.

Following Andy's leadership, more than 90 percent of the TCU football team came to Ignite on a regular basis. And while, on the field, those student-athletes were praised for their eye-popping talent and play-making abilities, at Ignite, they were part of the group. They were members of the body.

"[At Ignite], they're not football players," said Ignite co-creator Kelsey Taylor. "They're just part of the family. They're just solid guys who love Jesus. It's awesome that the quarterback of our football team wants to be involved because he's so busy all over the place."[9]

The third and final aspect of Andy's definition of Church deals with personal responsibility: **Church is how your character shows and how you live your life.** Matthew 6:21 says, "For where your treasure is, there your heart will be also." In church one Sunday, a pastor of mine interpreted that into a modern-day context: "where your money goes, so does your heart." Depending on who you are, "money" might be replaced with "time," "energy," "attention" or "all of the above." Our actions, how we live, will show the world what we *actually* love and value. If we value the Church, our lives should give others a clear picture of that.

In Andy's rookie year with the Bengals, he and his wife, Jordan, established The Andy & JJ Dalton Foundation—extending the influence of the Church into both the Cincinnati and Fort Worth communities by providing rewarding experiences to seriously ill and physically challenged children.[10]

> *Our actions, how we live, will show the world what we actually love and value. If we value the Church, our lives should give others a clear picture of that.*

"With our foundation, we work with sick children and kids with special needs, helping them with different things," Dalton said of The Andy & JJ Dalton Foundation. "Maybe it's a disease they're fighting, or whatever sickness or illness they're going through. But at the end of the day, that's not the ultimate cure. The ultimate cure is Jesus. And that's the point we're trying to get across, whether it be the kids or whether it be the parents or the family. We're not helping solely to give money or solely to give the kid one day that they can be happy. We're helping because we want them to see the love that Jesus has for us."[11]

Jesus gave the Church an incredible responsibility before He ascended to heaven: "to make disciples of all nations" (Matthew 28:19). There are so many different aspects to this—preaching, teaching, serving, nurturing, loving, etc.—that if we tried to accomplish this as individuals, we'd almost certainly fail. That's why we have each other; that's why the Church exists. The Enemy, the devil, wants us to be alone. He tries to isolate us because, as Proverbs 27:17 says, "As iron sharpens iron, so one person sharpens another." My *Life Application Study Bible* says this: "It is human tendency to overestimate what we can do by ourselves and to underestimate what we can do as a group…working together, the Church can express the fullness of Christ."[12]

Coach's Corner

I grew up attending a Catholic school and going to mass every Sunday. I attained the sacraments—Baptism, Confirmation, Eucharist, Penance and eventually, Matrimony—in the Catholic church. One of my earliest memories was lining up during grade school to attend an all-school mass. After grade school, I attended a Jesuit (a Roman Catholic order) high school, an institution that my father taught in for more than 40 years. Throughout my childhood, I never missed a Sunday service because I knew that, if I did, I couldn't take communion (Holy Eucharist) until I attended confession and repented of my sin of missing the service. To me, this was what I knew to be "church."

In my mind, church was pretty boring. The services seemed rehearsed and routine—they had the same structure from start to end. Except for a few good songs and the occasional inspiring message, I never took much of an interest in church, and because of it, I stopped attending regularly after high school. I became disenchanted with church, and once the obligation was gone, I lost all desire to attend. Although these experiences growing up set the foundation for my spiritual building block and provided me an opportunity to learn about Jesus, my heart wasn't receiving and accepting His message.

> **"Working together, the Church can express the fullness of Christ."**

As a young adult, I stopped growing in my faith completely. Time after time, I strayed from opportunities to develop spiritually. At my first job out of grad school, at Northwestern, I had the privilege of serving under head strength coach Larry Lilja, who was a great man of God. Although he led team Bible studies through the Fellowship of Christian Athletes (FCA) in the same building where I worked and invited me to attend, I repeatedly turned down his offers. Again, God put godly people and influences in my path, but my heart wasn't ready. I wasn't progressing in my faith, nor was I trying to. I didn't want to be part of the "family of God."

This resistance lasted for several years, until I met my future wife,

Jennifer. Oddly enough, one of the things that attracted Jen to me was my spiritual foundation. At that point in her life, she was seeking—she wanted to know more about this man named Jesus.

After dating for about a year, I began to wonder if Jen was "the one" I was supposed to marry. I had some doubts, and because of my spiritual upbringing, I decided to bring them before God. I found a Catholic church in Chicago and committed to attending regularly as I sought God's wisdom on my future with Jen. After about a month of services and prayer, I felt confirmation from God: she was the person for me. Through the Church, God began to show me all the wonderful qualities Jen possessed and how they worked together with my own character and personality. He opened my eyes to the beauty that had been in front of me the whole time. From that point on, the dynamic of my relationship with Jen changed. She was no longer just "my girlfriend;" she was "my future wife"—the one who God made for me. God showed me more and more of Jen's great character traits, and within a year, we were engaged and on a new adventure to Minneapolis.

About a year and a half later— although Jen wasn't Catholic—Jen and I performed our marriage nuptials in a Catholic church in our hometown of Milwaukee, Wisconsin. I wasn't yet a devout follower of Jesus, but a change was occurring in my life at that time. Jen and I had just committed our lives to each other in the presence of God, and on top of that, for the first time in my career, I was surrounded by grown men who were more than just Christians in name. While working with the Vikings, I interacted with players, coaches and staff members who were at the top of their professions *and* authentic followers of Jesus. And I watched them closely. I didn't ask questions, just observed their interactions and behaviors. I wanted to see if their faith and values were actually visible in their everyday lives. As a result, I started taking advantage of opportunities I'd previously neglected.

As part of this progression, Jen and I started exploring different churches around the Minneapolis area. We'd settled on a Catholic church, but we still stayed open to searching. I was doing my best to support, encourage and assist Jen in her journey of pursuing Jesus while also continuing my own personal journey of faith in Him. Upon the recommendation of one of our players, wide receiver Qadry Ismail, we attended our first non-denominational Christian church. The emotional speakers, lively worship and relevant sermon topics clashed against the routines and rituals of which I'd become so familiar growing up. It was a bit of a shock, but it was also refreshing. Although it was a one-time experience, it opened my eyes to new ways to worship God. And it began to reshape my view and understanding of "church."

Within a few days of that 1998 NFC Championship loss to the Falcons (if you forgot, see Chapter 6: Self-Talk), I was hired as the head strength coach for the Ravens. One of my first tasks was to hire an assistant strength coach. With the recommendation from Ravens' defensive coordinator Marvin Lewis, I hired Chip Morton, who had previously served four years as the head strength coach for the Carolina Panthers. Despite having more experience than me, Chip consistently demonstrated humility. In the three years we worked together, he never gave his opinion unless asked, nor did he have a "know it all" attitude. He understood the daily grind of managing the weight room and the art of working with professional football players. Most importantly, he understood and respected our roles. This earned my respect.

Beyond an appreciated colleague, Chip was a Christ-follower and a daily, up-close-and-personal example of a godly man. As I mentioned in Chapter 8, Chip gave me the example I needed to overcome the temptation to scalp my allotted Super Bowl tickets. Because of the professional respect I had for Chip, my eyes and heart were open to observe his Christian walk and to observe how his life differed from those who didn't follow Jesus. By this time, I was *asking* questions. Morton answered them all—as did kicker Matt Stover. As I mentioned earlier, Stover graciously gave me a study Bible to help quench my thirst for knowledge.

As I sought to learn more about Jesus for myself, the Ravens team chaplain referred me and Jen to a nondenominational church (Bridgeway Community Church) in Columbia, Maryland, similar to the one we'd experienced in Minnesota. They taught relatable life lessons based on the stories and principles of the Bible. During this time—for maybe the first time in my life as a church attender—I was really *pursuing* God. I wasn't just going through the motions. As a husband, father and professional, I sought answers to the "real issues in life"—purpose, morality, eternal destiny, etc. In that context of pursuit, in the presence of the body of Christ, God presented me with a choice.

At one of the Sunday services, as was customary, the pastor outlined the message of the gospel. He explained how God had paid the price of our sins through Jesus Christ and extended forgiveness, grace and new life to us. If we were prepared to admit our failure, ask for forgiveness and receive Jesus' mercy and grace, God would welcome us into His family—not because of anything we could do, but because of what He already did through Jesus. That Sunday was the first time I really felt challenged in a church—and I knew I needed to make a decision. I needed to take a stand. I could no longer follow God "halfway" or as a "lukewarm" Christian (Revelation 3:16)—I was either in or out. By God's grace, my heart was ready to trust in what Jesus had done for me. Believing as best as I could at the time, I recited a prayer the pastor shared and received Jesus Christ that day.

> *That Sunday was the first time I really felt challenged in a church—and I knew I needed to make a decision. I needed to take a stand. I could no longer follow God "halfway" or as a "lukewarm" Christian (Revelation 3:16)—I was either in or out.*

Without that prayer, I don't know where I'd be in my relationship with God today. The Church gave me a pathway to a new life in Christ—a decision that completely changed my future and the future of my family. On that particular Sunday, I was there by myself. I was still experimenting with different churches, trying to find the right place to bring my wife and young daughter, Hailey. After that day, though, we started attending that church as a family. A few weeks later, Jen also responded to God's call and committed her life to Christ in that church. From that day on, we've been profoundly blessed to have the foundation of Christ in our marriage and home.

Perhaps the greatest joy for me and Jen comes from watching our children grow in their spiritual building blocks, which, in large part, is due to the influence of the Church. Both Hailey and Aidan committed their lives to Jesus at our church outside of Cincinnati and were actively engaged with youth ministries growing up. In high school, they both became active members of Young Life, a nonprofit organization that helps students and young adults grow in their faith through study, service and leadership. Their "church" took place in our basement, at their friends' homes, in local restaurants, at local retreats and on road trips.

As parents, we always tell our kids to "do good" and "make good choices." We want what's best for our children, and we know, for the most part, the path to that life is paved by sound decision-making. Youth today are bombarded with traps—depression, suicide, academic and peer pressures, and pornography are just a few of the many challenges they face daily. Jen and I do our best, but as parents, we can only do so much. The reality is that it takes a community to help them win these daily battles with the Enemy.

In John 15, Jesus said, "I am the vine; you are the branches. If you remain in me and I in you, you will bear much fruit; apart from me you can do nothing" (v. 5). On our own, we can try to "be good;" we can try to live our lives with consistent character. But, as this verse tells us, the only way to live a truly *good* life is to abide in Christ. Like a branch attached to a vine, we need to stay close to Jesus and the people of God. If we do that, as Jesus said, our lives will "bear much fruit." Jen and I are extremely grateful for the Church body that helped connect our children to God and raise them in the way of Jesus.

One of my proudest moments as a husband and father was when Jen, Hailey and Aidan all made their own decisions to get baptized. This milestone in their spiritual journey represented an admission of their faith to their community. In the presence of the Church body, they wanted to acknowledge their sins and express their desire for repentance. Jen and I were baptized at birth and had been following Jesus for many of our adult years, but it took the initiative of our 14-year-old son to get us to take the plunge together as a family. Hailey, who'd been baptized at age 15, assisted with the dunking of Aidan, Jen and myself. Right after I stepped out of the baptism tank, soaking wet, Jen ran up to me and gave me one of the most passionate kisses of our 20-plus years of marriage. A deep satisfaction welled up in my heart knowing I had helped cultivate a strong spiritual foundation in our home that would bring us all eternal rewards—a deeper, more impactful victory than the Super Bowl I'd been a part of earlier in my career. The Holy Spirit was awakened in all of us that day.

> **Because of the body of Christ, God has generated a spiritual impact in my life that I know will last for generations to come.**

It's hard to describe the feeling of watching all the seeds planted over the years bloom in such a beautiful way. God had placed countless people in our lives—some of whom were with us that day—who each played a role in getting us to that moment. From those early days in Catholic mass, God had worked in my life through the Church. He'd crossed my path with other believers—Larry, Jen, Qadry, Chip, Matt—and through the God-given encouragement and wisdom I received through those people, God shaped both *my* spiritual life *and* the lives of my family.

In my mind, connection with the Church may be the single greatest legacy we can leave for our families. Because of the body of Christ, God has generated a spiritual impact in my life that I know will last for generations to come. Now, as a member of the Church body, I have decided to write this book to share the Good News of salvation. I don't consider myself an "evangelist" in a formal sense, but I want to use my God-given abilities to serve Christ and (hopefully) help enhance the physical, mental, social and spiritual growth of His body of believers.

Foundation Building Tip

Church isn't a building; it's a people—it's the body of Christ, the local and universal family of believers. Like Andy said, "Church is who you surround yourself with, how you interact with people, how your character shows and how you live your life." As "iron sharpens iron," we need the Christian community to feed, strengthen and encourage us to become more like Jesus, the head of the Church. The Enemy wants us isolated, but only through *connection* with the body of Christ can we fully develop our spiritual building block.

Make church attendance a priority, whatever that may look like. Whether that's Sunday morning, a mid-week small group or a shared meal in your home, engage and seek God with other followers of Jesus. As Jesus said in John 15, "[He] is the vine; [we] are the branches." The only way to bear fruit is to abide in the vine. The only way to do good—and experience the love, joy and peace God offers—is to *stay connected.* The Church, the body of Christ, connects us to the true vine. Invest in a community who can lift you up, build into you and offer encouragement.

Your Workout

1. Do you attend church on a regular basis? If so, why? What does your church attendance look like? Is your "why" more based on routine, or is it a true reflection of the body of Christ? If not, what's keeping you from gathering with other believers?

2. In what ways has the Church strengthened your spiritual building block? If possible, list specific examples.

3. Do you have people in your life to hold you accountable, to sharpen you "as iron sharpens iron"? If so, who are they? How might you deepen those relationships even further? If not, who could you ask to enter into that relationship with you?

4. How does church attendance and time spent in Christian community affect the way you interact with others? How have those relationships changed your character and how you live your life?

Extra Workout Challenge

Church can happen anywhere. Here are some examples for initiating Church in your home, workplace and community:

1. Initiate church in the home by gathering in God's name. Lead your family in prayer at mealtime or bedtime. Spend intentional time encouraging each other and holding each other accountable.

2. Initiate church in the workplace. This can be done in many ways:
   • Encourage a co-worker through prayer
   • When appropriate, share a message that stimulated or encouraged you
   • Invite someone to church
   • Act in a peaceful manner toward a difficult co-worker

3. Initiate church in your neighborhood by spending time with people through invitations to gather, like a cookout or a game night, or volunteer your time for a favorite cause.

SPIRITUAL

CHAPTER 16: PURPOSE

"Many are the plans in a person's heart, but it is the Lord's purpose that prevails." (Proverbs 19:21)

After 20 years of coaching on three different NFL teams with hundreds (if not thousands) of different players, the memories start to blend together. Yes, there are definitely certain moments that stand out (overtime losses, playoff wins, significant breakthroughs), but it usually takes something unique for a memory to stick. It might be a certain emotion or particular smell or a peculiar detail—some additional sensory experience to strengthen the memory. At the beginning of my second season with the Vikings (1997), for instance, it was the pain I felt in my hands.

In Minnesota, one of the strength coaches' pre-practice rituals was to warm up the quarterbacks. This had never proved too difficult a task— just play catch with them until they loosened up enough to practice safely and effectively—but during that 1997 season, the "simple" task took an unexpected turn.

We had a new quarterback on the roster, a back-up we signed in the off-season who'd last played in Philadelphia. While our head strength coach paired up with starting QB Brad Johnson, I partnered with the new second-stringer. I'm not exaggerating when I say the ball *literally hummed* through the air when he threw it. I can still hear it. Yes, I was still fairly new to the NFL, but I'd never experienced anything like it—and to this day, I never have. He took a few steps back, like he was dropping back in the pocket, eyes focused on the target (me), and let it rip. With every repetition, the sheer velocity of each throw increased the already growing pain in my palms and fingers. It took all of my focus not only to catch the ball, but to get my hands in a proper position as to not sprain a joint or break a finger. As someone whose job was to lift weights all day, this seemed noteworthy. Next time around, I brought gloves for protection.

To that point in his career, this quarterback had already built a reputation in the NFL. He was known around the League as the "Ultimate Weapon." His name was Randall Cunningham.

An All-American out of UNLV, Cunningham was drafted by the Eagles in the second round (37th overall). After playing sparingly as a rookie, Cunningham earned the starting job in the second half of the 1986 season. By 1988, he earned his first Pro Bowl appearance, becoming the first black starting quarterback in the Pro Bowl in NFL history.[1] In a three-year period (1988-1990), Cunningham earned three Pro Bowl appearances, an MVP award from the Pro Football Writers of America (PFWA) and brought the Eagles to three postseason appearances (after a six-year playoff drought, nonetheless).[2]

By that point, Cunningham had revolutionized the game of football—specifically the quarterback position. Unlike many QBs before him, Cunningham had a unique capacity to pass *and* run the ball. Because he always kept defenses on their toes, he was one of the first true game-changers in NFL history. Offenses rearranged their schemes to fit his skillsets; defenses threw out their game plans to try to slow him down.

As a dual-threat signal caller, Cunningham preceded the direction of the game today. His style of running was unparalleled. He moved well in the pocket to not only avoid defenders, but to make plays. He moved the ball with his arm *and* his legs and set the stage for other mobile quarterbacks like Steve McNair, Kordell Stewart, Donovan McNabb and Michael Vick. By the end of his career, Cunningham became the all-time leading rusher for a quarterback with nearly 5,000 yards (in addition to nearly 30,000 passing yards).[3]

Despite the accolades, Cunningham's last years with the Eagles were less than smooth. After tearing two ligaments in his knee in the

1991 season-opener, Cunningham's career took a turn for the worse. Although he returned to the field in 1992 to lead the Eagles to another playoff appearance, after the injury, his speed and athleticism weren't the same.[4] Cunningham's next few seasons were defined by injuries and an offensive system shift that pushed Cunningham into a back-up role. To finish the 1995 season (his last year with the Eagles), the then-three-time Pro Bowler was benched for the team's last 12 games.[5]

On top of the injuries and decreased role, claims started to spread from former Eagles' teammates and coaches that Cunningham was self-centered, aloof and not a team player.[6] Once a fan favorite in Philadelphia, those days were now in the rear-view mirror. Following the 1995 season, Cunningham visited a comedy club in Philly to enjoy some laughs with the rest of the audience. But even there, he couldn't escape the criticism. After being acknowledged by the club's master of ceremonies, a barrage of "boos" broke out among the crowd. That's when Cunningham knew his time in Philadelphia had run out. A few months later, by intentionally choosing not to offer him a new contract, the Eagles made Cunningham's realization official. After 11 seasons in the NFL, Cunningham announced his retirement from football in August 1996. The last thing he said publicly as an NFL quarterback was that he'd "lost his love" for the game.[7] Later, Cunningham would say he "didn't want anything to do" with football.

In the summer of 1997, less than a year after his retirement, Cunningham was throwing bullets to my gloved hands. Minnesota head coach Dennis Green was in the market for a back-up quarterback, and when he found out Cunningham might be available, he made a call. A few days later, Cunningham was a Viking, and he made an impact right away. After Brad Johnson got sidelined, with Coach Green facing pressure to win a playoff game, Cunningham delivered. With incredible enthusiasm, I watched Cunningham orchestrate an improbable 23-22 comeback in the Wild Card Round of the 1997 NFC playoffs—leading the team to score 10 points in the

By all accounts, Cunningham had revitalized his NFL career. He was a different quarterback—and it wasn't just the stats and accolades telling that story.

final 90 seconds of the game. It was the biggest playoff comeback by a visiting team since 1972—and more importantly, it was the Vikings' first postseason win in nine years.[8]

The following year—as you read about in Chapter 6 (Self-Talk)—I witnessed Cunningham engineer not only the best year of his career (3,700-plus passing yards, 34 passing TDs), but also one of the greatest regular seasons in Vikings' franchise history.[9] Cunningham led us to a record-breaking 15-1 record and an NFC Championship berth while posting a League-leading 106.0 passer rating and being named a First-Team All Pro.[10]

By all accounts, Cunningham had revitalized his NFL career. He was a different quarterback—and it wasn't just the stats and accolades telling that story.

One of Cunningham's former Eagles' teammates, wide receiver Cris Carter (who was now with the Vikings) admitted in an ESPN interview his dislike for Cunningham when they'd played together in Philadelphia. After Cunningham arrived in Minnesota, though, Carter's tone changed. His feelings for his new teammates took a 180, and the new QB-WR became fast friends.[11] After bracing for the "Cunningham of old," whose reputation preceded him, the Vikings were thrilled with the updated version of "The Ultimate Weapon" they received instead. Less than a year past his unfortunate exit from Philadelphia, Cunningham was not only a new football player, but a new man.

So, what changed during Cunningham's time away from football? How did Cunningham transform himself to pull his career and his legacy out from the bench to an All-Pro starter once again?

From August 1996 (Cunningham's retirement) to April 1997 (Cunningham's signing with the Vikings), two noteworthy events occurred in Cunningham's life.

First, naturally, Cunningham had a career change. While he worked as a studio analyst for TNT, he started his own marble, tile and granite company. He had some excess marble from the construction of his home in Las Vegas, so he hired a staff and opened a marble and granite shop. In a matter of months, Cunningham's life shifted from playing in packed stadiums, fans cheering his name, to grinding marble all day and responding to requests for customized kitchens.[12]

Second, Cunningham reconnected with his faith. He began attending a Bible study on a regular basis with a group of friends, often hosting them in his home. Through his engagement with Scripture and the encouragement of like-minded friends who cared about him, God began to work in Cunningham's life. Looking back on the end of his time in Philadelphia, he began to recognize the anger he experienced as a back-up. With prayer and perspective, God helped Cunningham reframe that season in his mind.

"I had so much anger inside for sitting the bench or for just not being treated the way I thought I should be treated," Cunningham told *Sports Spectrum*. "The Bible says there's a time to mourn, a time to laugh, a time to weep, a time to cry—there's a time to tear down and there's a time to build up. That was my tearing-down time."[13]

Cunningham's personal relationship with God was revived. God replaced Cunningham's feeling of rejection with reception. In studying Scripture, Cunningham learned to submit to God's authority and the people He placed in leadership roles in Cunningham's life. In that humility, God began to build Cunningham back up. Through encouragement and mentorship from other Christian friends, former teammates and pastors, Cunningham saw God's hand in his life more and more. Just a few months removed from NFL superstardom, this was Cunningham's new reality: Christ and kitchens.

Cunningham left the NFL without any intention of returning, but almost immediately, people started asking him, "When are you coming back?" Initially, he shrugged off the inquiries, but over time, curiosities about a comeback began to grow in his own mind. Instead of making a quick decision based on his own intuition, Cunningham now felt compelled to seek God's will for his next steps. In his heart, he didn't necessarily want to return to football, so he got down on his knees and prayed a very specific prayer to God: "Lord, if it's Your will that I should go back and play football, I'm willing to follow that. You know my heart better than I know myself. If it's Your will, have teams call me up, and I'll take that as a sign that You want me to get back

> *In the humility of getting benched, losing the respect of his fanbase and an unexpected retirement, Cunningham sought God, and God showed him a new plan. God revealed a new purpose for Cunningham's life.*

into football." It only took a couple days for teams—including Dennis Green and the Vikings—to start calling.[14]

As Cris Carter noted about Cunningham, "When he came to Minnesota, the number one thing in his life was his faith." God worked in Cunningham's life, and he changed. In the humility of getting benched, losing the respect of his fanbase and an unexpected retirement, Cunningham sought God, and God showed him a new plan. God revealed a new *purpose* for Cunningham's life.

Purpose answers some of life's fundamental questions—things like, "Why am I here on this planet?" and "What am I supposed to do with my life?" Purpose provides clarity and identity when life and people (and ourselves) try to pull us in all sorts of different directions. With purpose, we can keep our focus and concentration. With focus and concentration, we can block out noise and distractions, and we can more effectively and intentionally move toward peak performance. O.G. Mandino's book, *University of Success*, puts it like this:

> *"We all know that purpose makes a difference; a clear picture of what we wish to accomplish and the determination to reach our goal strengthens our power to achieve it. It can make the difference between success and failure, frustration and zest for living, happiness and unhappiness. Strong lives are motivated by dynamic purposes; lesser ones exist on wishes and inclinations. The most glowing successes are but the reflections of an inner fire. Multitudes of people, drifting aimlessly to and fro without a set purpose, deny themselves such fulfillment of their capacities, and the satisfying happiness which attends it."*[15]

Purpose is *essential* for peak performance ("...such fulfillment of their capacities..."). When we move throughout life with direction, when we actively pursue something, we can overcome almost any difficulty or obstacle in our way. As long as we keep our eyes on our goal, on our aligning purpose, trials and hardships won't deter us; they'll only make us stronger. As the Nietzsche quote that I mentioned in Chapter 1 says, "Those who have a 'why' to live, can bear with almost any 'how'."

For many of us, including myself, the problem isn't necessarily *following* your purpose; it's *discovering* what it is. Since humans often have different ideas of what our specific purpose could (and should) look like, it's key to bring in an outside perspective—a perspective of greater wisdom and understanding. Purpose requires a spiritual element because, ultimately, your purpose in life is only truly realized when you understand *God's* purpose *for* your life. As Proverbs 19:21 says, "Many are the plans in a person's heart, but it is the Lord's purpose that prevails."

> **"Strong lives are motivated by dynamic purposes; lesser ones exist on wishes and inclinations. The most glowing successes are but the reflections of an inner fire."**

Of the five "constant factors for true success" in *University of Success*, two of them are "purpose" and "spirituality." Purpose helps us move toward a goal—to combat aimlessness and feel like we're "going somewhere"—and spiri-tuality aligns us with the "greater purposes of life and the Author of those purposes." As the book puts it, "[One] must sense somehow the pervasive currents of God's existence and recognize his own existence in those currents, too...It is not the disparity of the outlook or vocation which counts, but rather the fact that [we] are in tune with life and its Maker."[16] In other words, it doesn't matter *what* we do, but rather *how* we do it and *whom* we do it for.

When you draw closer to God, you find out more about yourself: why He made you the way He did, what He wants you to accomplish in your life, and perhaps, most importantly, who He wants you to be when you are the best version of yourself. Like Cunningham's life, God often uses difficult circum-stances to bring about our most drastic changes. I'm reminded of

> **It doesn't matter what we do, but rather how we do it and whom we do it for.**

this truth found in Romans 8:28 which states, "And we know that in all things God works for the good of those who love him, who have been called according to his purpose."

Cunningham's retirement allowed him to step back and align his purpose to God's plan. God had worked on Cunningham's heart. He was a more mature, appreciative and grateful person. Vikings players and coaches noticed Cunningham helping and encouraging the starting quarterback, Brad Johnson, whenever possible. Cunningham had evolved from a prima-donna quarterback to a team player. He grew to understand contentment and humility. Even as a back-up quarterback, Cunningham was accepted by teammates as a leader.

Once we discover our purpose, the next step is *stewardship*. Stewardship and purpose go hand-in-hand. Purpose provides concentration and power; stewardship provides the map for how I can use my gifts and talents *for* that purpose. Success is knowing God's purpose for your life and managing (or "stewarding") your gifts and talents to fulfill that purpose. Until we know why we're here and what we're called to do, we'll never be able to fully utilize and steward our gifts and abilities in the best possible way. Without purpose and stewardship, we'll never be able to fulfill our maximum potential.

Like purpose, stewardship starts with knowing and understanding yourself. When you understand your strengths and weaknesses, you can then maximize those strengths and minimize those weaknesses.

> **Success is knowing God's purpose for your life and managing (or "stewarding") your gifts and talents to fulfill that purpose.**

In Jesus' "Parable of Talents" (Mathew 25:14-30), a man prepares to go on a journey and entrusts his servants with his money ("talents"). Two of the three servants went right to work and invested the talents to produce a profit. On his return, the man affirmed their production by stating, "Well done, good and faithful servant," and gave them more responsibility. The third servant did not produce a profit, but instead "played it safe" and buried his share in the ground. As a result, his master calls him "lazy" and reprimanded him for his self-centeredness.

When we faithfully respond to opportunities to accomplish God's purpose, He rewards us. Like the good servants in the story, at the end of the day, when we pass from this life to the next and are face-to-face with God, don't we all want to hear the words, "Well done, good and faithful servant"? God has given each of us different gifts, talents, and other resources according to our ability and he expects us to use them effectively. The more abilities and resources we have, the more responsible we are to use them in a manner pleasing to Him.

After returning to the NFL with the Vikings, God had even bigger plans for Cunningham. While his on-field performances were impressive, Cunningham's greatest work was accomplished off of it. When he first entered the NFL, he was a self-described "prideful" individual. Now, motivated by the strong, godly men who had mentored, encouraged and taught him how to recognize his spiritual gifts, Cunningham had a desire to do for others what had been done for him.

When I was with the Vikings, there are a couple of moments with Cunningham that, for some reason, I've never forgotten. Before one of our games, I specifically remember Cunningham boarding the team bus in a suit and sitting in the seat in front of me. He looked at me directly and said he was "dressed for Jesus" or something to that effect. It was an off-handed comment, but it stuck with me. He wasn't looking for fashion ratings on ESPN, but he wanted his attire to reflect his honor for Christ. On another occasion, I remember Randall joking with our head strength coach, telling him he wouldn't do proper repetitions in an exercise until the coach read the Bible. Scripture had such an impact on Cunningham's life that he couldn't help but share it with those he cared about. Again, these were comments made in jest, but I wasn't a Christian at that point in my life, so they stood out. Looking back, I can't help but wonder if these memories planted a seed that eventually helped lead me to Christ.

During the 2001 season, I was reunited with Cunningham when he signed with the Baltimore Ravens. In Baltimore, he started a Bible study with team leaders and future Hall of Fame players, Rod Woodson and Ray Lewis. For 30 minutes each week during the season, they met to study and discuss *The Man God Uses* by Henry Blackaby. The study had such a positive impact that Woodson called Cunningham years later, thanking him for what he did in his life during that year.[17]

Cunningham played his last NFL games in Baltimore, and although he never saw the on-field success again that he saw during that remarkable '98 season, he ended his career on a much better note. In August 2002, Cunningham reunited with the Eagles by signing a one-day contract to officially announce his retirement from football.

Seeking God's purpose and direction has led Cunningham to a life of meaningful fulfillment. The small Bible study Cunningham hosted at his house on an interim basis has grown to become a 1,000-plus-member church[18] of which he is now the pastor. Cunningham leveraged the talent God gave him to serve the bigger purposes of his life, and now, on a weekly (if not daily basis), thousands of people are reaping the benefits.

Coach's Corner

In the NFL, no job is ever really secure. Player, coach or staff member, under contract or not, you never know when your time with an organization—and corresponding livelihood in that location—might come to an end. Like I did, you might spend several years in one city, only to have it all turned upside-down on a Monday in early January: "Black Monday."

As I've mentioned already, Black Monday is the first day after the NFL regular season ends (usually the first or second week of the calendar year), and it marks the beginning of the vicious litany of coaching staff firings across the NFL—particularly among teams with losing records. There's a reason people in the League refer to the NFL as the "Not For Long" League. Like most of my colleagues, I've felt the wrath of Black Monday more than once: in Cincinnati with Marvin Lewis and in Baltimore with Brian Billick. On both occasions, I'd been with the organization for nearly a decade.

In Chapter 11 (Community), I talked about this transition when I was with the Bengals, but at that point—although the firing was a shock—I had a reference point for what to expect. The first time it happened, though—in Baltimore with Coach Billick (2007)— I had no idea what I'd fallen into. For the first time in my career, I no longer worked in a structured athletic setting. For 12 years, part of my identity had been wrapped up in professional football, and in one day, all of that was gone. It was a very humbling experience.

Like Cunningham's first retirement, I felt God calling this "timeout" in my life. In his perfect timing, I knew he had something planned—I just didn't know what. With an uncertain future, I prayed. I prayed with my wife, my friends, my church and by myself. Although each prayer had its own nuances and specifics, the main themes were the same: clarity and direction.

I started—also, like Cunningham—by creating my own business in the private sector that required a whole new professional skillset. Instead of training professional athletes, I worked with "average Joes." Instead of multi-million-dollar training facilities, I knocked on doors of local gyms, health clubs and parks to find places to train clients. Instead of players coming to me for training, I had to compete with rival personal trainers for business and with club members for equipment that was far from "state of the art." Instead of a rigid schedule, I chaotically ran from one training session to the next trying to keep up with my workload while managing the daily grind of being an entrepreneur. And the biggest challenge: instead of having a team of men around me working toward a common goal, it was suddenly me, myself and I. Or so I thought.

> *Before my identity as a "strength coach," "Super Bowl champion" or even "husband and father," I was a child of God.*

One of the groups I trained was affectionately known as the "Howard County Housewives." This contingent consisted of middle-aged adults (mostly women and a few courageous husbands) who lived in Howard County, Maryland (where I lived). Working with this population allowed me to use my gifts and talents to coach, teach and encourage *those around me*—a much wider population than NFL athletes.

By faith, I used my gifts and talents to take on an entirely new role serving a new population. In obedience, I persevered through the challenges of being an entrepreneur. As a result, God strengthened my spiritual building block and showed me that my purpose of glorifying Him extended far beyond professional athletics—an awareness that brought incredible joy and peace. I had a stronger connection to *whose* I was rather than *who* I was. Before my identity as a "strength coach," "Super Bowl champion" or even "husband and father," I was a child of God. As Randall put it, this "tearing-down" time pushed me to put less value into my worldly title and more into my identity in Christ.

As I talked about in Chapter 5 (Education), this chapter in my life also helped fortify my mental building block. I earned certifications in massage therapy and Active Release Techniques (ART) that wouldn't have been possible without time away from the NFL.

After the NFL bypassed me for a second year, I continued to evolve my business and was hired as the director of strength and conditioning for the inaugural season of the United Football League (UFL). To help the UFL players get ready for training camp, I prepared a strength and conditioning manual for the entire league. Given the comprehensive nature of professional success, beyond just strength and conditioning (physical building block), I felt compelled to integrate material on mental, social and spiritual development. Although, based on the timing and platform, I decided *not* to include the other blocks in the manual, thinking about them brought these concepts to a new life in my mind. As a coach, I was prepared to put them into practice daily and, eventually, on to paper with this book!

The Holy Spirit was calling me to share what was brewing inside my heart–to steward what I was given toward my purpose, for the sake of serving others.

My plan B was God's plan A. Although it wasn't my first choice to step away from the NFL, God revealed his greater purpose for my life through this unique season. I may not have had direct confirmation from God in starting this new chapter, like Randall did before returning to the NFL, but through the process, God began to show me the plan He'd planned all along.

Just like an earthly father who gives his child a "time out," our Heavenly Father gives us time to work on our hearts and prepare us for the future. God used my time away from the NFL to encourage me to grow mentally through a new management position and further education, and deepen my faith by reaffirming my purpose and talents. Equipped with a new skill set, in 2010, I received an invitation to work with the Cincinnati Bengals as an assistant strength coach.

I was ready when called. Not only was I able to serve others in new ways, but I also had a fresh opportunity to observe professional athletes from the lens of the physical, mental, spiritual and social building blocks. With a keen and hungry eye, I was much more observant of the total athlete and the unique gifts and rituals they were utilizing to be the best in their field. Rather than place me in a position of authority as a head strength coach, God opened the door for an assistant position that lessened my workload and gave me more time to write this book. The Holy Spirit was calling me to share what was brewing inside my heart—to *steward* what I was given toward my purpose, for the sake of serving others.

This greater purpose God showed me, I'm convinced, wouldn't have been possible without God first pursuing a personal relationship with me. Growing up in the Catholic church, I tried my best to keep a checklist of religious rules—many of which were really good ones. I thought keeping the rules was the road to eternal life. I lived in a way to "make the cut-off," so to speak. As I found out later, God had a better, greater plan for my life than performance-based religion. While God cared about my behavior, He was (and still is) much more concerned about my trust in Him and His plan. I began to realize that I didn't want a religion, I wanted a relationship with God. I wanted a sense of peace, forgiveness of sins, freedom from guilt and a security about my eternity. I wanted purpose in my life. And that's exactly what God wanted with me—a relationship based on His terms, not mine, that promised peace, grace, love and purpose.

When I received Jesus into my life that Sunday in Baltimore (see "Chapter 15: Church"), at the time, I didn't think much of it. From my perspective, it was somewhat uneventful. Afterwards, though, subtle changes started happening in my life. I stopped swearing as much, started to give money to God (tithe), made it a habit to attend church on a weekly basis and read the Bible. I began listening to sermons and taking notes to remember and put the information into practice. My belief in Jesus began to change my behavior. And it couldn't have come at a better time.

Jen and I had just recently arrived in Baltimore. This was before Hailey and Aidan were in the picture. We were young, newly married, and adjusting to a new city, new home, new jobs and the news that we were pregnant with our first child. With the Ravens, I had more responsibility at work than ever before, and Jen's full-time sales job kept her busy around the clock. Yet amid that craziness—and corresponding relational stress—the Holy Spirit's work in my life began to carry over into our marriage. After accepting Christ in 2000 (our second year in Baltimore), God gave me the patience, love and gentleness to come alongside Jen in her own spiritual journey—and to do the same for our children. After the births of Hailey and Aidan, God led me to pray with them each night as I put them to bed. With a new end goal of directing my family toward Christ, God empowered to become a devoted husband, father and spiritual leader.

The real purpose of why I was put on this earth began to change—or, at least, it became clearer to me. As my relationship with Jesus deepened, I slowly became conformed into His image. I wasn't doing these things because I needed to "make the cut off," but because *I wanted to*—because I was truly grateful for God's grace in my life.

Wherever you're at on the journey of discovering and following purpose, God has a plan for your life. Often, when we are in the trenches, it can be hard to see how God is working, but God created you and gave you specific gifts and abilities for a *specific reason*—not just to serve yourself, but to serve *others* and glorify Him in the process. And the beautiful thing about that is, in doing so, you will actually achieve your peak potential. It all starts with trusting in Him. When you surrender your life to God—when you commit yourself to Him and His purposes, instead of your own—you open the door to a much greater power and strength than you ever could've come up with on your own. God wants you to seek His purposes—not to rule over you like a dictator, but to give you a deeper, richer, fuller life in Him. In doing so, you not only achieve peak performance, but you gain the blessings of peace, joy, love and contentment that flow from it.

Put simply, this is the purpose of this book—to help you discover your strengths (and weaknesses) and steward them accordingly toward God's purpose for your life. If you're struggling to discover what that purpose *is*, ask God. Pray and ask what He wants for your life. Look for His guidance and have faith that He is directing you. Take an assessment of your strengths, your abilities and your passion. StrengthsFinder and Uniquely You are a couple resources that have helped me on my journey, but there are a countless number of other tests, tools and tips out there that might work better for you. In what unique ways has God gifted you, and how might you use that to serve and love God and those around you?

> **God wants you to seek His purposes—not to rule over you like a dictator, but to give you a deeper, richer, fuller life in Him. In doing so, you not only achieve peak performance, but you gain the blessings of peace, joy, love and contentment that flow from it.**

Seek out God's purposes through the other elements of the spiritual building block—by reading the Bible, praying and going to church. Each one of these provides us access to God, and in turn, communication with Him about His will for our lives. Scripture, prayer and church all serve the same ultimate purpose in our lives—to be with Jesus, to become more like Jesus and to do what Jesus did. His life provides us the perfect example of what it means to follow God's will with your life.

If you're struggling to surrender to God and His will for your life, know you're not alone. Trusting God through life commitment is a major (and difficult) step toward recognizing your truest, deepest, most satisfying purpose in life. The Enemy, other people and your own mind will try to sidetrack you with lesser, secondary pursuits—promising you satisfaction and happiness. Don't listen to those voices! As Joshua 24:15 says, "**Choose for yourselves this day whom you will serve,** whether the gods your ancestors served beyond the Euphrates, or the gods of the Amorites, in whose land you are living. But as for me and my household, we will serve the Lord."

Knowing my purpose for being on this planet has provided me with peace. I know God has a specific plan for my life that is within my nature, persona and gifts—one that is far better than anything I could've dreamed up myself. I don't need to alter my personality or the crux of who I am, but I do need to keep my focus on serving God and being obedient to His calling. Regardless of whether I am training professional athletes, weekend warriors or the "average Joe," I move ahead using my unique gifts and talents to glorify Him.

Foundation Building Tip

Peak performance *is* following God's will for your life. We may have our own plans for our life, "but it is the Lord's purpose that prevails" (Proverbs 19:21). God's plan will ultimately come to fruition, so the best thing we can do for ourselves is to get on-board with His will and use our gifts and abilities to serve Him and His purposes for our lives. And, as we know through Scripture, He will not let us down.

Maybe you didn't recently get fired or retire from your career, but you will still benefit if you take a "time out" to seek God. He is entrusting you with unique abilities and wants you to use them to serve His purpose. Ask him to reveal your gifts and how He might want you to leverage them to serve His Kingdom. You don't have to quit your job or take a sabbatical (necessarily), but you will need to dedicate time to unplug and be attentive. Like Cunningham, you may simply want to ask God to open a new door or offer you favor so you know which direction to head forward.

Your Workout:

1. Has God ever put you in a situation to reevaluate your purpose? If so, reflect on this disruption and what God may have been trying to communicate to you through it.

2. In what unique ways has God gifted you? What skills, abilities and passions had God continuously placed on your heart? If necessary, take an online assessment of your strengths and/or spiritual gifts.

3. Think for a moment about those gifts and talents. In what ways are you using them to accomplish God's purpose for your life? In what other ways might you be able to serve God and others through these gifts?

4. Negative influences—laziness, procrastination, fear of failure, other people, etc.—can hold us back from stewarding and developing our talents to the fullest potential. Is there anything or anyone holding you back from using your gifts to accomplish your purpose? If so, what or who is it?

Extra Workout Challenge

1. *Compose a list of five gifts or talents you have been given (the five things you do best!).* I recommend taking a spiritual gift profile assessment to help identify your talents, interests and passions. Several years ago, I took an assessment at UniquelyYou.org. The highest-ranking gifts for me were encouraging/exhorting, showing mercy and teaching. Knowing my gifts allowed me to find a rewarding vocation. Strengthen your spiritual building block by using the unique talents on your list to the fullest extent possible in whatever you do.

My Gifts:

1. _____
2. _____
3. _____
4. _____
5. _____

2. *Write down your purpose.* For me: "I want to help people get from Point A to B by using my gifts and talents to improve their physical, mental, social and spiritual development." Place that statement somewhere noticeable so that you will frequently be reminded of that purpose. Use this as a measuring stick to determine whether your choices move you closer or further from your goal.

My Purpose: _____

_____
_____
_____
_____
_____

WE ARE ALL COACHES

The term "coach" didn't originate as a title. Before a coach referred to a person, it referred to a vehicle in 16th century Europe—a horse-drawn carriage with a specific purpose of transporting a person *from where they are to where they ought to be going*.[1] Although this definition has morphed and changed during the past 500 years, the truth of its original meaning has remained: the role of a "coach" is to push, motivate, strengthen, encourage, *carry* others from "point A" to "point B."

By this definition, coaches aren't limited to sports—or any specific training field—either. Coaches can be teachers, parents, siblings, spouses, teammates, friends, co-workers and really everyone in between. We often even need to coach ourselves! It's less about the *title* and more about the *action* and *responsibility*. If there's a willingness to help others, anyone can apply the principles in this book.

As coaches (or potential coaches), we have an opportunity to help people identify gaps in their performance and correspondingly move them further along the performance curve. As parents, spouses, co-workers and peers, we can inspire positive change and help others build a solid foundation. Coaches have a unique job of influencing others toward their full potential in all phases of life. That's why coaching isn't limited to sports or education or relationship—coaching is holistic. Real, lasting change—both in ourselves and in others—comes from a conscious effort to daily grow physically, mentally, socially *and* spiritually.

Developing building blocks is a simple concept, but that doesn't mean it's simplistic. As you probably already know, it's much easier to *set* a goal than it is to *achieve* one. As humans, we have a built-in tendency to choose the path of least resistance. It's easy for us to get comfortable with the status quo and neglect self-improvement. Living in a culture of immediate gratification has only increased our desire to seek (and expect) rewards that are even more instant. As a result, we're constantly pulled away from crucial elements of development like discipline, rest and self-reflection. Our days are filled with tasks and activities that wear us down instead of building us up. That's why real, substantial growth is so rare! If it was easy, everyone would be doing it.

As coaches, change starts with us. It's true in professional football, and it's true for you and me. Empower those around you to grow not only through your words, but through your *actions*. As College Football Hall of Fame coach Grant Teaff said, "That which we teach, we must live. We need to be a walking sermon."

The power to change is preceded by the desire to change. As Marvin Lewis said, "If you change your habits, you can change your life." Make your motto to improve every single day. Find a way to grow in each building block one step at a time. Remember, life is a journey, not a race. It's a compilation of daily decisions, daily choices to say, "I will" or "I won't." While every day might not look like a "win," it's about the bigger picture—is your trajectory moving up the performance curve or down it? It won't be easy, but it will be worth it.

Throughout his Hall-of-Fame career, quarterback Kurt Warner took daily initiative to strengthen his foundation, and he gradually moved from his Point A to his Point B. Building on the base of the four blocks, Warner made the impossible possible. No other future NFL MVP, Super Bowl champion and Hall-of-Fame quarterback has entered the NFL from such a humble starting point as Kurt Warner. An undrafted, 26-year-old provided an example for others with similar aspirations and became a living representation that "nothing will be impossible with God" (Luke 1:37, ESV).

The Enemy wants nothing more than to "steal and kill and destroy" (John 10:10) both us and our building blocks. If you recognize this—and acknowledge the One who comes to give us "life to the full" (also, John 10:10)—you'll empower yourself (and others) to reject anything other than the life of love, joy, peace, faith and hope that God desires for you.

ACKNOWLEDGMENTS

As any author knows, writing a book never happens in a vacuum. It requires the combined talents of *many* people serving in various capacities along the journey. This book wouldn't be in your hands without the encouragement, wisdom and support I received from friends, family and colleagues—to put my thoughts on paper, to develop my ideas and to share them with a broader audience. I had to rely on some uniquely gifted people to get the job accomplished, and to them, I owe my deepest and fullest gratitude.

Thank you to all those who helped read, edit and offer perspective on the many, many drafts of this book. To Ben Creamer, Lisa Dean and Dawn Palazotto, for your time and insight. To Brian Sienko, for your limitless patience and expertise in design and layout. To Chris Folmsbee and Jeff Zurcher, for believing in my message and, in wisdom, guiding me through the process. To Ken Moyer, for your patience, time and willingness to help me develop this message for an audience. To Clif Marshall, for your encouragement and giving me an opportunity to share this message with other coaches. To Ron McKeefery, for your encouragement and guidance in getting my thoughts onto paper. To Dave Michener, for your creative content development, editing, and constant support, encouragement and friendship.

Thank you to The Core Media Group and to everyone there who helped bring this book across the finish line. When Jen and I were struggling with the publication process, God brought you all to us when we didn't even really know what we were looking for. As He always does, He gave us what we needed when we needed it. To Robert Walker, for your wisdom and guidance, and for overseeing the process until the end. To Nadia Guy, for your creative design and for visually capturing the heart of this book. To Kevin Horner, for your critical insight, incredible dedication to this project and for brilliantly and creatively bringing our thoughts and ideas to life on paper.

Thank you to all the people who saw something in me, gave me opportunities and changed the course of my life during my coaching career. God put the right people in my path at the right times. To Mick Weber, for hiring me as a graduate assistant at Illinois State and starting me on my coaching journey. To Bill Foster and Larry Lilja at Northwestern, for guiding and mentoring me in my first full-time paid coaching position. To Steve Wetzel and Dennis Green in Minnesota, for welcoming me into the ranks of professional football coaching. To all the former players, coaches and colleagues mentioned in this book, for allowing me to share your story and make this book a reality.

Thank you to my wonderful, supportive and encouraging family. I couldn't have written a single word of this without you. To my parents, Angela and Gerald Friday, thank you for providing me with the resources, tools and love to build my life physically, mentally, socially and spiritually. To my kids, Hailey and Aidan, thank you for your patience throughout this process and for all the time and energy you sacrificed to allow Mom and I to work on this book. To my beautiful wife, Jennifer, thank you for coming alongside me in this process and providing invaluable insight. You completed my thoughts in an articulate and purposeful way. As we both know, our foundational commitment to God through marriage provided the basis of this book, and it's been a privilege growing alongside you on this journey.

Finally, to all of the "coaches" in my life—past and present—thank you for taking me from Point A to Point B and molding me into the man I am today.

NOTES

Preface
1. Life Application Study Bible (include pg. #)

Introduction: The Four Building Blocks of Performance
1. https://www.kansascity.com/sports/spt-columns-blogs/va-he-gregorian/article1272729.html
2. https://www.espn.com/nfl/player/stats/_/id/1682/kurt-warner
3. https://www.espn.com/nfl/game?gameId=190912014
4. https://www.profootballhof.com/players/kurt-warner/biography/
5. Sports Illustrated – "All Things Possible"
6. https://dancingwiththestars.fandom.com/wiki/Kurt_Warner
7. All Things Possible. Talk about a humbling experience. That's about as humbled as you can get, to go from being in an NFL camp… to stocking shelves for $5.50 an hour, which was minimum wage. Pg 78
8. Kurt Warner, First Things First: The Rules of Being a Warner, (Tyndale House Publishers, 2009), pg. 34
9. Kurt Warner with Michael Silver. All Things Possible: My Story of Faith, Football, and the First Miracle Season, (HarperOne Publishers, 2000).
10. https://www.youtube.com/watch?v=MZypGn5AnFM
11. Kurt Warner with Michael Silver. All Things Possible: My

Story of Faith, Football, and the First Miracle Season, (Harper-One Publishers, 2000).

12. http://chrisbrauns.com/2014/10/four-questions-every-thinking-human-must-answer/

Chapter 1: Fitness

1. https://www.profootballhof.com/players/ray-lewis/
2. https://www.pro-football-reference.com/boxscores/200009240rav.htm#all_player_offense; Record: https://www.pro-football-reference.com/boxscores/200010220cin.htm#all_player_offense
3. https://www.youtube.com/watch?v=DX8ZeA7ahDg
4. Jeff Duncan, Paying the Price, The Times-Picayune (Date unknown)
5. Michael Siver, Burden of Proof, IN: Sports Illustrated presents Champs! Baltimore Ravens Super Bowl Champions 2001, 2001 Time Inc., pg. 64
6. Bob Glauber, Ray Lewis at 37; God juice Keeps Him Going, Newsday, August 25, 2012.
7. Ibid.
8. https://www.newsday.com/sports/football/ray-lewis-at-37-good-juice-keeps-him-going-1.3927221#
9. Bob Glauber, Ray Lewis at 37; God juice Keeps Him Going, Newsday, August 25, 2012.
10. Ibid.
11. Department of Health and Human Services. Physical Activity and Health: A Report of the Surgeon General. Atlanta: U.S. Department of Health and Human Services, Centers for Disease Control and Prevention, National Center for Chronic Disease Prevention and Health Promotion, 1996.
12. Ibid.
13. Fit For Life: The Annapolis Way, by Heinz Lenz and John Murray, Leisure Press, 1985.
14. Arch. Intern. Med. 168:154, 2008).
15. Specialized Strength Training: Winning Workouts for Specific Populations, Wayne Westcott and Susan Ramsden, Exercise Science Publishers, 2001. pg. 38
16. https://time.com/5324940/americans-exercise-physical-activ-

ity-guidelines/

17. Twilight of the Idols (1889) 'Maxims and Arrows'

18. https://health.gov/sites/default/files/2019-09/Physical_Activity_Guidelines_2nd_edition.pdf

19. Forbes,G.B. (1976). "The adult decline in lean body mass," Human Biology, 48: 161-73

20. Keyes, A., Taylor, H.L. and Grande, F. (1973). "Basal Metabolism and age of adult man, " Metabolism, 22: 579-87.

21. https://biblehub.com/commentaries/1_corinthians/9-25.htm, MacLaren's Exposition: 'Concerning the Crown' 1 Corinth 9:25

Chapter 2: Practice Habits

1. David Kindervoter, John Randle: Pro Football Hall of Fame Class of 2010, Bleacher Report, August 5, 2010. Brian Murphy, Vikings Guard Steve Hutchinson says John Randle was a Hall of Fame Teacher, Pioneer Press, August 7, 2010. https://www.profootballhof.com/news/notes-and-quotes-john-randle/

2. https://www.pro-football-reference.com/players/R/RandJo00.htm

3. David Kindervoter, John Randle: Pro Football Hall of Fame Class of 2010, Bleacher Report, August 5, 2010.

4. https://www.danpink.com/2012/03/the-power-of-habits-and-the-power-to-change-them/

5. The Power of Habit by Charles Duhigg

6. https://www.twincities.com/2019/11/30/vikings-legend-john-randle-humbled-by-selection-to-nfl-all-time-team/

7. Mark Craig, Class of 2010 Enshrinee: John Randle, Official Pro Football Hall of Fame Yearbook, 2010-11.

8. Ibid.

9. Dave Campbell, Relentless John Randle to Enter the Hall of Fame, Desert News, August 6, 2010.

10. David Kindervoter, John Randle: Pro Football Hall of Fame Class of 2010, Bleacher Report, August 5, 2010.

11. Coleman R Griffith, Psychology of Athletics, (Charles Scribner's Sons, New York-London 1928), 68.

12. "Practice periods which exercise a single skill beyond twenty or thirty minutes without rest are unwise. That is, the time

spent over and above twenty or thirty minutes is wasted time, provided we are thinking first of economy of learning." Pg.91

13. Coleman R Griffith, Psychology of Athletics, (Charles Scribner's Sons, New York-London 1928), 89.

14. Avi Karni, etc al ... The acquisition of skilled motor performance: Fast and slow experience driven changes in primary motor cortex. National Academy of Sciences, Vol. 95, February 1998.

15. Email conversation with Christopher D. Green, author of Psychology Strikes Out: Coleman R. Griffith and the Chicago Cubs

16. Conversation with Dr. Gordin

17. Email conversation with Christopher Green

18. https://www.vikings.com/news/john-randle-brett-favre-share-stories-over-pregame-drive

19. The Power of Habit, Charles Duhigg

20. Marvin Lewis direct quote

21. St. Confessions of St. Augustine, Modern English Version, Hal M. Helms, Paraclete Press, Orleans. Massachusetts. 1986

22. The Power of Habit, Charles Duhigg

Chapter 3: Nutrition

1. https://www.pro-football-reference.com/leaders/pass_long_single_game_playoffs.htm

2. https://www.profootballhof.com/players/shannon-sharpe/

3. https://www.pro-football-reference.com/years/1990/draft.htm

4. https://broncoswire.usatoday.com/2017/06/24/denver-broncos-news-shannon-sharpe-hustled-final-roster/

5. https://www.cantonrep.com/sports/20181202/hard-work-pushed-shannon-sharpe-out-of-brothers-shadow-to-pro-football-hall-of-fame

6. https://broncoswire.usatoday.com/2017/06/24/denver-broncos-news-shannon-sharpe-hustled-final-roster/

7. Colin J. Loiter, How Does Shannon Sharpe Remain Football Fit? NFL.com, Oct. 16, 2014.

8. The Carnitine Miracle, Robert Crayhon

9. Ibid.

10. "Fed Up" documentary on Netflix

11. https://www.cantonrep.com/article/20110807/
    News/308079925
12. Jen Murphy, Football Player Leaves the Field, Not the Gym,
    The Wall Street Journal, December 21, 2010.
13. Ibid.
14. https://www.mayoclinic.org/healthy-lifestyle/nutri-
    tion-and-healthy-eating/in-depth/art-20043983
15. https://www.verywellfit.com/is-skipping-breakfast-best-for-
    weight-loss-3496232
16. Jen Murphy, Football Player Leaves the Field, Not the Gym,
    The Wall Street Journal, December 21, 2010.
17. 1. Duke University Diet & Fitness Center, 1997, 2. Nancy
    Clark's Sports Nutrition Guidebook: Eating to Fuel Your Active
    Lifestyle, Nancy Clark
18. Sue James Baltimore Ravens Nutrition Handout 2006
19. Jen Murphy, Football Player Leaves the Field, Not the Gym,
    The Wall Street Journal, December 21, 2010.
20. https://www.mayoclinic.org/healthy-lifestyle/nutri-
    tion-and-healthy-eating/in-depth/art-20043983
21. Melvin Williams
22. Colin Liotta, How does Shannin Sharpe remain football fit?
    NFL.com Oct 16, 2014
23. https://www.health.harvard.edu/heart-health/can-a-healthy-
    lifestyle-reset-your-genes
24. The Western way of life has limited instictive, corrective
    choice.' Source: Applied Kinesiology, pg. 152.
25. https://www.ncbi.nlm.nih.gov/books/NBK470561/
26. Strength training for the aging adult. Strength-training pro-
    grams meet the demand of the new aging generation, who will
    invest in maintaining youthful health, mobility and physical
    grace. By Wayne L. Westcott, Ph.D. 2. Ballor, D. L., & E.T.
    Poehlman (1994). Exercise training enhances fat-free mass
    preservation during diet-induced weight loss: A meta analytic
    finding. International Journal of Obesity, 18: 35-40. 4. Brehm,
    B., & B. Keller (1990). Diet and exercise factors that influence
    weight and fat loss. IDEA Today, 8: 33-46. 19. Tuft University
    Diet and Nutrition Letter (1992). An IQ test for losers. 10: 6-7
    (March).

27. https://healthynestnutrition.com/food-impacts-focus-concentration-learning/
28. Ephesians 3:17-19, NLT

Chapter 4: Rest

1. https://www.foxsports.com/nfl/story/cincinnati-bengals-marvin-lewis-new-practice-schedule-102615
2. https://www.footballoutsiders.com/stat-analysis/2016/2015-adjusted-games-lost
3. https://spec.lib.miamioh.edu/cradleofcoaches/brown
4. https://web.archive.org/web/20120609023051/http://aol.sportingnews.com/ncaa-basketball/story/2009-07-29/sporting-news-50-greatest-coaches-all-time
5. "Preparing to Win" by Bill Walsh
6. Paul Brown with Jack Cleary, The Paul Brown Story, (Atheneum, 1979), 78.
7. https://www.medicalnewstoday.com/articles/320172#the-three-stages-of-gas
8. Adrenal Fatigue; the 21st Century Stress Syndrome, James Wilson
9. https://www.medicalnewstoday.com/articles/320172#the-three-stages-of-gas
10. Recovery Training in Australia, Angela Calder, This was a presentation.
11. Personal conversation
12. https://www.theguardian.com/sport/ng-interactive/2017/aug/02/usain-bolt-fastest-man-ever-lived
13. Admin, Sleep to Be an All-Star: Why Athletes Should make Sleep a Priority in their Daily Training, Fatigue Science, Sept 3, 2013. https://www.fatiguescience.com/blog/infographic-why-athletes-should-make-sleep-a-priority-in-their-daily-training/
14. Al Sidra Media, Usain Bolt says Sleep is Perfect Cure for Early Season Slump, 2012.
15. Van Cauter, E., Kerkhofs, M., Caufriez, A., Van Onderbergen, A., Thorner, M. O. and Copinschi, G. A quantitative estimation of growth hormone secretion in normal man: reproducibility and relation to sleep and time of day. J. Clin. Endocrinol. Metab., 1992, 74: 1441–1450.

16. Am J. Clin Nutr. 91:1550, 2010 (for whole bullet point)
17. The Oxford Handbook of Sleep and Sleep Disorders, Charles M. Morin and Colin A. Espie
18. https://www.kqed.org/science/26331/how-electric-light-changed-the-night
19. http://www.risesci.com/about Rise Science, a company that uses sleep to push athletes to peak performance.
20. Personal conversation, Jeff Kahn, CEO Rise Science. He said the following: "Have your ghost writer look up Till Ronenberg who writes a book called internal time."
21. https://www.sleepfoundation.org/how-sleep-works/stages-of-sleep. https://www.sleepfoundation.org/circadian-rhythm
22. National Sleep Foundation's Sleep Health Index. https://www.sleepfoundation.org/press-release/lack-sleep-affecting-americans-finds-national-sleep-foundation
23. https://health.gov/myhealthfinder/topics/everyday-healthy-living/mental-health-and-relationships/get-enough-sleep
24. Success over Distress, Wayne Topping
25. In: Institute for the Study of Labor.
26. The Productivity of Working Hours, John Pencavel, pg.37, April 2014
27. "The Ruthless Elimination of Hurry" by John Mark Comer

Chapter 5: Education

1. https://www.si.com/college/2017/03/17/northwestern-wildcats-first-win-ncaa-tournament
2. https://americanfootballdatabase.fandom.com/wiki/List_of_Big_Ten_Conference_football_champions
3. https://www.adminplan.northwestern.edu/ir/data-book/v45/3.01-total_enrollment.pdf
4. https://www.chicagotribune.com/news/ct-xpm-1995-02-01-9502010038-story.html
5. "students who are anxious, angry, or depressed don't learn; people who are caught in these states do not take information efficiently or deal with it well. (Emotional Intelligence, pg.78)
6. Your Miracle Brain by Jean Carper
7. http://www.ncaa.org/about/resources/research/mens-basket-

ball-probability-competing-beyond-high-school
8. ESPN Radio (10/12/15)
9. https://www.chicagotribune.com/news/ct-xpm-1995-02-01-9502010038-story.html
10. NU media guide: https://s3.amazonaws.com/sidearm.sites/nusports.com/documents/2018/10/10/1819_B1G_MD_Guide.pdf
11. 1996-97 Northwestern Basketball Media Guide.
12. Jump Shot: Evan Eschmeyer. Lauren Price
13. Mostly personal conversation. Other source: What ever happened to...Evan Eschmeyer. The Daily Northwestern Matt Baker, May 15, 2006
14. Personal communication
15. https://dailynorthwestern.com/2006/05/15/archive-manual/what-ever-happened-toevan-eschmeyer/
16. Personal communication. Other sources: Jump Shot: Evan Eschmeyer by Lauren Price
17. Lauren Price, Jump Shot: Evan Eschmeyer, Northwestern Magazine, Winter, 2008.
18. https://activerelease.com/
19. John Kiely, Historic Performance Podcast #98
20. Ibid.
21. Personal conversation with Oliver Terrell; Neuroscience, Carnegie Mellon
22. Why Learning Leads to Happiness
23. Education and Health: Evaluating Theories and Evidence

Chapter 6: Self-Talk

1. https://www.vikings.com/team/legends/timeline
2. Ibid.
3. https://www.pro-football-reference.com/teams/atl/1998.htm
4. ESPN NFL Analyst Cris Carter discusses pressure in an NFL Championship game, Mike and Mike in the Morning, ESPN Radio, Jan 23, 2012.
5. Ibid.
6. Lou Tice, Personal Coaching for Results, (Thomas Nelson Publishers, 1997).
7. "The Role of Self-Talk in the Awareness..."

8. Daniel Goleman, Emotional Intelligence: Why it Can Matter More Than IQ, (Bantam Books, 1995), 89.
9. The Role of Self-Talk in the Awareness of Physiological State and Physical Performance
10. Blanchfield, Hardy, etc., Talking Yourself out of Exhaustion: The Effects of Self-Talk on Endurance Performance, Medicine and Science in Sports and Exercise, May 2014, 46(5): 998-1007.
11. The Role of Self-Talk in the Awareness of Physiological State and Physical Performance
12. "The Role of Self-Talk…"
13. https://www.promisesbehavioralhealth.com/addiction-recovery-blog/cris-carter-from-addiction-to-superstardom-in-the-nfl/
14. https://www.startribune.com/sobriety-vikings-turned-carters-career-around/191301091/
15. https://www.promisesbehavioralhealth.com/addiction-recovery-blog/cris-carter-from-addiction-to-superstardom-in-the-nfl/
16. ESPN radio Mike & Mike Sept 23, 2015
17. Ibid.
18. https://www.espn.com/nfl/player/stats/_/id/21/gary-anderson
19. "Heart of a Champion: The Story of the 1998 NFC Champions". NFL Yearbook. 1999.
20. https://www.espn.com/nfl/player/stats/_/id/10/cris-carter
21. https://www.pro-football-reference.com/leaders/rec_career.htm
22. Personal Coaching For Growth
23. Born to Win
24. Ibid.
25. Kent Hughes, Disciplines of a Godly Man, (Crossway Books Publishers, 2006)

Chapter 7: Emotion

1. https://www.espn.com/nfl/player/stats/_/id/2136/jamal-lewis
2. https://www.pro-football-reference.com/leaders/rush_yds_single_game.htm
3. https://www.baltimoreravens.com/news/the-caw-watch-a-hilarious-trivia-night-with-jamal-lewis
4. https://vault.si.com/vault/2003/11/10/2105-yards-the-chase-is-

on-the-ravens-jamal-lewis-with-a-new-maturity-and-sense-of-purpose-is-leading-the-nfl-in-rushingand-stalking-the-single-season-record

5. https://www.pro-football-reference.com/leaders/rush_yds_single_season.htm

6. https://www.espn.com/nfl/player/gamelog/_/id/2136/type/nfl/year/2003

7. https://vault.si.com/vault/2003/11/10/2105-yards-the-chase-is-on-the-ravens-jamal-lewis-with-a-new-maturity-and-sense-of-purpose-is-leading-the-nfl-in-rushingand-stalking-the-single-season-record

8. Walter Payton, Never Die Easy, pg. 86

9. Personal conversation with Dr. Peter Ganshirt

10. Inner Skiing

11. Ibid.

12. How Emotions Influence Performance in Competitive Sports. Richard Lazarus

13. Talking Points Week 6: Plan A,B,C, Positive Coaching Alliance (www.positivecoach.org)

14. Dr. Ganshirt

15. Ibid.

16. Ibid.

17. Lazarus, pg. 233

18. Dr. Ganshirt

19. Richard Lazarus, How Emotions Influence Performance in Competitive Sports, The Sports Pyschologist, Human Kinetic Publishers, 2000, 14, 229-252.

20. Lazarus, pg. 243

21. How Does Sport Psychology Actually Improve Athletic Performance? A Framework to Facilitate Athletes' and Coaches' Understanding. Chris J. Gee. Behavior Modification 34(5) 386–402 © The Author(s) 2010

22. https://www.si.com/nfl/2016/10/30/raiders-record-most-penalties-nfl-game

23. https://www.teamrankings.com/nfl/stat/penalties-per-game?date=2006-02-06

24. Jamison Hensley, With 21 penalties, 2 Ejections, Ravens Spin Out of Control to Worst Start Ever, Baltimore Sun, October

10, 2005.

25. Dr. Ganshirt

26. Lazarus, pg. 241

27. Lazarus, pg. 235

28. Lazarus, pg. 245

29. Emotional Intelligence 2.0, Travis Bradberry

30. https://www.simplypsychology.org/defense-mechanisms.html

31. https://www.sports-reference.com/cfb/schools/northwestern/index.html

32. https://www.sports-reference.com/cfb/schools/northwestern/1995-schedule.html

33. Personal communication with Dr. Peter Ganshirt

34. Lazarus, pg. 233

35. Lazarus, pg. 240

36. Lazarus, pg. 243

37. Lazarus, pg. 237

38. Dr. Ganshirt

39. Inner Skiing

40. Ibid.

41. Inner Skiing, pg. 4

42. Dr. Ganshirt

43. Lazarus, pg. 242

44. Life Application Study Bible

45. Wedding at Cana (John 2:1-11). Jesus clears the Temple (John 1:12-25). Nicodemus Visits Jesus at Night (John 3:1-21)

Chapter 8: Wisdom

1. https://www.pro-football-reference.com/teams/clt/index.htm

2. https://www.pro-football-reference.com/teams/clt/2005.htm

3. https://www.youtube.com/watch?v=LgwXjf9cbIs

4. https://www.youtube.com/watch?v=LgwXjf9cbIs

5. https://www.pro-football-reference.com/years/2005/kicking.htm

6. Geoff Colvin, Why Talent is Overrated, Fortune Magazine, Oct. 27, 2008.

7. Ibid.

8. Search for Significance by Ravi Zacharias

Chapter 9: Character

1. The Ultimate Irony, Don Banks, CNN SI, 1/4/01
2. a.) https://www.pro-football-reference.com/teams/oti/2000/gamelog/ b.) https://www.pro-football-reference.com/teams/oti/1999/gamelog/
3. Dilfer makes his mark, Mark Cannizzaro, ESPN.com, 11/16/00
4. https://www.stadiumsofprofootball.com/stadiums/nissan-stadium/
5. https://vault.si.com/vault/2000/11/13/13
6. NCGA Golf, Kevin Merfeld
7. The Ultimate Irony, Don Banks, CNN SI, 1/4/01
8. Mike Lurie, Dilfer Stays Lose Despite Abuse About Weak Offense, CBS SportsLine.com, January 11, 2001.
9. Growing Kids God's Way
10. https://www.vikings.com/news/a-football-life-production-shocks-john-randle-in-a-good-way-19970667
11. NY Times, Sports of the Times; For Collins and Dilfer, a Matter of Faith, Dave Anderson, 1/28/01
12. Life Appl Study Bible, pg. 380
13. Unwanted Champion: Super Bowl winner Trent Dilfer ponders his next Job, David Ginsburg, Associated Press, July 23, 2001. https://www.baltimoresun.com/sports/bal-dilferarchives1001-story.html
14. Dilfer gets his shot at Baltimore, Joe Vardon, The Daily Record, Wayne & Holmes County, Ohio, October 16, 2005
15. https://www.espn.com/nfl/player/stats/_/id/649/trent-dilfer
16. Jamison Hensley, Seattle's Dilfer Returns to Town, Baltimore Sun, November 21, 2003.
17. Joe Vardon, Dilfer Gets His Shot at Baltimore, The Daily Record, October 16, 2005.
18. Aaron Wilson, Dilfer Apologizes to Billick, Russell Street Report, October 4, 2007.
19. Kenneth Boa, The Leadership Bible, (Zondervan Publishing, 1984), 646.
20. Aaron Wilson, Dilfer Apologizes to Billick, Russell Street Report, October 3, 2007.
21. Associated Press, Niners QB Dilfer Regrets Harsh Words

Against Ravens' Billick, October 3, 2007

22. Aaron Wilson, Dilfer Apologizes to Billick, Russell Street Report, October 4, 2007.

23. Ibid.

24. Ibid.

25. Associated Press, Niners QB Dilfer Regrets Harsh Words Against Ravens' Billick, October 3, 2007

26. Dilfer Ready to face Tampa: Thankful for his years as a Buc, QB returns a Ravens hero, David Leon Moore, USA Today, 1/15/01

27. Mere Christianity, C.S. Lewis

28. A quote from my friend, Pastor Dave Michener

Chapter 10: Relationships

1. https://www.youtube.com/watch?v=lWGKmOVIcTc

2. https://www.espn.com/blog/nfceast/post/_/id/80996/20-year-rewind-how-the-cowboys-passed-on-randy-moss

3. https://www.espn.com/blog/nfceast/post/_/id/80996/20-year-rewind-how-the-cowboys-passed-on-randy-moss

4. Cris Carter, Going Deep: How Wide Receivers Became the Most Compelling Figures in Pro Sports, (Hyperion Publishing, New York).

5. Ibid.

6. Ibid.

7. Ibid.

8. ESPN interview (maybe)

9. https://www.promisesbehavioralhealth.com/addiction-recovery-blog/cris-carter-from-addiction-to-superstardom-in-the-nfl/

10. https://www.brainyquote.com/quotes/gary_hamel_528654

11. Becoming a Person of Influence, John Maxwell, Jim Doran

12. https://bleacherreport.com/articles/741234-10-best-wide-receiver-rookie-seasons-in-nfl-history

13. https://www.profootballhof.com/players/randy-moss/

14. Clayton Hicks, H7 Network

15. Cris Carter, Going Deep: How Wide Receivers Became the Most Compelling Figures in Pro Sports, (Hyperion Publishing, New York).

16. SermonIllustrations.com (Dr. Bernie Siegel, Homemade,

May, 1989)

17. pg. 178 Emotional Intelligence

18. Life Application Study Bible

19. Chip Scoggins, Moss: I would Love to Come Back to Minnesota, Star Tribune, March 16, 2011.

20. Brenton Weyi, Why Successful People Leave Their Loser Friends Behind, Addicted2Success.com, April 25, 2013.

Chapter 11: Community

1. https://www.nytimes.com/2001/01/31/sports/pro-football-baltimore-celebrates-its-super-bowl-victory.html

2. https://www.pro-football-reference.com/teams/rav/2000.htm

3. a.) https://www.espn.com/nfl/player/gamelog/_/id/1196/type/nfl/year/2000 b.) https://www.espn.com/nfl/player/gamelog/_/id/930/type/nfl/year/2000 c.) https://www.espn.com/nfl/player/gamelog/_/id/389/type/nfl/year/2000

4. https://www.pro-football-reference.com/teams/rav/1999.htm

5. Zoom conversation with Ravens team

6. https://www.pro-football-reference.com/teams/rav/2000.htm

7. Super Journey: Diary of the Ravens World Championship Season. Produced by the Baltimore Ravens in conjunction with the Publishing Group of NFL Properties. 2001. Pg. 84

8. Alone Together by Sherry Turkle

9. https://www.nytimes.com/2018/01/17/world/europe/uk-britain-loneliness.html

10. https://www.brainyquote.com/quotes/helen_keller_382259

11. SB Zoom Call

12. https://www.si.com/nfl/2020/12/23/nfl-rumors-houston-texans-interested-in-marvin-lewis

13. Celebration of Discipline: The Path to Spiritual Growth by Richard Foster

Chapter 12: Love

1. Tim Keller, Meaning of Marriage

2. C.S. Lewis, The Four Loves

3. "Inner Ache of Loneliness," Ravi Zacharias

4. Ibid.

5. Tim Keller, Meaning of Marriage

6. Ibid.
7. John Mark Comer, Loveology

Section 4: Spiritual Building Block
1. An Answer for Every Question by Michael Ramsden. RZIM (Ravi Zacharias International Ministries)
2. http://chrisbrauns.com/2014/10/four-questions-every-thinking-human-must-answer/

Chapter 13: The Bible
1. https://www.espn.com/nfl/player/gamelog/_/id/13766/type/nfl/year/2014
2. https://www.pro-football-reference.com/years/2014/defense.htm#defense::tackles_combined
3. Ed Valentine, Daily NFL draft profile: Vincent Rey, MLB, Duke, SBNATION bigblueview.com, March 30, 2010.
4. Conversation with Vinny
5. The Seven Laws of the Learner, Bruce Wilkinson
6. Coley Harvey, Why Vincent Rey's Voice is Often all that's Heard at Bengals Practice, ESPN, August 28, 2015.
7. https://www.pro-football-reference.com/players/R/ReyxVi00/gamelog/2012/
8. https://www.baltimoreravens.com/news/reports-linebacker-vincent-rey-works-out-for-ravens
9. https://www.espn.com/blog/cincinnati-bengals/post/_/id/14345/bengals-vincent-rey-walter-payton-man-year-nominee
10. Conversation with Vinny
11. https://www.quotes.net/quote/17664

Chapter 14: Prayer
1. Jobs Related Almanac for stress? (in Times-Pacayune 10/24/2000). USA Today for injuries (Skip Wood, 11/30/2001)
2. Davies ME, et al Cumulative medical history of prospective NFL players over a decade, medicine and science in sports and exercise, 1997; 29(5):5191
3. Tim Keller, Prayer

4. https://www.newsweek.com/faith-healing-133365
5. https://www.gq.com/story/troy-polamalu-pittsburgh-steel-ers-super-bowl
6. Ibid.
7. https://www.bible-history.com/geography/ancient-israel/cities-jesus-visited.html
8. Clarence Macartney, The Word that Conquers God, In Classic Sermons on Prayer, compiled by Warren Wiersbe, (Hendrickson Publishers, 1987), 17.
9. Life Appl. Study Bible, p. 2141.
10. Tim Keller, Prayer
11. Life Application Study Bible, Pg. 2153

Chapter 15: Church

1. FCA article (September 2013)
2. Ibid.
3. https://www.pro-football-reference.com/years/2011/draft.htm
4. Stefan Stevenson, Andy Dalton Provides a Greater Faith for TCU Horned Frogs, The Dallas Morning News, December 25, 2010.
5. Stefan Stevenson, Faith Lifts TCU Football Player: Quarterback Andy Dalton will leave Spiritual legacy at School, The Ledger, Saturday, Jan 1, 2011.
6. Direct quote
7. Stefan Stevenson, Andy Dalton Provides a Greater Faith for TCU Horned Frogs, The Dallas Morning News, December 25, 2010.
8. Direct quote from Andy
9. https://www.dallasnews.com/sports/tcu-horned-frogs/2010/12/25/andy-dalton-provides-a-greater-faith-for-tcu-horned-frogs/
10. FCA article (September 2013)
11. Andy, personal conversation
12. Life Application, 2136-2137

Chapter 16: Purpose

1. https://www.pro-football-reference.com/players/C/CunnRa00.htm

2. https://bleacherreport.com/articles/2899647-former-nfl-mvp-randall-cunningham-hired-by-raiders-as-team-chaplain
3. Ibid.
4. https://www.espn.com/fantasy/football/ffl/story?id=3577512
5. 1995: Started first four games … Source: Minnesota Vikings 1998 Media guide. "Unlike the look of disappointment Cunningham often showed when he was benched in 1995 by Eagles coach Ray Rhodes and several times before by then-coach Buddy Ryan" Source: The Former Eagle has Landed, Pioneer Press, 9/27/99. As is usually the case for players toward the end of their time with a franchise, Cunningham battled injuries and was benched for performance. The team's fans never fully appreciated Cunningham's contributions, many Eagles observers say. https://theundefeated.com/features/black-quarterback-randall-cunningham-was-unlike-anything-the-nfl-had-ever-seen/
6. Ray Richardson, The Former Eagle Has Landed, The Pioneer Press, September 24, 1997.
7. https://apnews.com/article/4104e508d299723d9a3fcdc-9589c495a
8. https://www.pro-football-reference.com/teams/min/playoffs.htm
9. https://www.espn.com/nfl/player/stats/_/id/8/randall-cunningham
10. https://www.pro-football-reference.com/players/C/Cunn-Ra00.htm
11. Ray Richardson, The Former Eagle Has Landed, The Pioneer Press, September 24, 1997.
12. https://vault.si.com/vault/1996/03/18/on-the-rocks-its-good-that-randall-cunningham-now-has-a-marble-and-granite-shop-because-employment-as-a-starting-quarterback-may-be-over
13. "A Time to Heal" by Roxanne Robbins (Sports Spectrum)
14. Ibid.
15. Kenneth Hildebrand, How to make the most of your abilities, In: University of Success, OG Mandino, pg.89
16. Howard Whitman, How to Fashion your own brand of success. In: University of Success, OG Mandino, pg.15
17. Laying it Down: How Letting Go Brings Out Your Best by Randall Cunningham

18. https://www.reviewjournal.com/local/henderson/
remnant-ministries-led-by-pastor-randall-cunning-
ham-adds-youth-facility/

Conclusion: We Are All Coaches

1. https://www.etymonline.com/search?q=coach